You Can Read Me Like a Book

You Can Read Me Like a Book

Maureen Lipman

LONDON   NEW YORK   SYDNEY   TORONTO

Typeset in Plantin by Selwood Systems, Midsomer Norton and
printed in Great Britain by Butler & Tanner Ltd, Frome and
London

For Dr Jeffrey Gawler and
Mr Fary Afshar, with gratitude

Acknowledgements

LOUISE DIXON: Beyond the call of editorial duty – with scissors and glue, tact, skill, insight, taste and a liberal peppering of mirth and fag ash, she made software into hard opinion.

JACQUIE GRANDITER: Who laid out this book in sheets, scraps and tattered notelets, then cajoled, wheedled and finally shamed me into joining them. The deciphering and endless retyping was done with love, tea and sympathy.

ROBSON BOOKS: In publishing terms, small really is beautiful.

GOOD HOUSEKEEPING: For the healthiest circulation a girl's bloodstream could have.

SHE MAGAZINE: For the good times, when we still spoke.

JACK: My rock, without whom I'd be a one-parent family living in fear of John Redwood.

ZELMA: Without whom this book would still be part of a rainforest.

For the company and perpetually illuminating smiles of Gwen Watford, Jeffrey Chiswick, Reggie Grenfell, Virginia Graham, Judy Scott Fox, Anthony Bowles, Roy Castle and Morris Fishman.

Contents

Pro's Log

No, but where did they go? The Chinese Year of the Rooster and Year of the Dog? I can't believe the Pig has come round so soon when I've scarcely brushed up the matzo crumbs from Passover. What in the name of Dim Sum has happened to make the earth turn quite so rapidly and thus impel the *Guardian* birthday column to embarrass me so *frequently*?

Yet, there I was, only a few months back, standing before a distinguished gathering of Chinese and English business persons, after a banquet to celebrate the passing of the Dog and the coming of the Pig, saying slowly, painstakingly and very phonetically 'Djew dar gia shin nien how! Djew nien shune li!' in the desperate hope that it came out meaning 'Good Luck in the Year of the Pig' and knowing for certain that, with my luck, pronunciation and sense of pitch, I could be saying 'You all look like dogs and I just ate like a pig.' Still, nothing ventured . . .

The food was miraculously good and I was able sincerely to compliment the Dorchester Hotel and Michel Roux on their achievement and to remind the distinguished gathering of the man who walked into a restaurant and said, 'I want a plate of bacon, eggs and chips – but I want the bacon fatty and limp and lying in a pool of fat, the eggs broken, hard and overcooked and the chips soggy and cold.'

The restaurateur says, 'But, sir, I can't serve a meal like that!'

'Why not?' says the customer, 'you did yesterday!'

Albert Roux, born in the Year of the Pig, gave the toast to the outgoing Dog, (me – why are you laughing? – oh, all right,

1

let's get all the barking, frothing and on heat jokes out now, shall we?). Albert's speech was refreshingly brief and was accompanied by repetitive stroking of his nice round obelisk of a belly. He ended by saying cheerily 'And now I finish my speech because I must go to ze leetle boys' room.'

Jane Asher, Joanna Lumley and I are all well-known Dogs of 1946. Jane, a red setter perhaps, though cleverer; Joanna, a standard poodle or perhaps a collie; and me, perhaps a mongrel out of borzoi and spaniel. I have a lovely picture of Jane and I, age twenty in the pages of *Honey* magazine in russet tones, both sporting the new shaggy hairdo. It was supposed to be a contrast of two very different up-and-coming actresses but, not for the first time, I'd decided to become a natural redhead overnight. I love this picture more than I can say. Such youth, such optimism – such a fake!

Actually it's not a Pig, it's a Boar and for those born in the Year of the Boar this will be a time for reaping benefits from past efforts, a period of relaxation, pleasure and self-indulgence, a time of impulsive spending and good will all round – but watch your weight!

Famous Boars include, without a trace of irony, Sir Richard Attenborough, Sir Robin Day, Ronald Reagan, Henry Kissinger, Donald Sinden, the Duke of Kent and Brian Clough.

So, now what of Pigs? The Year of the Boar will, I'm told, bring hard work, humour, wit and a ready smile and, according to the ancient astrological chart in front of me, you will find all of these qualities in abundance if you continue to read the book you are now reading. Wow! Extraordinary! Karma!

Oh, apparently, the Pig can also be extremely gullible . . .

Dramatis Personae

First Person: 'I':   Actress, writer, speaker, avoider and sloth. A woman in her late forties. 'I' is mentioned enough times to warrant accusations of ego and mania. In 'I' 's defence, if 'I' was substituted by 'we', 'us' or 'one', then us would be in grave danger of making an ungrammatical prat of one.

Jack: Him indoors. Supportive spouse, concierge, foot warmer, fish fryer. A man whose idea of a good night out is staying in. Writer by profession and seemingly by osmosis, he is at present sporting his first beard since Amy, then aged two, pointed at Rolf Harris on the television and said 'Daddy'.

Amy: A daughter of twenty-one years. Looks fourteen, thinks 114. Professional worrier and shoulder to all with tear ducts. Student. ABBA aficionado. Artist, emotional Loch Ness, and occasional parent to 'I'.

Adam: A son. Nineteen years. Yawning Gap Year ahead. China and India have been mentioned. 'I' have told him both continents are bursting with North London students in GAP clothing but so far have failed to deter him. Apparently, one more word about him and I'm a dead 'I'.

Zelma: A mother. No, *several* mothers. Seventy-

3

two years, looks fifty. Could be something
to do with the portrait of her daughter she
keeps in the attic. Zelma continues to
spread joy and mirth, not entirely inten-
tionally, through the lives of everyone she
buttonholes. Typical exchange culled from
my diary:

 'Wednesday, 21st. Shirley Black suggested we have dinner at the Waldorf
tonight. Zelma says "Ooh, can I come? It'll
be a lovely way of spending my last night."
Shirley: "Oh, are you going back to Hull
tomorrow then?" Zelma (blithely): "No.
Monday." '

Jacquie:
 A personal secretary to 'I' and Him. Forced
to work for a man in a flapping brown velour
dressing gown and a woman with 'abandon
ship' programmed into her brain cells. If
you ever buy and read this book, it will
be entirely because the personal secretary
finally snapped and padlocked her em-
ployer to a rosewood desk.

Sally:
 Works as 'I' 's assistant in long runs in the
theatre and short runs on TV. Sally is raven
haired, looks like a Gauguin painting and
is an Espanophile who can sniff out a Tapas
bar on an industrial estate in Bradford. Sal
knows when I'm running on a reserve tank
and her pockets look like one of Paul Dan-
iels's flak jackets. Rescue remedy, Vitamin
C, Ginseng and mustard jostle for space
alongside tubs of cottage cheese and bottles
of aqua vitae on days when bacon butties
and Nescafé are the only available fodder.
Sal sees all and Sal says *nada*. Sal is also
visibly with child and, delighted though I
am for her, I can't bear to contemplate a

Sally-less existence in showbiz.

Carmela: Who cooks and cares for us all and looks after the house while I pretend to work. She was sent by the Mary Poppins School of Housekeeping Department in Heaven. Her daughter, Jasmine, would like me to mention that Carmela is her mother.

Pushkin: Upholstery and fabric recycler. Female. Nineteen years. Feline. Tabby. One tooth, hardly any thyroid. Now down to seven or eight meals only per day. Seemingly immortal. My friend, Lizzy, swears the vet gave us back a new cat after the thyroid op.

1

Actor in the House

Good Housekeeping

In 1983 an untried and untested columnist was commissioned to write a thousand words on a subject of her choice for the dashing new magazine, *Options*.

The subject on which the untried columnist decided to test-pilot her writing skills was my kitchen. For yes, gentle Poirot and Morse followers, I *was* that columnist. At the time I was renovating Château Rosenthal in Muswell Hill, gateway to the North Circular, and my handbag, my pockets, my sleeves and my mouth were bursting with fabric samples, offcuts of lino, crumpled brochures for white enamel taps offering 'Swan-Necked Versatility' and white Circotherm ovens offering all-round cookability and self-cleaning sides (would that I could have found such sides for my son!). On the subject of kitchen accoutrements, I was a Mastermind. 'Bong – Lipman, London. And your special subject is ... Waste Disposal Grinder Noises ... and you have thirty-secondsstarting *now*.'

In short, I had a nouvelle cuisine before that became a meal which only covers one third of your plate. A Smallbone fitted kitchen. One of the early models. Drag-finished in canary yellow with tiled work surfaces in cobalt blue, courtesy of a tile shop you needed a second mortgage just to phone. (I'd never used the words 'epoxy resin' before. Not together at any rate.) I had Amtico flooring in oak-look 'random plank', trendy down lighting, wobbly pine circular table and chairs and blue gingham café curtains and tablecloth. When finished, it looked exactly as I'd dreamed it would. Like a cross between Monet's restored house at Giverny and the set

of the old *Mary Tyler Moore Show*. Since then, on birthdays
and at Christmas, everyone who knew me added yellow
plates, blue china, yellow and blue egg-cups and I even
managed to buy, mail order, a free-standing wood carving of
Clint Eastwood in denims and yellow shirt, which *really* made
my day.

So, fade out and fade paintwork, the years rag-rolled by
and the truth and the woodwork began to reveal themselves.
I, the kitchen expert, the *maven*, even (What! you don't speak
Yiddish? Fear not. You will.) was forced to admit, Spock-
like, that I hadn't always been right. Let's be honest, I'd been
fifty per cent extensively, expensively wrong.

First off, there is no such thing as a fitted kitchen. They
don't. On the whole, *you* fit in with *them*. It may be that all
you've ever dreamed of is an American fridge large enough
to marinate a yak in and a wall oven high enough to avoid
traction, but if you've only got one-and-a-half integral walls
and a dining area, then you too will end up with a gnomic
fridge which spews out family-sized foodstuffs – Mount Etna
style – each time you open the door, and an undercounter
oven with integral grill, under which you crouch, squint,
steam up your glasses and up from which you have to be
forcibly winched. Both appliances will, however, fit in to
'housing units'. Boy, if there were as many housing units for
humans as there are for dishwashers then the Cardboard City
would be as anachronistic as the Forbidden City.

What matters, I now know, is not the streamlined look so
beloved of gas commercials and sitcoms. No, what matters is
to have a place to store cutlery and crockery, a place to chop
very near to a place to tip and wash, a place to serve close to
a good sized double oven, with easy clean – no, *ludicrously*
easy clean – hob which I'm afraid means ceramic for hygiene
and halogen for speed and a fridge the size of Demis Roussos.
Oh. And forget white, for anything. It chips. On *taps* it doesn't
chip – it peels, revealing dull, leprous brass beneath. And,
while we're at it, if you can stretch the budget, get a water
filter because the entomology in the water supply is yet to be

revealed, and it's about to be re-overfluorided.

Talking of floor riding, he – lover, househusband, new man, MCP, or hunk who came to read the meter and never left – may worship the ground beneath your feet, but will he sweep and mop it? Mine will – but he's old enough to have done National Service and anything's fun after polishing your kit-buckle for four-and-a-half hours. If he won't, then buy something easy on the feet, and patterned to the point of camouflage so *nothing* shows. Ceramic tiles? You want to run downstairs at 3.00 am for a hot milk and a diazepam only to develop toes like Ranulph Fiennes? I don't care how much you adored their glazed splendour during that week in a villa in Ischia – they don't work in Esher.

So. Painted kitchens? Gorgeous. What fun to change the colour scheme every four years. Oh yes? *And* the plates, and the cloths, and the tea towels and the little Delft pottery village over the plate rack? Terracotta and slate with distressed stencils, or more likely, water dye all over the washing machine, china all chucked in the skip and a distressed home-maker.

One more word. Sinks. The bigger, the better. One bowl big enough to bath a two-year-old or baste an endangered species in, one small with waste disposal if you're still on speaking terms with your bank manager, and proper draining boards built in. Forget the 'Oh you just drain in the sink and transfer to the dishwasher' routine. It's a fallacy. The dishwasher's always full, the sink's always waiting for the dishwasher to empty and you've got to have somewhere custom built to stock three days' pans, haven't you?

Recently, an age-old grudge against a work surface of stained tile grouting resurfaced. Out went the tiles and in came Corian. Ah. Now you're talking. Slate-blue, speckled man-made stuff, it flows over the work surface and, without a murmur, transmogrifies itself into a white double sink with a blue stripe. I must confess to a sinking feeling when the new draining area held on to quite so much water. The fitter said: 'Yeah – well, they're not really built to drain. As such. It's more for an area of definition.'

I gleamed dangerously. 'An "area of definition", eh? Listen, mate. If I'd wanted an area of definition, I'd have put two sodding white *arrows* by the sink! Make it drain!'

Also it's not fantastically good at taking hot things on its gorgeous surface and, furthermore, it's gorgeous surface is already unbelievably scratched, but it does look wonderful against the new butter-cream of the units and blue wash of the walls.

Goodbye Circotherm oven with variable grill element, I want to cook a chicken and have a piece of toast and Vegemite at the same time, thank you very much, and 'Hello, Good Housekeeping Institute? Can you tell me what's the best performing electric double oven on the market today? No, it *doesn't* have to slide into an undercounter hob – if it cooks nicely it can stand in the middle of a two-acre pig farm!'

Finally, and most financially trying, every Sunday night, my son and his father carried ten bags of dripping, dog-chewed garbage, in the dark, round the back of the house, squeezed juicily past the car and wet-footed it down the drive to the road. This placates the dustbinmen into taking them away on the Monday. This is called life in Haringey: highest rates in England, no wheelies. Enter Natasha the trasher, stage left, escorted by Mark the demonstrator. Out comes Natasha's drawer, in go two bags of Rosenthal refuse. 'Prrrrrr' goes Natasha and reduces said refuse to one-third normal size. Whaddya think of it so far . . . ? Rubbish, only smaller.

Then it was done. The whole thing took a week and two days. Day one: my mother stood in the midst of workmen, plumbers and piles of used mugs and said, 'Ooh, I love anything like this . . . You know . . . workmen – and a mess.' Days three and four: agreed upon original colours and textures then changed mind in night. Much sighing from daughter Amy. 'It's all horrible – why do you always have to *change* things?' Day seven: son Adam, home from school, blinks myopically and, whilst extracting salt and vinegar crisps from drawer, says, 'There's a big chunk chipped out of the crisp drawer. Wasn't Me!'

Me? I feel genuinely ill throughout the whole operation – something to do with the heart of the house developing an irregular beat? Jack, the writer, writes 'Scene 1', then nothing but cheques.

Once it *is* done you never notice it again. As long as you continue to go out to work, that is. It's when you stop and 'stop in' that you start to notice things. My enforced 'noticing' came after a spell in hospital when I was forced from a supine position to re-examine the disintegration of my surroundings. Sick woman – sick building syndrome.

For years, on every visit, my mother has had to stare into my mystified, uncaring face when she utters, as only she can utter, the inevitable: 'Oooh, that small toilet's in a shocking state, Maureen, why don't you get George to do it with some nice blown vinyl?' and, 'Hasn't your kitchen scuffed, can't believe it can you, all that money, it's not worth doing it again, is it?' and, 'That rug will stop walking if you get some Rug Grip' and, 'I bet you'd never get a green carpet again, would you? They're all the same, they go a horrible shade of grey, don't they? Have you noticed?'

Well. I did. Notice. Everything. She was right. About *everything*. It's just that I'd never focused on it before. Things like 'Rug Grip' never impinged on my day-to-day existence. 'Just say no to rugs' was my maxim. 'Blown Vinyl' was surely a Sunset Boulevard hooker? It's all to do with shovelling your own sh-you-know-what ... and if you've delegated all the household tasks, then you don't see chipped paint and fulminating Hotpoints. Other people see them, and other people don't give a tossed salad how rundown they are as long as there's a Christmas bonus. Once you're clean out of acting and take over the Marigolds yourself, you become a woman who's cleaned up her act.

Not Such Good Housekeeping

The truth is that it's some time since I did my own Hoovering, dusting, washing, cooking, cleaning and ironing – no, sorry, not ironing, honesty prevails, I never ironed. Not seriously, anyway. Once in a blue and starchy moon, I ran the big, heavy, man-made, steam-bellowing bastard over collar or cuff for long enough to turn it brown and pungent, but a big, damp basketful of sheets, shorts and shirts in the company of *Afternoon Theatre* was never really my idea of a regular riveting Tuesday, Wednesday or any other day of my permanently crumpled week.

As it happens, for one blissful year, Carmela has been taking care of us in a kind, unobtrusive and humorous way. I could not fault her – and between you and me I have a Ph.D and a Chair at the University of Flatbush in faulting people. Washing comes back the same size and colour as it went in, the plants tend to live without going brown and crisp and every so often a mean kedgeree appears on my late night table, with extra stock. One small drawback. Carmela's five-week annual holiday in Spain happened at exactly the same time as I was opening for a five-week run in a new play at Greenwich. The triple threat: Housework, Theatrework and the Blackwell Tunnel.

I started out with a hastily acquired replacement from Colombia, explained the mysteries of the vacuum cleaner, the washing machine, the dishwasher, the fact that one child rose at dawn and the other slept till two and neither understood the principle of the hanger as a means of keeping piles of clothing off the carpet. The replacement nodded and smiled and even brought along her niece to nod and smile with her. Then, after four or five days of picking up the rudiments of the job, they both disappeared without trace.

At this point, I did what any actress approaching opening night in a heatwave and suffering abject terror, nervous dyspepsia and regular Blackwall auto fumes would do. I put on a pair of Marigolds, picked up a J-cloth and, murmuring my lines from Act II Scene 3, attacked the forgotten art of housewifehusbandry.

Sweeping the kitchen is not that difficult, but it's a lot trickier without a brush. Our brush resembled a Chinese crested puppy. Its bristles were reduced to single figures and a follicle. My sweeping was not only ineffectual but sounded like one of Ginger Baker's basic drum riffs. I got on my knees with dustpan and brush, stood up too quickly and Ginger Baker took over in my skull. I'd been housekeeping for twelve minutes and I was a sick woman. I then did what any mature woman would do. I spent £48.50 at Hardware City on state-of-the-art twin lines – a long-handled brush and pan and a Dustbuster. Meanwhile, the washing machine was beckoning me. I went over and filled it jauntily with clothes, then gazed cluelessly into the two powder compartments: left for pre-wash, right for main wash. Or was it the other way round? I put on my glasses to find my reading glasses and consulted the household file which revealed a distinct lack of a Hoover 1100 manual. So. I was a woman with a manual deficiency. What did I do? I rang my mother. She was thrilled by my inadequacy.

'Well, mine's a top-loader but I'm sure your left is pre-wash and your right is the main wash,' she exclaimed. 'That's what I've always done. Oh. Wait a minute though ... No. The one on the right is the pre-wash – or is it? Ooooh, I don't know, now, it's *ages* since I've been to your house ... let me think ... no, I was right – it's the left. Ooooh, I don't know though – haven't you got a ball?'

Once I'd established that the ball in question was neither crystal, anatomical nor social, I located the orb and filled it with detergent from a new-fangled reduced-sized container. In my day, packets were bigger and more economical each week till you had to have luggage wheels and a muscular friend to get them home. Still, I popped it in, softly humming 'After the Ball Was Over' and the washing machine washed *all* day every day until the powder dispenser fell out permanently in a fit of ball-induced envy and a man had to be called in. After he'd relieved me of half the price of the original machine, the tumble dryer began to make a noise like a puppy parted from its mother before it's fully weaned. 'Grow up, you useless prat,' I screamed and shut it in its room. Well, you know, if you go to them *every* time they cry . . .

The shopping and cooking I managed with hope if not enthusiasm and at 3 o'clock I knocked off for an hour of pre-theatre dozing, during which I mentally went through all the tasks I hadn't managed to do, like changing the towels, dusting and/or polishing, sticking the Toilet Duck up the family toilet – Toilet Duck! I ask you! What's wrong with a swig of Domestos? Always kept our toilet germless enough, but oh no, nowadays each toilet sits there batting its eyelid and saying 'I suppose a duck is out of the question?'

The net result of all this Ducking and driving was that I suggested to Jack that we move. The man who invented *Moving Story* looked aghast, as well he might. After all, the last time we moved, I'd managed to be at rehearsals all day and he'd managed to fall down the cellar trapdoor and sprain his foot. It was fifteen years ago and I'm not sure the dust is quite out of our crevices. Still, always game for an adventure, we had the house valued and delegated a friend of a friend to keep eyes to the ground rent for a suitable property. Only thing was that every time such a property came leafleting through the letterbox, we were too busy, too unsynchronized, too unsure of the area or too bone idle to bother. When the first clematis appeared in the front borders, I booked a decorator, a curtain maker and Wham Bam Terence Conran, I'm back in the world of tiny squares of fabric and the old cheque book is flapping open and shut like a catflap in a kitchen with a whole salmon on a low table.

I can't help noticing that in my last book there was a chapter called 'Sofa So Good'. It's about the impossibility of trying to buy new sofas after the cat had single-pawedly decimated the leather Chesterfield that came with Jack. Since then I've had the experience of ordering a three seater, a two seater and a wing chair and stool which I saw and admired in a furniture shop in Hull and had delivered 200 miles in fabrics of my choice. In fact there was a particular New Year's Eve party when the furniture arrived just before the guests and questionnaires were handed out as to the suitability of it for a living room. The no's had it and the kindly furniture shop owner took the whole thing back, some 200 miles and, in the fullness of time, sold it on to other householders with more taste and less guests.

There was nothing wrong with the sofas – it was just a terrible choice of fabric. By me. I chose it from a 4" × 4" scrap of pink, green and cream stripe. Innocent as I was in the undercover world of overcovers, I didn't suspect that in between the striped area shown on the sample, was a massive area comprising a khaki stripe bigger than the cream, pink and turquoise stripes put together. Consequently, I had foolishly and irreparably ordered two khaki sofas for a turquoise and cream room – making the whole look like a couple of camouflage tanks in a swimming pool. That was three years ago.

Since then, I haven't had the courage to re-order more sofas. I just can't take the decision. I've seen the ones I want. They're in a shop called 'Recline & Sprawl' at the bottom of Kings Road. They know me well in there. I pop in occasionally, look, measure up, take leaflets, mutter something unfathomable and leave. Then Jack does the same. Then Zelma pops in for a chat and a sit down. Then I return and go through the whole preamble again. It's neurotic, pathetic and lunatic. What we in the householder trade call the three 'ics'. And frankly, it's making me ic! (*sic*).

What's more, I've discovered that if I choose a very, very, very tightly woven fabric, then the cat doesn't shred a tear. Which narrows the choice down to a mere three thousand or so (all at £49 a metre!). Bless her, how much longer can she ... you know ... I mean, at nineteen, with one tooth and dodgy haunches ... you know? Still, she bobs along merrily, as my chum Lizzy is wont to say, and you can rest assured that if I splurge out on the £49 per metre, cat-proof, hand-woven by fallen women in Kurdistan, she'll wait for it to be delivered and, as the popping wrap is peeled away, give a strangled cry of disdain, like a guest at a New Year's Eve party, and expire on the velvet pile.

So, now I'm sitting on the floor looking at the walls.

Finally I get up and send for Roy Callow from Cornwall, a gentleman to his bootcaps, and a human poultice to a woman in a state of decorative turmoil. The samples, both fabric and paper, have reached a surfeit, a pinnacle, of indecision. The overmantel mirror is stuck with them, like so many Christmas invitations. There are checks behind the bedhead and stripes buddied to the pictures. Some of the samples have been there for years – the pictures get dusted and the samples re-stuck behind them.

I set a date for Roy's arrival and when he arrived I looked him in the eyes and said pathetically, 'What do *you* think?' Like the most seasoned psychotherapist he managed, by a painful process of elimination, to find out what I *didn't* want, and from there to try out samples of what I did want. Throughout, he lived with us, and when he finally left we were all bereft. Amy would ring from Manchester, saying, 'Is Roy still there?' and when we said yes, 'Oh – it's not fair – and I have to be here!' Adam, Jack, Roy and I solved every political and artistic dilemma every night over dinner. 'Roy knows everything,' said Adam one night. On VE weekend, when Roy had been repainting the paintwork, after a dodgy colour choice on my part, Jack took his violin, Adam his electric guitar and me my spoons and we serenaded him with songs from the forties.

Now I've got a dining-room washed in terracotta pink. It's fab. So good that when Mother saw it she made a single solitary and rather high-pitched 'Hmmmm'. I snapped out the light in fury and we all had to grope our way into the hall. I've a verdigris and cream dragged living-room which only took four or five days to get the right shade and a bedroom which frightened the both of us.

'This is the wallpaper, Roy,' I beamed. 'And I'm going away for four days. So put it up wherever you like, OK? Oh, and that blue we chose in the bathroom. It's wrong. It should have been "pigeon" and we got "duck" ... er. Bye.' The man's a saint. Saint Roy. I'm gonna get him canonized if I have to buy my own cannon.

Roger White, also from Cornwall (I suspect the hint of whimsy makes me feel secure), has brought curtain fabrics and I've chosen the bedroom and the living-room. Not that there's anything wrong with the living-room curtains; it's just that if I keep them I'll be unable to choose sofa fabrics for another four years. So something has to change to galvanize me and I think the change has to come from my pocket. I couldn't quite choose anything for the dining-room to go with the new terracotta walls, so I had the old ones cleaned, which cost the equivalent of my parents' first house. When we tried to hang them, we realized they were now four inches too short. I complained bitterly to the dry cleaner who came round a couple of weeks later and gently pointed out to me that the hooks had been replaced four lines too far down the heading and the curtains hadn't shrunk at all. Now the clean old curtains are crushing up nicely on the dining-room table, the new ones are in Penzance, the windows are curtainless and we're eating in the hall.

I'll tell you what – we'll move. And not to any of those derelict shells so beloved of *Gnomes and Gardens*: 'Jocelyn and Fern Dwyer-Anspliss stumbled upon this turn-of-the-century apricot distillery and with a little help from designer Selwyn Holmes Profiterole, they've turned it into a quasi-Florentine/Byzantine olive drab and tangerine working pottery and salvage store and home to Jocelyn and Fern's four children, Tristram, Flossie, China and Reject, three Afghans and a free range llama.'

Whoever's house we buy is going to have to have *exactly* my taste and to have refurbished the whole place but six months ago. I'm not changing a brass knocker! The only sample I ever intend to see again will be in the doctor's surgery with a cloth over it!

Meanwhile, I shall hand over the Hoover to Carmela, put on a blindfold and plunge back into the scruffy, chipped and highly over-painted world of show business.

Surprise Partly

Mother was going to be seventy. It was inevitable to everyone but mother. The line to Hull crackled with suggestions.

Me: Would you like to go to a health farm?
Mother: Nooooo! What for? I'm all right. I'm not even thinking about it.
Me: Would you like me to send you and Amy to Jersey for a week?
Mother: Nooooo! I don't want you to send me any-where. Honestly. I mean it. I'm just going to forget it. Why spend all that money for nothing?

Anyone less schooled in the art of the subliminal message could have accepted her emphatic denial as mere emphatic denial. After forty-six years at the Humberside College of Advanced Sub-Text, this cum laude graduate started planning the surprise party immediately.

Invitations were sent out a few weeks before the event: 'It is Zelma's Seventieth Birthday on 15 April. Zelma thinks no one knows this but herself and a man who once worked at Somerset House . . . For once, Zelma is wrong.'

It warned guests to enclose receipts with gifts, because the exchanging of them would be the best birthday present of all, and, when RSVPing, if Zelma, who was now staying with us, were to answer the phone, to please say they have phoned for her recipe for Stuffed Monkeys. No, it's not what you think – Zelma isn't a taxidermist. Heavens, no. She won't even take a mini-cab. No, Stuffed Monkeys are her speciality biscuits which are deliciously chewy, sit just above your windpipe for about a week and have as much resemblance to anything simian as I do. But I digress.

At this point, caterers were consulted, the event priced and the host and hostess given a warm milk and brandy. A hasty phone call secured the support of Judy Bastyra, neighbour and cookery writer. A planning meeting was planned and the codename 'Smiley's People' was agreed upon. The next time Judy rang and said 'Re Smiley's People', I thought she'd gone raving mad and said so.

There is no one on earth more blessed than I with good friends. Lynn is my Californian friend. We go running together of a morning when she hasn't got a bad knee and I haven't got a migraine, which means roughly the Wednesday before St Agnes Eve. This day we ran to The Balloon Shop and, £32 later, we ran out of money and ran home. The Balloon Shop! I ask you! Recession-ridden East Finchley shops opening and closing like a bridegroom's pyjama bottoms (you should pardon my language) and The Balloon Shop is thriving. (Since I wrote this it's gone up, up and away!)

The cake. A three-act drama involving dozens of eggs and a concept. It was to be a large Marks & Spencer's carrier bag with humorous lettering on the theme (Mum's relationship with the Customer Service Department being somewhat closer than Richard's relationship with Judy) of refundable cake. Lynn would make it. I would ice it. Astrid, my artistic American friend, would supervise. (By this time Zelma had arrived in London, so we had to tell her we were going for a run. A five-hour run. With a dozen eggs.) We arrived at Astrid's with no icing sugar and a migraine. Astrid iced. I sipped herbal tea with Nurofen and went off to my evening performance at the theatre, leaving Astrid to clear up a kitchen which looked like William Hill's after Grand National Day. Like I said, I'm blessed with my friends.

By now, the phone was ringing on a regular basis. I'd invited all her Hull friends whom I knew would be in London staying with their children, plus old friends of ours, plus the odd friend of hers who didn't mind getting on a dawn bus from Hull on a Sunday morning, plus my globetrotting brother from Brussels and his five children from the five corners of the world. This, with eight shows a week and one hard-pressed secretary, Jacquie, was faintly more foolish than challenging Anneka to a 'Who's got the tightest bum?' competition. There were seventy acceptances and that was before the 'I've got a guest staying ... Can I bring ...?' syndrome raised it to eighty-four.

Tables, chairs and helpers were hired, glasses and crockery borrowed and a speech written in between Acts I and II. Every time the phone rang at home, one of us grabbed it and immediately went into the garden, which was fine in mild weather but insane in the middle of a thunderstorm. The condemned woman appeared not to notice our indifference to inclement climes.

The birthday itself was a couple of days before Party Day. She was thrilled with her presents. She loved her cards and was only temporarily miffed by the lack of her son's presence and presents on the day. How could we tell her that that weekend all seven of them were coming over? And that he and his wife had given up an all-expenses paid trip to Hawaii in order to be with her? Still, by the evening, she was in merry mood as I drove her to see *Crazy For You*, the hottest ticket in town.

'How was it?' I asked later.

'Ye ... es, it was very good, you know, nice but daft. The scenery was *wonderful*!'

'How about the show itself?'

'Ye ... es ... you know ... it was a musical ... What can you say? Far-fetched.'

Two days to go and she still hadn't tumbled it. She met her chums for lunch at Selfridges, but the cat was still in the bag. Incredible. Driving her to town with Amy, I heard myself say, 'Jacquie's daughter is coming on Sunday.'

'Coming where?'

The British Museum came into sight. 'To ... to ... the exhibition!' I blurted.

'What exhibition?' Mother was on to it like a lurcher.

'The Georgia O'Keefe'/'The Turner' said Amy and I adamantly and simultaneously.

'I thought you had people to brunch,' she accused. I had earlier embarked on a fib that Tom Conti was coming over. This was to ensure that when Lynn took Zelma over to another friend, Lizzy, for Sunday morning coffee, she would dress as a woman of certain years might well dress for scrambled eggs with Shirley Valentine's rejuvenator.

'Yes ... Well ... *afterwards*! Oh, I don't know! I'm tired! We'll see!'

One night before the day after, I brought home a card from a friend. After another frantic day and twenty-two phone calls, I wasn't thinking and gave it to her. 'I'm so sorry I can't be with you at your party', it said.

'What party?' said Zelma.

'*Whatalovelycard!*' I yelled, snatching it, 'I *must* show Jack, *Ja-a-ck* ...' I ran from the room, stuffed the card behind a radiator and tried to give myself mouth-to-mouth resuscitation.

I slept fitfully and woke up stiff-necked like a meerkat. Mother came down. She wasn't well, she wasn't sure she could go out, she wondered if she should phone Lynn and cancel ... Poor woman, we had her dressed, made up and out the door before she could blow on her porridge. It was 10.15 am. At 10.30 am the massed brigade of Mothers in Support of Women with Mothers descended on Muswell Hill.

Salmons with cucumber scales fanned out beside Thai salads, tri-coloured rice and watermelon baskets of fruit salad. 'Groan' said the table. Flower arrangements flowered, three charming Irish girls set up a helium pump in the hall and balloons ballooned, and the cake was smuggled in, Astrid still licking food colourant from her leggings. Ice clattered into a dustbin, wine cooled. The sun came out, outside furniture was hosed down, inside furniture arranged by me and re-arranged by Jack . . . A hush fell. One o'clock prompt and the first guests crept stagily in . . . the story of Zelma's where-abouts was told seventy times, Jack positioned himself on the stairs with the video, Adam tried to tell him how to use it. 1.40: no sign of Lynn and Zelma. I rang Lizzy. She said they'd gone to a deli in St John's Wood . . . my heart began to Lambada . . .

'Quick, they're here! Everyone into the two rooms save Geoff's family and ours. She's walking down the road.'

'It won't start! It won't work!' – Jack on the video.

'Turn it on, dad' – Adam on automatic pilot.

'RRRRing!' – the door bell. My heart and I opened the door and Louie Ramsay ducked in hissing 'She's seen me, I'm late, oh shit!' before being yanked into the kitchen.

This time, when the bell rang, it was Zelma. 'Geoffrey! Phillip! Mei-Mei! Joey!' her voice could get no higher, but did. Then out burst the Hull contingent. 'Nora! Ruby! Rae! Helen! Aaaargh!' Jodrell Bank must surely have been on the alert . . . 'David! Kim! Aaagh! Look at the baby!' Lynn and I hugged each other. 'We did it, we did it!'

In my speech I ran through her early life; her first stage role at The College of Commerce School in *The Marvellous History of St Bernards*; her appearance, 'Oooh, I was beautiful! I had the most gorgeous curly hair!'; her first boyfriend; her first job at the aircraft factory when all the men would whistle the Laurel and Hardy theme as she walked through their ranks, head down, face purple; the time, shortly after her marriage to my father, when he took her to a film at the Regal Cinema, found the film boring enough to head out for a game of snooker, then went home and couldn't for the life of him think where the hell the wife could have got to.

There were tributes, too, for her bravery and care looking after Dad, then her sister-in-law, Rita, till the end, and special greetings, surprisingly enough, from the Customers' Exchange Point at Marks & Spencer's, Debenhams and Binns of Hull, and the makers of Radoxon and Woolworths' 'Pic 'n mix'.

A video machine was then brought in, to her patent horror, with a label which read:

> No, you won't have to shlepp it back to Hull, it will
> be driven!
> Yes, you will be able to work it.
> Yes, it does have a device like Lily's got, for recording
> while you are away.
> Yes, there *are* tapes included!

Her delight was now transparent, so Jack added, 'and the first instalment's due in July!'

(It worked. Since Zelma moved into her new flat, there isn't a single inhabitant who hasn't been subjected to the twin indoctrination ceremony of the video of *Re: Joyce!*, an interval of tea and cake, and *My Seventieth Party*, starring Z Lipman. I try not to think about it, as I get a bit hot around the ears.)

The final presentation was six advanced driving lessons to lessen the chance of, once again, backing out of the drive into her own back wall, involving lengthy insurance actions on car and wall.

The loveliest part of the video is the sight of everyone who knows and loves her, rocking with laughter and clutching at each other with recognition. And no one laughed more than the Golden Girl herself.

Déja View

Synchronicity, agree my Chambers and Oxford dictionaries, is to coincide in time, but how random is it? Whenever my holistic daughter and I exclaim our amazement at some impossible coincidence, you can rely on her scientifically inclined sibling to say 'Yes, but think of the billions of times it *didn't* happen.'

Take last week when I went to the dentist for the regular scale and polish. When I say regular, I mean as in annual or even bi-annual if the press haven't started describing me as 'brunette, brown-toothed Beattie'. In uptight mood, then, I was parking my car in Sloane Street, when I was accosted by a chicly dressed stranger who said in accented tones, 'Oh my goodness! Just the person I wanted. I am a fan of yours – we are coming to see your play. But tell me – have you got a second...?'

'Well, actually, I'm late for the dentist and...'

'One *second*. You see my son is being Bar Mitzvahed and I need to have some satin shoes dyed to go with the dress – where do I go?'

I told her. She wrote it down. I said, 'Must dash, I've got a ...' I pantomimed madly towards my mouth and escorted my firmly gritted teeth into the grit removery.

Later that same day, I was driving home with a zingingly confident mouth when I was accosted again, this time by a black velvet dress in a shop in Chiltern Street. No, really – I mean *accosted*. It waved its wide satin collar at me saying 'Pay your card right and you can have me' in a velvety voice, until my Honda juddered to a halt two and a half streets away like

27

Circe and Ulysses on wheels. Once inside the shop I knew that serious damage was about to be done, since almost every other garment in the shop was waving at me in similar fashion.

No time to take off boots, leggings and 'body' – the designer pinned me into the dress regardless of them. At which point a customer came in, to choose, it goes without saying, a dress for a Bar Mitzvah and it took all of twelve seconds' resistance before I was beside her discussing the vagaries of various velvets. The assistant came up from the bowels of the boutique, Willie Mossop style, only French, to triumphantly display a bale of exquisite lilac, rose and cream lace. No sooner was it across her bosom than I heard my mouth exclaim, 'No. It's ageing. Makes you look like Miss Haversham.' Willie Mossop was not best pleased. The bale he carried was nothing to the baleful look on his brow.

It ended spectacularly with me, in leggings, leg warmers and heavy boots, modelling a forest green velvet, floor-length gown (which they had in my size but not, alas, in hers). It looked great on us. 'You're my second Bar Mitzvah of the day,' I told her archly. 'I was just parking my car when . . .' It was at this point that I remembered I'd fed my parking meter enough to do forty minutes worth of sartorial damage only.

There may have been funnier sights in the Baker Street vicinity than a woman with a numb lip in floor-length halter-necked green velvet pinned at the back, lace-up boots, leg warmers and flapping green parka legging it two blocks waving a five-pound note at passing strangers and muttering ' 'Ave you got change of a . . . ?' but frankly, I doubt it.

Two dresses and a three-piece trouser suit later, I drove, fuelled by guilt, through the rush hour in the rain in the vain hope of seeing my son for eighteen minutes before setting out for the night shift at the Old Vic. To quell my racing mind, I turned on the radio to hear a familiar tune. An overfamiliar tune. One which had gone irritatingly around my head for the months of out of town touring pre-London previews and short-lived West End run. I wasn't *in* the musical but my husband wrote the book and still has the bitten nails to prove it. The song I was listening to was from the score of a little missed musical entitled *Bar Mitzvah Boy.*

'So what?' said my son as I plonked down the evidence of a sort of Karaoke Kismet at work. 'How many times have you spent the day sanding Norwegian wood and turned on the radio to hear "Lily the Pink"?'

He's right, of course. Still, we girls continue to marvel at the vast eternal plan which has us erroneously seeing an old friend in a crowd twice in one morning, only to actually bump into the friend later on the top of a bus, or wake up thinking of the sender of the very first letter you open, or finish your loved one's unexpected sentence simultaneously, then both say 'That's weird'.

There are countless stories of twins separated at birth who turn up to meet each other, aged fifty, in the same dress, having both married a man called Zebediah, lost a finger in a mincing machine and called their dogs Giblet and mostly we take these claims with a pinch of Lot's wife but I must tell you that I witnessed my husband's meeting after thirty years with a cousin, Alex, with whom he'd been very close as a child and who'd left for Israel in 1948.

When they met they were wearing the same jacket. More interestingly, they were both in the middle of reading books about Blackpool landladies, both had pictures of Manchester trams on the wall and, best of all, they both collected rhinoceroses. What's more, I felt the same age-old familiarity with Alex that I felt the day I met his cousin, Jack.

My brother, who out-scepticizes his nephew, my son, was once running to take an elevator in a hotel in Canada. 'Hold the lift!' he called to the young, male inhabitant of the lift. Once inside, the Canadian commented on his English accent and asked where he lived. When Geoff told him he was originally from Hull in Yorkshire, the Canadian said, 'I believe I have a distant cousin in Yorkshire – don't suppose you know him – name of Geoff Lipman.'

And it goes on even when you're not looking for it. Last week at a photo shoot for my new television series, *Agony*

Again, the make-up artist failed to turn up (Coward! Couldn't face the challenge, eh?) and a lovely New Zealander called Fiona Fletcher was beeped in on her mobile. While she erased and improved me we talked holiday, as you do.

'I'm driving down to Cornwall for a week,' I told her.

'Oh, I've just got back from showing my parents Cornwall. They originated from there and wanted to see my grand-father's birthplace. Whereabouts are you going?'

'Oh, it's a tiny place inland called Helston, just a quiet hotel and...'

'That's where he was born! We've just been given the freedom of the "City" of Helston. My grandfather was the boxer, Bob Fitzsimmons, the undefeated champion of...'

'Wow! Wait till I tell Jack that...' I didn't know whether to be more excited about the coincidence or the boxer. Jack used to box in his youth and was quite promising but had to give up because his mouth kept bleeding so badly – sometimes even before he'd been hit. The mystery was solved when his trainer discovered that the connection of buck teeth and his own defending glove was what the blood letting was all about. I think he gave up his attempt at a world title round about then. Coincidentally.

Bridling Visibly

Apparently most women rush to get married for one reason only. No, not the shotgun, but the show gown. No matter whether they have been living with their partner for seven years, had several children and a change of washing machine, when it comes to the formalities themselves it's the old, flowing symbol of purity, plus train, starting price £800 which they covet and desire.

Let's take a stand on ceremonies. If you are concerned about buying a dress you can be married in but wear again afterwards, don't be. You won't. Wear it again. You'll *almost* wear it, then sentiment will take over and you'll wrap it lovingly, or if the marriage turns out to be a fiasco, viciously, in polythene, until the day comes for your daughter to walk down an aisle. Then you'll proffer it, bashfully, to she who scours your everyday wardrobe for everything from 'kinky' boots to 'grandma' vests and she'll hurl scorn over your lack of style and get married in black rubber jodhpurs and a chin ring.

Don't invite everyone you are working with at the time to the exclusion of those you think you've grown out of, because in a couple of years' time you'll have grown out of this lot too. Your childhood chums will be there through thick and even thicker if you'll let them. Do invite all ages and generations and mix them up in the table plan. You'll be amazed how well mothers and daughters get on when they're not related to each other.

Make sure your speech makers at the 'do' can speak. Very

little is worse than the lurching best man cracking endless 'in jokes' about the groom's ability to drink a yard and a half of lager out of a suit of armour on fishing trips to the Orkneys. Speeches should be written, not improvised, and sincerity is as important as humour, unless you happen to be marrying Bob Monkhouse, in which case you can sit down and shut up for an hour and a half. Don't let the groom knock the future mother-in-law. It's *booring.* Nor send around a collection plate to send her on holiday, '... and don't forget, the more you give, the further we can send her!'

Do try, as a parent, not to inflict your own tension and nervous dyspepsia on your child. Let them have their own. Remember Neil Simon's *Plaza Suite* when daughter, Mimsy, in full bridal gown, locks herself in the bathroom and refuses to budge in spite of the tears, travails and damn near cardiac arrest of both parents? Finally, the groom is the one to prise her out of her self-imposed prison with the words 'Mimsy. Cool it.'

I've seen fathers gripping their daughters' arms so tightly that the blood drains out of their lacy wrists. I've heard them audibly whispering, 'Smile, for Christ's sake, just keep on smiling!'

It is important for the couple to be allowed to marry in their own style, unless a purely traditional ceremony is agreed upon by all. So when a friend of your father's suggests a baronial manor with four-poster beds and 400-year-old tapestries for the honeymoon at a reduced rate because there's a Furtwängler Appreciation Convention on that week, it may be best to politely refuse and stick to the Don Pepe in Torremolinos. My husband and I ended up in Bognor Regis for that very reason. In February. I mean, it's good to have something to look back on and laugh, but a *honeymoon?*

The Presents. Have a list. I thought having a list was bourgeois and demeaning. I didn't realize in those balmy post-60s days that it was also time-saving and commonsense.

Thus, I received twenty-two stainless steel platters and a lot of abuse from salesgirls when I tried to return them to the wrong shops.

This may seem obvious, but do marry someone you like. Love is a devilish cocktail of chemicals and conditioning and your hormones are in no condition to sift judgement from pleasure. If Ms/Mr Right at the engagement party is cursory to your parents, patronizing to your friends and over-monopolizes you at the expense of your personal growth, then they are Ms/Mr Seriously Wrong. There are thousands of women, and undoubtedly some men, out there who honestly believed at the altar that they, and only they, could alter their loved one by the application of diplomacy, understanding and the laying on of hands.

This is known as a mercy marriage and, since it exhibits both arrogance and lack of self-esteem, refuges are full of the casualties of such unions.

Finally, let me confess to you bonny and blushing brides and grooms that for twenty-four years I have been asked, *ad nauseam*, what is the secret of keeping a marriage contentedly bobbing along, particularly in a showbiz setting, for so long.

It's like saying to the winner of the lottery, 'How did you do it?' There's no recipe, no magic ingredient, although humour helps. A little pride in each other, a lot of patience, your own front door, the odd shared interest, a healthy ability to argue without sulking, and a healthy but not overly-lecherous libido ... My husband doesn't dance, doesn't drink, doesn't know a brown sock from a green one and holds his breath alarmingly when reversing a car, but he laughs at my jokes and he's always the man I'm glad to be leaving the party with; and I apologize for ending with a preposition. Like Pompidou, he is a man with a centre.

Also, if you are planning on having children, don't marry one. And don't invite *me* to the wedding because I tend to start crying when the invitation arrives.

A year ago the actor George Baker married my dearest

friend, Louie Ramsay, his screen wife in the Wexford mysteries. It was a marriage made in Devon, as I said, rather
contrivedly, on his *This Is Your Life*, and my non-appearance
as Matron of Honour at their wedding is one of my more
impractical jokes. Louie has been part of our lives since we
spent three happy years together at the Old Vic in 1970. She
was 'Best Woman' at our wedding and we were best friends
to her when she went through an incredibly painful divorce,
which left her breathless but determined to rebuild her life
and renew her self-confidence. All of which she did quite
brilliantly. Simply, to know Louie is to love her and I for one
was alarmingly confident that her co-star, George, would do
just that when he recovered from the loss of his beloved wife,
Sally, the year before.

When they actually announced their intention to marry,
and, further, asked me to speak at the wedding, I was over-
whelmed with pride. I knew I would be in Edinburgh, where
I was directing my first play, but planes fly near to Wiltshire,
don't they? I would be there. Wild horses wouldn't stop me
... no, but wild kippers might ... the date of the wedding
was Yom Kippur – the most holy day of the year in the Jewish
calendar and the one I always adhere to. Wherever I am (and
I've been in some funny bloody places, I can tell you), I fast
for twenty-four hours to atone for the rotten things I wish I
hadn't done all year. It does me good and I need to do it. I've
fasted on a film set in Dublin, a rehearsal room in Waterloo,
a *pensione* in Italy and a clapboard villa in Connecticut. As
Joyce Grenfell recalled when she was trapped in a lift for
some hours, 'Wherever we are, we are always in the same
place, because we are always in the presence of God.' Or, as
Jack wrote in *Bar Mitzvah Boy*, when the thirteen-year-old
performed his Bar Mitzvah portion standing on his head in a
playground, 'Hamacoum means "place" meaning *every* place,
meaning everywhere, meaning God. God means anywhere,
everywhere. A synagogue, a bedroom, a battlefield, a playground ... you did the full portion Eliot? ... In my view,
Eliot is now Bar Mitzvah.'

Even with Hamacoum, I couldn't make it on the day, a combination of migraine and Atonement, which some might say are the same thing, and the groom Mr Baker himself delivered my speech from the hall staircase in my absence. I understand it was a devastating impersonation and brought the house down:

> I'd like to state that, with the possible exception of the groom and the best man, if there is another person in this room, town, county or universe who is happier for this particular bride than I am, I would like to challenge them to a nude wrestling-in-chopped-liver match, and I would win.
>
> For no one else on earth, with the possible exception of Harrison Ford, would I have travelled on Yom Kippur, the Day of Atonement, so far and so hungrily to see someone given away. Only Louie, bless her, could have so arranged things. After I'd gone through months of agonizing phone calls:
>
> Ring, ring ... 'Well, has he phoned?'
>
> 'No, honestly, Mo, there's nothing in it, really. We're just happy to be good friends ... really, Mo, no. I'm just so happy that he feels he can rely on me as a friend.'
>
> Ring, ring ... 'Well, have you heard from him?'
>
> 'Oh, just a note from Australia, he's having a very nice time with his family.'
>
> Ring, ring ... 'Well, is he back? Have you seen him?'
>
> 'We're having dinner.'
>
> 'Aaagh. I knew it!'
>
> 'No, Mo. Honestly! Just to chat about his holiday.'
>
> Ring, ring ... 'I didn't find out about his holiday but I found out he loves me ... and we're getting married.'
>
> Tears were streaming down my face, my chest, my knees. 'Oh, Lou. When?'

'25 September – and you have to be my Matron of Honour.'

Tears hit my sandals and squelched over the parquet. 'Oh, Lou. There's nothing on earth that would stop me. 25 September did you say? OH MY GOD! I was right, nothing on earth – that just leaves Heaven, Louie – it's Yom Kippur, I can't come!'

So I rang Rabbi Hugo Gryn – a man you could lay on an open wound – and told him my predicament.

'Well, Maureen,' he said, after a sage suggestion or two. 'Let us look at the word Atonement. Look at it carefully,' he said. 'It could also be read At-*one*-ment and from what you've told me, that one-ness was meant and is in itself a blessing.'

And no one who knows these two people could doubt that today is a blessing, nor that their happiness is not at one with all that is good in life and all that is meant. I haven't known George very long, but I think that to know him at all is to love him.

As for Louie, I've known her since 1969 and all my life since we met at the Old Vic and survived John Dexter together. We both had parts in that epoch-shattering musical, *Tyger*, the story of William Blake – can there be anyone here who can't summon up at will six or seven of their favourite numbers from *Tyger*? Louie and I have essayed the roles, probably our most definitive and well-loved characterizations of the Second and Third Randy Women. We represented Blake's erotic conversion when he wrote for sexual help to a box number. It was a plywood box on wheels containing we Three Fantasies, who, after a heavy baked bean supper in the Old Vic canteen, teetered out fragrantly and sang libidinous verses.

I was wearing hot pants and Louie was in wall-

to-wall black bondage leather and stilettos. Harold
Hobson had to be put on a life-support machine.

We were together for three hilarious and wonderful years at the National and she was Best Woman
at my marriage to the man who's at this moment
busy atoning for both of us somewhere in West
London.

At the wedding, Louie made the day by singing
'Happiness is Just a Thing called Mo'. I wanted to
return the compliment today, but it's not so easy
with her given name.

> Happiness is just a thing called Louie
> Sainsbury's Puff-Puff Pastry is too chewy.
>
> Happiness is just a thing called Louie
> I'll meet yer half past five outside the brewery.
>
> Happiness is just a thing called Louie
> Weddings always render me boo-hooey.
>
> Happiness is just a thing called Louie
> Napisan stops diapers smelling pooey.
>
> Happiness is just a thing called Louie-sh
> 'Ame that Jack can't be here but he's Jewish.

And if those phone calls ever stop, I'll be dev-
astated. All those phone calls – she's, bless her, the
world's number one apologizer.

Ring, ring . . . 'Is that you, Mo? Oh, sorry! Is this
a bad time? Oh God, I'm such a fool. Sorry, you
must be eating. Sorry, Mo – won't take a minute . . .
Look, I'll ring again when – I'm *so* sorry. Look, I'll
ring you back when you . . . Oh, it's Louie, sorree,
darling – senility – you know how it is . . . '

I've got it!

Happiness *is* just a thing called Baker
And now I'm off to square things with my Maker.

Well, I've seen the video of George reading my speech and he's a dead ringer for me. In fact, if Bob Hoskins ever gets tired of the BT ads, there's comeback potential in having a very tall, very butch Beattie with a west country burr and a Panama.

Let It All Hang In

I was sucking the toe of an ex-presidential candidate recently, when the mobile rang. I switched on the descrambler and in a heavy Columbian accent said, 'chello'. It was someone asking me to talk about my recent conversion to Islam on a morning television show alongside a heavy metal rock star who'd given up smoking Odor-Eaters, and an international cover girl who recently admitted on national TV that she'd been abused as a toddler by the village nit nurse.

I mean, what in the global village is going on? Is it really better out than in, as the defrocked bishop said to the soft porn actress, or has confession become nothing more than a sound career move?

Let she who is without stones throw the first sin. Well, all right. Some years ago I participated in a programme called *Mothers by Daughters* and to my amazement, whilst talking quite animatedly to a sympathetically inclined Bel Mooney, my eyes filled up to the brim as I touched on something touching and I blubbed all over my lilac mohair sweater, without missing a cue or slipping a syllable. In fairness, I had no idea I was going to do it. I thought it would just be a few affectionate quotes and the odd deadly impersonation. But no. I learned something that day: that nothing makes better television than slow pain on fast exposure.

'Do you want to stop?' asked Bel, sincerely.

'No-o-ooo. I'm OK ... sniff ... sorry ... no, carry on, really, sniff, I'm fine ...' The show, of course, must go on and even if it doesn't, they can edit round the gap. Let's face it, I must have been aware, even in my lachrymosity, that

39

cracking good TV was being made. I've never had such a mailbag, before or since, and all from people identifying with feelings that I had thought were entirely personal. 'It was so wonderful to hear someone actually saying what I'd only ever *thought*.' 'I couldn't believe what you said about your mother. It could have been me talking!'

Which left me wondering. Should it take a revelation from a total stranger to reveal your own heartache? If so, then, what are best friends for? And priests? And shrinks? And good literature? And *mothers*, for God's sake?

Here we are, the generation who buy our magazines for headlines like 'The great swallowing debate: should we or shouldn't we?' and 'Your orgasm: is it enough?' Who supply boysenberry-flavoured condoms to our sixteen-year-olds and shout 'Gerremoff' at oiled Chippendales. And really, we are no more able to communicate our deep-seated problems than were our great-grandparents. Or perhaps we just can't distinguish between fact and faction – truth and *True Confessions*.

Look at the sales of *Hello!* It's almost a guarantee that appearing in this schmaltzy update of *Photoplay*, in the company of your partner and progeny, in the shade of your own collection of porcelain artichoke steamers, will ensure that, within days of publication, your husband will have bolted with the second cousin of the ex-King of Mesopotamia, your children will be in drug rehab learning to get in touch with their forceps delivery, and your daily will be selling your sordid story to the dailies. Nevertheless, the rich and the near-rich will continue to queue up for entry – 'Oh yes, I'd be happy with the black smudgy pages at the back. *More* than happy' – and the public will continue to buy their copy the second it hits the newsagent's lower shelf. They want to conjecture. They want to empathize. How Cindy Costner is coping. Has Liz's face caved in? Has Ivana played her last Trump? Will Princess Stephanie have anything in common with her bodyguard after the afterbirth? Morbid curiosity is the weekly lure, whilst prurient curiosity is the order of the daily.

A few weeks ago I had the dubious pleasure of watching something called the *Sally Jesse Raphael* show on Sky (no I *haven't* got it but I have politically incorrect friends who have) and there was a riveting interview with three women with hair like surf spray, skirts like pelmets and six of the most perfectly symmetrical and unnaturally inflated mammary glands ever gathered together in one space at one time. The interview, accompanied by giggles and close physical contact from the participants and spontaneous applause from the studio audience, concerned the affair of the second pair (SP) of breasts with the husband of the first pair (FP) of breasts while she, FP, was drying out in an addiction clinic, and the ensuing close friendship which developed between the a-four mentioned women. The third PoB was there, I presumed, because she was the best friend of SP and because she was interchangeable with either of the other two. We didn't actually see the obscure object of their desire, the husband, but we heard him 'down the line' admitting that he found the friendship of the two women 'kinda weird'. The audience and Sally Jesse just *lurved* it though, and whooped and 'whe-heyed' their approval for the women's up-front, as it were, confession. 'I wuz blind, but now ah see...'

Yes. Betty Ford has a lot to answer for, apart from the Liz Taylor/Larry Fortensky (now ya see it, now ya don't) marriage. At these clinics they teach you to get in touch with yourself, to clean up your act, to take responsibility for your own life – then, like Liza Minelli, you can go out and incorporate it into your stage act.

I mean, *must* we know what amused Mona Lisa? Whatever happened to imagination, for Heaven's sake? I'd be just as happy to believe that she was suppressing a grin at something her mother-in-law said over the fuselli, or that she'd found a way of clenching her stomach muscles just to give her something to do while that Mr da Vinci went on and on telling those terrible old jokes of his than any

amount of pedantic speculation on with whom she may or
may not have spent the previous night in a cabana on the
Lido.

How much more interesting and satisfying to kiss and *not*
tell, or even kiss and tell something completely different.
What's so appealing about revealing? The child who will
loudly and ingenuously inquire, 'Mummy, why has that lady
got a beard?' will not necessarily answer as frankly when you
ask whether she likes school or not. 'I like the jelly!' she
may say, and we'll all laugh and ignore the fact that it's a
diversionary statement.

Once in the public eye you quickly learn to field the inevitable questions asked by the public at large ... like 'How do
you learn your lines?' (the thespian equivalent of asking Albert
Roux how he turns his oven on), and the inevitable, 'Has
anyone ever told you how much younger/prettier/thinner you
look in real life?' (Yes. Everyone. And I'd much rather look
younger, prettier and thinner to twelve million viewers.) And,
'How do you manage being a wife and mother *and* an actress?'
Answer: badly.

Then there are the questions that journalists ask you, to fill
a small gap between an article about Regal colonic irrigation
and a colour picture of Dawn French on a day bed. They
come accompanied by a faxed replica of the same questionnaire as completed by Mariella Frostrup in last week's
issue and the Dalai Lama in the week's before, and a fulsome
note from the journalist saying, 'I know you must be very
busy with requests like these, but ...' Usually one fills 'em in
last thing at night with *Eurotrash* corroding the brain on the
cathode ray tube, a plate of banana on toast and the prospect
of a day off.

Q: *What word or phrase do you most overuse?*
A: 'Yes.'
Q: *How does a girl know when she's really a woman?*
A: 'When she compares her wage packet with a
     fellow doing the same job.'

Q: *What really bores you?*
A: 'Questionnaires.'

Not too difficult the questions. Not overly interesting the answers. But what would *you* do if you received the *Express* Questionnaire, as I did, a few weeks ago? 'It is lighthearted,' said the letter, 'and in the best possible taste.'

Oh yes? It began with an aphrodisiac question which I could easily have answered by pleas to the poacher to lay off killing the rhino for the lacklustre quality of its horn, but I doubted whether too many poachers read the *Express* and those who did would write me off as a leftist 'My hair extensions are not tested on voles' loony. I left a gap in which I doodled a drunken-looking frizzy-haired beast whom I later christened Afro-dizzy Yak, and continued downhill.

The second question was: *Barbara Cartland and Debbie Reynolds waited until their wedding night. Where and when did you lose your virginity?* Now the truth might be interesting since he was the handsomest man I've ever seen, before or since, and I was so flattered and shattered that he chose *me* that to this day I swear I was unconscious throughout, so instead I wrote: 'I was queuing up in Waitrose for a pound and a half of coley for the cat's tea, when I happened to notice it was gone. I rang King's Cross Lost Property only to be told that anything not reported missing for thirty years would probably have been sold.'

The next question was *Do you think sex cures insomnia?* Since the truth is that my old man can fall asleep mid-sentence, mid-flossing – mid-riff even – and I tend to require forty or fifty minutes' good solid mental filing of every worry, panic, deadline or fear of retribution I have in the world before I slip soundlessly into full, threshing about REM, I thought long and hard before writing, 'I find my insomnia is at its peak whilst I'm having sex.'

I was beginning to enjoy this: next please.

How many lovers do you admit to? I counted them up. It was enough to send my mother into a retreat from which she would only emerge dressed as the Invisible Man. On the other hand it was pathetic compared to most of my girlfriends with whom I'd shared many a bragging, comparing and scoring night on the Glühwein. How many lovers do I admit to? I took the Bic between my teeth and wrote 'I admit to all my lovers, and so far they've been very understanding about it.' The nice thing about this questionnaire was that patently no one was ever going to use one word of my cocky replies. Onwards.

What is the most flattering thing you've ever been told in bed? I would have loved to give them 'You are the best', but, instead I wrote, 'Darling, he's done a fabulous scar!'

By now I was in great danger of having what can best be described as a good time . . .

'Whoever loved that loved not at first sight' quoth Shakespeare. Do you believe in sex on the first night? Thoughts of this took me back to the handsomest man I ever met, and I had to put my head in the ice-making compartment of the fridge. I came out covered in Ben & Jerry's blueberry and pistachio, but otherwise fine and wrote, 'Personally, I'm usually so nervous on a first night – what with the critics and the reviews and everything – that I try not to have sex until after the curtain call.'

And now for the next question in this crucial cultural assessment of man's most basic, pre-Sharon-Stone-age, instinct: *If you woke up in the morning to find you had changed sex, what would be the first thing you would do?* Yes, you got it in one: 'Phone my wife.'

So, penultimately, *Where and when was your most memorable sexual experience on holiday?* 'There's no comedic competition here, it was, without question, the breakfast buffet at the King David Hotel in Jerusalem. Don't believe me? Don't knock it till you've tried it . . . and perfectly permissible between consenting adults in the privacy of someone else's dining-room.

And now the end is nigh and as I reach the final question: *When do the partners you have had sex with* (sic) *say they lost their virginity, and . . . and . . . do you think they were lying?*

Clearly what is patently wrong with my erstwhile happy sex life is that I never took a clipboard to bed with me. So I'm forced to fabricate again and devil take the hairy palms: 'Mostly they say it was Michaelmas Eve 1964 after a heavy Lamb Pasanda and a crate of Advocaat 'neath an inky sky, in the back seat of a Reliant Robin.' *Do you think they were lying?* 'Partially, and partially squatting.'

I can't help wondering as I post off the coupon, whether *anyone* answered this absurd questionnaire earnestly and, if so, why? Looking back through all of the ones I've kept over the years I came across a slightly more original question than usual. It said 'Can you sum yourself up in not more than fifteen words?' and, underneath, someone, who I can only assume was me, had written: 'She told everything and revealed nothing. With laughs.'

Personally, I think one of the unsung virtues of our times is stoicism. I'm all for a bit of quiet bottling up. It may stall your career, it may even decimate your dreams and eventually come out as a cluster migraine, but it stimulates the creative juices and saves the kids the embarrassment of turning on the telly, opening up the tawdry tabloids or being persecuted in the playground when Mummy's felt the need to tell that nice radio psychiatrist that she used to have afternoon love-ins with Cary Grant dressed as an oven-ready chicken and that she began life as a stevedore called Dwayne in Nantucket.

The Return of
'Raising Arizona'

I wonder if any of you remember the piece called 'Raising Arizona' from my last book, *When's It Coming Out?* It concerned a young man who stopped me in the street in Muswell Hill and told me that the love of his life, an American girl called Robyn, was going back to Arizona and that he didn't think he could live without her.

He was, in a tentative but sweet way, asking me for £400 to cover the trip. Robyn was mortified by this gentle high-waymanism and, not for the first or the last time, I ended up taking their address with the intention of helping them.

Back at the house, I was in tears, recounting to the family Robyn's reply when I said, 'What are you going to *do* with him in Arizona?'

'Oh, I dunno,' she'd smiled shyly. 'Just love him, I guess . . .'

'They could be Romeo and Juliet,' I'd blubbed.

'Or Bonnie and Clyde,' replied Jack gently.

'Run after them,' said Amy dramatically. 'It's a unique opportunity to change someone's life.'

'Why didn't you just tell them to sod off?' said Adam, all heart.

So. What did I do? First I lost the address, then I wrote about it for *She* magazine and at the end I said, 'My fee for writing this should cover your air fare . . . Write to me.' Months later, on Irish TV, I told their story and waited to hear. Nothing happened.

Last year I received a letter, stamped Arizona. It was from Peter:

Dear Mrs Lipman,

Hi, this is a letter from the skinny hippy boy who stopped you in the street and asked you for money. As you see from the postmark, I did make it to Arizona.

Robyn (my lover) went back to the US, as planned, a few days later and then, I don't know how, but after about two months I managed to get the air fare together and left with the rucksack on my back. It was a very exciting and packed time of experiences. When I landed in the US without any money, the customs officers zeroed in on me and were going to deport me on the next flight which was scary. However, in the end I convinced the head guy to let me stay and on I went to Phoenix.

It was great to be with Robyn and we spent a few weeks getting back together before we married on 2 July 1992. Then we went through another palaver trying to get the paperwork done so I could stay. Of course eventually it was and we could get on with our lives.

Now I work as a clerk in a hospital and Robyn has gone back to University to study and become a psychotherapist. These have been the happiest times of my life and so you could say this is one of those 'and they lived happily ever after' stories. We get along together really well.

I feel there are a few things I should say about me asking you for money. I don't know that it was right or wrong and it's not a thing I've done before or since. It seemed a good idea at the time.

The fact that you didn't feel right about giving money was fine with me and totally understandable. In the same shoes I would probably have done the same. What was really neat for me was that you took the time to listen to my story and had empathy with it. That was really important and gave you a place of fond remembrance with me for ever.

Despite my impositioning you, you listened and offered me this, and that's what's needed in the world.

Well, I don't mean to preach. Apparently you said that this meeting had remained in your conscience, wondering whether you did right or not. I wanted you to know it was right because that was the way you felt at the time.

Well, I guess this is all I have to say.

I hope that you and your family are in good health and wish you luck in whatever you do.

Lots of love,

Peter

I wrote back to him:

Dear Peter,

I can't tell you how delighted I was to receive your letter. It really gave the whole story a poignant and beautiful ending and I'm so pleased that you're married and happy. I'm doubly pleased because it confirms my faith in my own bullshit meter. In other words, I really knew that you were honest and that your intentions were all good just by talking to you. But I didn't trust my instincts and it's nice to know that they were right.

I'm sending you a copy of my book because in it you'll see your story under the heading 'Raising Arizona' which I originally wrote for *She* magazine. I kind of expected you to get in touch with me after the article was printed but I guess *She* magazine was probably not your kind of rag. Still, at least in my next book I can tell everybody the happy ending, if you don't mind.

Lots of love to Robyn. I hope the hospital work is interesting and will lead to other interesting work and please do keep in touch as I would very much like to know how you're getting along. I'm enclosing a little wedding gift.

All best wishes,

Maureen Lipman

Training Cats and Dogs

I've never had a dog. As such. We didn't have any as children because they were not Dralon-friendly. One Saturday night my dad, a tailor, brought home a pup which someone had brought into the shop, probably in lieu of payment for a Prince of Wales check hacking jacket or a bale of Terylene mix. The pup was black and white and had already shown its aversion to Morris Oxfords by sprinkling the passenger seat halfway down the road back from town.

My mother took one look at him and did the only thing a woman of mature sensibilities could do under such circumstances. She had hysterics. Furnishing fabrics, the life expectancy and spiralling costs thereof, were brought into play. Axminster carpets were invoked, mounds of shedding hair touched upon. Mention was made, more than once, of 'Who'd end up feeding it? Who'd have to schlepp it for walks?' and, most pertinent of all, 'Who'd be cleaning up its neverending lorry load of "you know what"?' This led to finger pointing at certain inhabitants of the house who never lifted them (fingers, that is) or cleaned out *jet black* rings from baths, or even Blanco'd their own plimsolls!

The innocent victims of these slanderous accusations began to bleat their protests. Their protests turned into full-scale demos. Satchels were flung. Doors slammed. Minor bashings ensued. 'S'not fair,' they wailed. 'S'like everything else in this house!' Everybody in their entire classes, their entire school, the whole world and Hessle Foreshore had a dog. Some had five! And terrapins! How could the accused possibly learn a sense of responsibility if they had nothing to be responsible

for? *Of course* they'd clean up after it ... or ... they'd train it
to do it in the garden – o-oh, bad move ... hadn't the garden
just been nicely asphalted over to prevent other dogs from
popping in, uninvited, to drop off their calling cards? *Cack
On My Asphalt*, a slim volume by a woman never parted from
her Domestos bottle, sprang to mind.

It was all over – bar the cowering. The puppy cowered,
Dad cowered, we cowered. A coward would've cowered
against such determined opposition. The dog dematerialized.
Dad sulked for a few days, his tail between his legs. Mother
told the same story with magnificent additions over the phone
for twenty-four hours. My brother was eventually lured back
with egg and chips and red jelly. I stayed in my room, sucking
the place where they'd *nearly* hit me until it turned into a
truly hideous blood blister which took weeks to heal. That'd
show 'em.

Of course I may not have been good dog material. I may
never know. I was always scared stiff of Alsatians. There was
a short cut through to the back of the houses which entailed
passing a fence, behind which prowled next door but two's
Alsatian. He had one job in life. To bark. And he was bloody
good at it. I can still feel my heart exploding as I tip-toed the
first few feet, then, at the first sounds of his jaw opening, ran
like a ripcord, making ambulance noises all the way through
to the back alley. I probably frightened the poor animal half
to death.

Years later, I grew inordinately fond of my landlady in
Stratford-upon-Avon, Peggy McDonald's, wonderful old
boxer, Suki. Whilst other actors swanned in and out the Dirty
Duck and swarmed the noticeboard for possible breakages
amongst star limbs, I sat home night after night with Peggy
and Suki, and there was never a merrier threesome. In a row,
our suppers on our laps – well, Suki's lap left a lot to be
desired but she made mincemeat of ours – we watched the
box and poured scorn on what we watched from sedentary
heights. Suki had character. She was, if anything, rather
grandiose with an airy, often slightly pie-eyed look which

suggested she might well have been at the cooking sherry whilst we were out. And I tell you, until you've been wakened in the wee small hours by a boxer's tongue all over your bare essentials, you haven't lived – and no, there will be no Mike Tyson jokes at this juncture, thank you.

No, dog-wise, I think I Peked with Emily. Emily, the Brontë-named Yorkshire terrier and downstairs inhabitant of our first married flat. It was a lovely, bay-windowed flat in Hampstead and the glass and chrome oval dining table and perspex chairs took pride of place in the bay overlooking the garden.

Emily's owners, Edith and Bryan, became friends and when we moved in Emily decided to make us welcome in her own way. She chose, curiously enough, to do this at meal times. No sooner did the tin opener come out or the gas fail to ignite – ah, those were the days – than Emily would step out and start what we could only describe as her 'Meandering Heights'. She would pad up the steps in a sort of jaunty, jowly way, for all the world as if contemplating a constitutional, glance round casually, sniffing the air and then, as if an interesting new thought had occurred to her, she would stroll, no I really mean saunter, across the front of the window, pause, yes, it had to be said, nonchalantly, then swiftly mount our kitchen steps virtually whistling with indifference. It was a class act, followed by her look of absolute 'have you gone raving mad?' shock horror when, inevitably, the contents of our plates found their way on to hers. Chaplin must have based a lot of *The Kid* on Emily.

The only pet to grace 'Schloss Rosenthal' save Zuckerman, the much chronicled tortoise and escapologist, has been the tabby bought for Child One when Child Two came along to screw up her entire life. Pushkin and the aforementioned assassin are now nineteen years old and it's hard to say which of them is more eccentric. Pushkin talks to me, sleeps – disastrously – on my head, wipes her nether regions on my script, waits by the garage for my car to return from the show, tells me when and how to brush her, lies cradled in my arms when I'm on my trampoline and decimates my tights.

She is fed, vetted and nursed by my husband and she only has eyes for me. Which is why I love her. Every fraction of upholstery in the house resembles shredded wheat, the chair legs are grated and I *still* love her. But I do have intensely disloyal thoughts sometimes about, sh! having a dog...

One of my favourite programmes in the Radio 4 series *The Lipman Test* was concerned with dog shows. I *know* that where our own personal obsessions are concerned we are all quite mad – but these people took the shortcake.

'He's a little Shitsu, aren't you?' yapped one owner. 'You know, a "coming and going" dog. They are actually the reincarnation of the souls of the dead monks of Tibet. That's how we like to think they are, anyway.' Makes you wonder what the poor monks spent all that time meditating for, doesn't it? To end up on the Shitsu-heap.

'I'm just grooming him out for the Show,' said another. 'When I'm finished he's supposed to look like a chrysanthemum.'

'That's what you call fulfilling his potential, then, is it?' I tried not to add.

Another woman was the owner, no, let's not beat about the bush, the *mother*, of a dozen or so Chinese Cresteds – sort of Oriental rats with quiffs. Her house sounded like a budgerigar convention. 'They're my whole life,' she trilled. 'My husband can go tomorrow, but the dogs – they're wonderful – I really love 'em.'

Dog shows are for bitches of all varieties and what goes on during and after them is the stuff of tragedy. Losers have been known to pour paint over the winners' transport home, to loosen their car wheels or worse. There was a famous dog-show winner who was apprehended for tampering with the goods. Every show dog must be the proud possessor of two testicles, both, obviously, descended into the scrotum. It seems that one of the show dogs had the underwhelming disadvantage of having just the one. Undaunted, his ingenious and determined owner did a home op with pliers, sutures and a glass marble, or, as we used to call 'em, glass foggies. No judge ever spotted the deliberate mistake (or even suggested a swap) and the little chap went from trophy to trophy until one fateful day, a bemused judge found himself feeling not two testicles, not one testicle, but, clunk, clink, three testicles! Game, set, match and, new balls.

One recent weekend when the temperature reached into the 90s, I understood for the first time why people speak the way-ay the-ey do in Tennessee Williams's pla-a-ys, largely because moving your lips is *exhausting*. Pushkin, being totally caparisoned in fur, took to lying flat on her side under the magazine rack, and worried us all by losing her appetite and thus most of her erstwhile haunches.

'What I do with my dog,' said the lady minicab driver as we hit Cricklewood en route to the BBC and air-conditioning, 'is drench tea-towels in cold water and lay them on him. It's a bit of a shock when you first do it, but he feels the benefit.'

I phoned Jack from my dressing-room with the news. His excitement was palpable. He couldn't get off the phone quickly enough. When I got home he had the air of a trainee conjurer about him. 'Sit down, love, have a drink,' then, 'Pushkin – come and show Maureen . . .' I can't describe what came into the living room. It was a Garfield produced by Spielberg. Draped wetly in a white linen handkerchief – you know, the crumpled linen look – she looked like the rolled-up napkin you get at the end of a Chinese meal. On legs. Her face said it all. 'I have not spent nineteen years of my life, 133 in your terms, gaining wisdom and maturity to end up in a wet T-shirt competition for amused householders in North London. I'm a cat, for God's sake!' She managed to get all this across to us whilst walking sideways, for some reason not unassociated with desperate embarrassment, across the room. She then finished off a meaningful performance with a haughty and somewhat ghostly leap on to a chair where she lay, tripe like, maliciously staining the cushion. It was one of the great silent performances of the age. Like a tiny sheikh. Sort of Yasser Arrocat, if you like.

It has to be said that she made no attempt to shrug the whole thing off. Instead she knelt down on the new kitchen cushions and remained there, drying out, kipping and looking like a tiny Pope kissing alien tarmac.

Perish the thought, but one day she'll perish and we'll bury her under the grapevine because all good grapevines should have a dead cat under them. She's slowing down and takes the stairs with stiff back legs. Sometimes she jumps optimistically on to the dressing-table and misses. Sometimes her eyes look cloudy. I'll never tell her I've always wanted a dog, or that one day I may throw catflaps to the wind and buy a pack of beagles. Then at last I'll be able to invite Mum over for Sunday morning beagles and licks.

Car Per Diem

There are few places in the world, save the obvious ones, where I can be alone. Take me to a remote island off the Albanian Peninsula and you can bet your last pfennig that a total stranger will grasp my arm and tell me I'm much thinner in real life and would I come and sign his wife's prosthesis.

It's not the price of fame. It's always happened. In Hull, everybody knew my dad and, accordingly, seemed instantly familiar with me. 'So this is your Maureen,' a voice would say, and a total stranger would lean down, make personal remarks about one or more of my features and pinch my cheek with a viciousness belied by the laughter which it provoked.

It's hereditary. Nowadays my children complain because I always pick people up on holiday. Not in a 'Toerr is Hugh, to forgive Divine' fashion, but in a 'Morning. Looks like brightening up a bit, doesn't it? Have you just arrived today?' sort of way, which by day three has become, 'Hi! We were thinking of eating at "El Ponderosa" actually, would you and your family like to join us?'

'You've done it *again*, Mum!' they hiss. 'Can't you understand, we don't *want* to mix with other kids – we just want to be with *us*!'

I gather people like tenors gather lilacs, only I do it in *all* seasons. The only place I don't do it is in my car. Pick up strangers, I mean. In fact I drive with my doors locked. For fear of kidnappers posing as windscreen cleaners. My car is my place of contemplation in a steady stream of chaos. Classic FM or Radio 4 to soothe and to inform, the familiar sights

of London, not flying but limping past me, a tin of barley
sugars, a parking ticket or two, assorted sticks of make-up for
last-minute re-application, nine or so unlabelled cassettes of
the words of plays I can no longer remember being in ...
another parking ticket ... all the collected memories of a
driving passion.

My Prelude by M Lipman, a slim volume of love songs
which have taken seven lean years to compose. 'She'll never
frown, never break down, this loyal companion will show me
the town ...' I often sing loudly and, it seems to me, flawlessly,
on solitary journeys in my Prelude and there's never been a
single complaint from her. She's always there for me.

Until tonight. For tomorrow I test drive a BMW soft top
and to say my Prelude feels threatened is an understatement.
Tonight she refused point blank to take me to Lizzy's. Or
anywhere. I looked up Irrational Possessiveness in the Hand-
book but it's not there...

Yes ... I've succumbed to the charms of a younger model.
I feel like Rod Stewart. I'm driving around the North Circular
trying to feel blonde. Now, the soft top is giving me delusions
of grandeur. The last time I travelled in one was when Lynda
Bellingham's husband, Nunzio, drove us both to Greenwich
last year. I dressed for the part. When they arrived I was
wearing figure-hugging 'trews', and a cross-over shirt knotted
under extremely 'pointy' breasts (popsocks, since you ask),
stiletto heels, a long headscarf tied around the back of the
head, Lollobrigida shades and a tiny vanity bag. I was smoking
through a holder and carrying a small fur dog under one arm.
You want attention? You goddit!

My own version is, according to legend and ledger, Mau-
ritius Blue and the hood slides down by some kind of electric
command. It has 17,000 miles on the clock, which is just six
thousand less than the mileage on Ronda's clock after seven
years, but this baby goes like Damon trying to sabotage
Schumacher! With the top down I get funny looks and pollution up my nose. I have to speak to myself severely about
playing Mendelssohn's Violin Concerto very loud like a total

poseur, or worse, learning my lines out loud on my way to work, courtesy of the tape recorder. The car is, as yet, unnamed but with DUL as the registration, then Dulcie can't be far from my mind as you know it. My fingernails have gone from operating the roof catches, and I occasionally worry about how I'll clean it now I can no longer drive through Kings Cross Car Wash and have a mug of tea and a bun at the end, but these are minor considerations when you are talking *lurv*. As for Ronda, well Ronda went with narry a backward glance to a new 'one lady owner'. I felt like King Lear.

Knowing Pains

I love my kids. I always have, but never more than now when they are so very tolerant of me.

I gaze at them with awe when they set off alone for foreign climes. I'm rapturously grateful when they tell me their plans and over the moon if they ask for the money for them, which on the whole they don't.

My gratitude is touching when they announce they will be coming home to eat and can they bring five friends. When they party in the garden, I watch them jealously through the windows and wonder wistfully whether what has just made them fall over with laughter would be even vaguely comprehensible to their mother.

I also love their friends. Nothing thrills me more than the sight of Will's size elevens spanning my hall or Melanie's Fiesta blocking my drive. I like to come into the kitchen when scores of coffee cups and a picked clean fridge herald an all-night, all-girls' sit-up and I cherish the sound of massed baritone mirth from the one hundred and seventy-eighth viewing of *A Life of Brian*.

I don't even mind being turfed out of my living-room because they need it for *Red Dwarf* and I'm tickled pink by the memory of Adam and Will celebrating the end of A Levels with tea and toast and the *Guardian* crossword. Rebellious bastards! And I'm reduced to a blubber by the sound of two six-foot lads teaching each other to cook and ride a bicycle respectively.

When I come home from a hard day in the mind-slamming world of sitcom, the sound of an electronic guitar from an upstairs room is music to my years. And the pleasure of one of them perched on our bed at night, tucking us in and kissing us goodnight before settling down to a video or two, is almost unparalleled.

Occasionally we sit, fogey-like, at the table while they clear up, apallingly, after dinner, or make us a coffee, and we watch them exchange derisory glances at one of our childish witticisms. At that point the fogeys have been known to get giggles of the 'church' variety and resort to a lot of mouth covering and shoelace tying.

I don't know where the time has gone, forgive the yawning cliché, since they needed us, looked up to us and totally tied us down. When, suddenly, did I become an amusing pet, inevitably putting my foot in it whilst trying (and failing) to be a cool parent?

'Thanks for doing so much of the clearing up, love,' I said to Adam last night.

'I *have* cleared up!' he countered defensively. 'Look at all the stuff in the draining rack...'

'No! I *meant* it!' I cried. 'I meant, "thank you".'

'Oh, sorry,' he grinned. 'I just found it amazingly difficult to accept that there wasn't an element of sarcasm in your statement.'

There was a lot of history in that response.

Meanwhile, the University Kid is home and we've managed to overcome the first powerfully charged weeks where we don't mention the state of her room for so long that it is *bursting* out of every sentence we utter.

'Did you sleep OK, darling?' ('In spite of the fourteen black plastic bin-liners full of books surrounding your unmade bed, darling'); and 'Will you be on the phone much longer, darling?' ('Because if you've got time to talk to Emma and Melanie and Emma Jane and Neal and Emma then you've got time to pick five tons of *ironed* clothes off the floor, darling!').

I've managed to learn all the important features like who goes out with whom and who used to go out with whom and who wouldn't be seen dead with whom. Also, I never ask any question concerned with the 'W' word. The four-letter expletive deleted word. I'll say it quietly in case anyone's listening if you *promise* not to repeat it ... 'work', because that is not what University is about, is it? It's nothing to do with essays and reference books and theses and lectures, it's about getting legless and getting off and getting together and basically learning to live without, well, me, really.

I was watching, as is my wont, a stunning programme on mountain parrots. The mating was spectacular, the brooding and hatching meticulous. Hungry mouths open to be fed, beak to beak, dowdy grey down waiting to be changed into glorious plumage. Such single-minded instinct to raise 'em, rear 'em, make sure they've got all *their* instincts right. Then, whoosh! One day, a gust of wind, a flap of orange-crested wing and, 'Ciao, fogeys, I'm off backpacking across Nepal. No thanks, I *don't* need any seeds, I've got plenty of my own, if you take my meaning, nudge, nudge, wink, wink.' And that's it. That was a late parrot. That parrot had ceased to be.

The strongest note of optimism is that it is only in one's own experience of parenting that one gains knowledge of how difficult we made it for our own parents. This was never more strongly illustrated than last week when Amy sat in the garden reading her father's latest play which revolves around a group of parents accompanying their offspring to their Cambridge interviews. Some time later, she called me over in a rather strained voice. 'Can I borrow you for a moment?' and I found her spilling over with the kind of sobs I dimly remember from her twelve-year-old school-days of 'best friend betrayal'.

'Poor Dad,' she sobbed. 'I feel so awful. I didn't know he felt so lost when I went off – I didn't know he felt like an old eskimo – I feel so terrible.'

By now, we were both awash – a not unusual phenomenon chez Rosenthal – the men just stare at us, more in pity than in sorrow. 'But that's how it is, darling. It's supposed to be like that. Dad's fine now, and there's a whole play come out of it and that's wonderful because it makes people think and understand. Other people's shoes – you know ...' I petered out, feeling embarrassingly avuncular – well, a*vaunt*ular, I suppose. Dangerously near to Sally Field'ism, the dreaded Mrs Gump. 'Lahf is lahk a box of chocolates, honey, y'eat some, 'n y'eat some more, 'n y' finish 'em off and you're sick as a hog in a compost heap!'

Still, when I think of every stage and its accompanying worry – 'Will they ever walk, will they ever sleep through the night, ever socialize, stop clinging to me, learn to read, learn to share, go to school by bus, ever go out, ever stay *in*? – I have to smile and shake my head in a way only American moms in movies ever seem to do. Everything in its own time, Maureen, the instincts are all there – all that's required of you is to be there and be consistent.

There is a tribe in the Kalahari Desert, I'm told by the fascinating book, *The Language Instinct* by Stephen Pinker, which builds complex sand sculptures to teach their babies to stand, to crawl and, finally, to walk. The children do these things, ultimately, at exactly the same growth stage as do any other babies in the world, but the parents feel as though *they've* done it for them. And the children let them take the credit. For a while anyway.

Good Risibility

The doorbell had just rung. It was a Sunday, our wedding anniversary and, for a treat, we were all watching Manchester United thrash Leeds United to within an inch of its FA Cup life. We were two goals up, so my husband went to the door. There was a slight scuffle, a thump and a half-strangled shout and I heard him moan, 'They've done us again!' Even after this, when he could have been lying in a bleeding heap of mugged citizen, it was hard for my son and I to tear ourselves away from Ryan Giggs' neat corner flicks, but we did. There in the hallway was a helpless Jack. Beside him is a large traffic cone covered in silver and white with the words 'Happy Anniversary' on the rim and an assortment of Jelly Babies and clotted creams stuck around the perimeter. Alongside is a large amber warning lamp. Flashing. And we can't find out how to turn it off.

'How did they get them in?' I asked, knowing immediately the identity of 'them'.

'Left them on the step and scuttled back to the car,' said Jack.

'Now what do we do?' I wiped away a tear. 'Our move, I guess.'

It was the culmination of a continuing saga of mutual harassment between consenting adults which began on a quiet weekend at the glorious culinary retreat of Chewton Glen in the company of two friends, the Morrows. On the drive down to Dorset we became mildly, then wildly, hysterical over the number of traffic cones bordering, abutting,

nay, even pie-frilling, the road. I shall become even more of
a bore on this subject later.

They were like a bad attack of acne – 'They'll only spread
if you pick 'em!' They were single file, double file, rolling
about, teetering in circles, copulating, breeding, suppurating
... Anyway, there were a *lot* of them on the Bournemouth
road and we four began to build up the sort of jokey scenario
which was very funny in an enclosed space hurtling down the
M3, but less so if I were to relay it to you now. Suffice to say
it involved Cone'n the Barbarian, Sir Arthur Cone'n Doyle
and Mr and Mrs Cohen and their son, Raffik. With a combined age of over 200 years in the car, all we needed, really,
was someone to settle us down with a boiled sweet and point
out the window cooing 'Look, darlings, moo cows!'

Once installed in the hotel, Jack and I left the Morrows
sleeping next door and went for a sedate swim and a leisurely
sauna. We were sitting in the jacuzzi, wondering, as ever after
two minutes, what the hell we were supposed to do *now*, when
we couldn't help but notice a by now familiar orange and
white striped plastic object by the poolside. 'Do you mind if
I borrow this for a while?' I asked the poolside receptionist.
Sometimes it pays to have a familiar and, let's be honest,
mad-as-an-orange face, because she agreed immediately and
offered me the loan of a bollard.

We crept past our own room, placed the cone outside
the Morrows, rang their bell and, giggling, crouching and
tiptoeing more than was strictly necessary, returned to the
safety of our room.

Throughout the next twenty-four hours that cone turned
up in more places than Judith Chalmers. It was in our bed
alongside a chocolate and a rose – what the chambermaid
thought I can hardly conjecture – it was under the breakfast
table, it accompanied us to a local tea shop and when we
waved it goodbye, we all felt withdrawal symptoms.

A week later, when it was little more than an after-dinner
story – one which, on the whole, received polite but glassy-
eyed smirks as opposed to hallelujah choruses of hilarity and

requests for telling the whole thing again from scratch – Jack received a bill. The bill came from the hotel. It was for a missing traffic cone and it was for £18.

Easy to say, after the event, but had *I* been there I *may* have viewed it with a small soupçon of suspicion, but Jack had no such compunction. He was outraged. A man possessed. A massive injustice had been perpetrated and straightaway he got on the phone to the hotel to rectify it.

'This bill I've received is preposterous! Unbelievable! We asked permission to *borrow* the cone from the pool and we put it back *immediately* after we'd used it! It was a joke! You seriously expect me to pay this ridiculous ...' There was consternation behind the Hotel Reception, as well there might have been, since the bill had been invented and typed on hotel stationery by none other than our friend, Mr Morrow, a fact which was suddenly, and with absolute certainty, comprehended by my husband as he studied the 'bill' he was brandishing.

It took a lot of grovelling, shrugging *and* forelock tugging to convince the staff not to call a manager, a lawyer – and an ambulance – but in the end he succeeded. It was, we decided, touché.

This part is a confession. Yes, it was me. I took it. The derelict and torn traffic cone I found under my Honda, some weeks later in the Waterloo Road. Under cover of darkness and spurred on by a spirit of vengeance, I popped it in the boot and, looking neither left nor right, sped home like a common criminal. Later that day, having first wrapped it in bandages of silver paper and tinsel and superglued Woolworth's 'pic n' mix' chocolates all over its surface, I left Jack to deliver it to the Morrows' pristine home in Finchley as a house-warming gift. The weather was wet, icy and one might even say inclement if one was the sort of toff who also said 'one'.

It emerged that their new house was situated down a long lane fronted by a barrier, erected specifically to prevent unknown cars driven by lunatics carrying gift-wrapped contraband traffic cones down ice-covered driveways. Braving life, limbs and any sense of dignity he ever had, he placed it in situ, then, mission accomplished, limped, slid, tottered and skeetered back to the car, losing the rest of his will to live on the way.

I might point out to those of you who are not practical jokers that the receiver of the said item *never* mentions to the sender that anything in any way unusual has arrived. The idea is to smile grimly, simmer a while and retaliate, if necessary, after years.

But, it wasn't years. It was the other night. The night we were going out to dinner with our friends, the Morrows. We drove over there to pick them up taking the warning lamp with us. When they walked out to greet us it was on the top of our car, flashing. No one mentioned it and we put it back where it had come from, on the way out. The following day we mailed them a box of forty-eight ice-cream cones from the freezer centre.

I'm not sure what the next move is, but I think, and here Jack's dismay is palpable, that it involves a megaphone, two traffic wardens' outfits, a search warrant and some very, very dirty boots. Suggestions welcome on a plain brown warrant.

I'm mad for practical jokes and I'll never give up when I'm one down and it's my turn. It depresses the hell out of my family when I get that bloodhound-brow look, because they can sniff trouble, and it comes in fancy dress.

In Eilat early this year we stayed at a very spectacular hotel called the Royal Beach Hotel. It just so happened that our trip coincided with an intake of French Algerians *en famille*, who were attending an advanced Noise, Nuisance and Nastiness Convention over the same time span. It was a movie, starring Midler, Danny de Vito and the Institute for Repulsive and Badly Behaved Minors.

They ran up and down in the lifts, they ran up and down the lounges, they jumped into the pool in battalions of eight and when they came down for Friday night dinner, you had

your work cut out not to bring a Sten gun. The women
seemed to be men in drag, wearing tight, short to the point
of 'mind if I park my bike there while I change my library
book?' Lycra skirts and low-cut bustiers appliquéd in gold
leaf. They had uniformly gravelly voices, knuckleduster jewellery and spikey maroon hair. It was an open audition for *Irma
La Douce*. Chorus work only. The men were square and
gilded, with ferocious tempers and the children had thighs
like pillar boxes and mouths to match.

Dinner was buffet-style and Friday night it was buffalo
style. I actually saw one gold lamé dragon push her way so
heftily into the dessert display that she came out with crème
caramel on both nipples. It was riveting. There was a
dispute at one family table of sixteen which escalated in
tone and tension till, finally, two titan viragos attacked each
other over the hors-d'oeuvres and had to be separated at
source by their mothers-in-law. It was alarmingly funny –
but the air was thick with the threat of machetes and the
waiters were in terror. If a main course dish didn't please
or suffice, there would be a scrape of chair and a man,
who was the same size standing up as he was sitting down,
would hurtle across the dining-room like a bullet and grasp
the poor waiter by his lapels, hurling curses the length of
the room whilst making murderous gestures with his cigar-
clipping implement.

We laughed long and hard over the French in some jolly
games of Scrabble with a couple of lovely Mancunians,
Dorothy and Ray, whom we'd met there. After they had
returned to England they received a letter from two of the
Algerian families, expressing their delight that they would
be finding themselves in Manchester quite soon and would
appreciate bed and board, as suggested by Mr and Mrs
Rosenthal, for themselves, their in-laws, their children and
the children's pet goats.

One of the many points of identification we'd shared with
Ray and Dorothy over the week's stay was a horror of our
parents' occasional use of Yiddish when we were children.

To say I looked 'blech' was more insulting than it ever was to say I looked pale, or wan, or even washed out, which implied something slightly interesting. To hear that so-and-so was 'grob' was infinitely more obscene than to say they were fat, and being told to 'fress' as opposed to eat, could put you off ever eating again. The worst for Jack and Ray – I had never actually heard this one, but, onomatopoeically, it's already engraved on my spleen – is the Yiddish for a certain type of pickled cucumber ... wait for it ... an ugeke – pronounced ug-eh-key. 'Go, fress those ugekes' meant a mass exodus from the table of anyone under twenty-five.

So it was with wry appreciation that on our return from Israel we found ourselves the recipients of not one, but *twelve* huge jars of ugekes. From Harrods, noch! Harrods Special Ugeke Deliveries Inc! I'm biding my time on this one. Fulminating and cogitating. It might be months, it might be years ... hmmm ... hmmm ...

One gag I thought had backfired on me was a letter I sent to Mr Derek Nimmo, or the Right-on Sir Derek of Nimmeau, as I prefer to call him. Derek and his wife, Pat, are chums of ours, and Derek revels in being sent up. Particularly by me. So when I read an article in *The Times* about entertaining at home, which claimed that his dinner parties had been revolutionized by the acquisition of an electronic place setting machine, I was delighted.

The article went on: 'We usually start with champagne, followed by white wine with the first course, water in a large glass, red wine with the main course in a decanter, pudding wine in another decanter, then port, cognac and cigars for the men while the ladies clear off on their own – never quite sure where they go, into the bedrooms, I think.' The guests to be electronically seated included Tarquin Olivier, Geoffrey Palmer and 'an Omani friend of mine who has the best cellar in Muscat of anyone I know'.

It was irresistible and I was inspired to write the following letter:

Dear Sir Nimmo,

I am writing this letter after reading your very nice interview in *The Times* on the subject of entertaining at home. I do not normally read *The Times* but I was peeling some string beans for my current employers' Salade Niçoise and needed something to rest the colander on. Once I had started to read about your exemplary manner of entertaining, I knew at once I was in the wrong position and decided to take the bit between my teeth and write to you applying for a job in your excellent household.

I do like to see things done properly and I am afraid, without pointing any fingers, that my current employers, Mr and Mrs Rosenthal of Muswell Hill, fall seriously short of those standards.

I have been in service now for some fifty-six years and I think you will find my record completely flawless. I spent several years in the employ of Mr Huntley and Mr Palmer, of high-class biscuit fame, and I wonder whether the Geoffrey you mentioned in your article could be the reprobate youngest son of Mr Palmer, now turned thespian. He was a very dear boy, but *would* he eat his greens? Mr Huntley personally helped me to climb the ladder from scullery maid to 'tweeny and, finally, to second server on silver salver. In fact, he was, like your goodself, the possessor of a magnetic placement board, of which he was very proud. Unfortunately, one day it was attracted by signals from his pacemaker and had to be surgically removed from his dress shirt.

Mr and Mrs Rosenthal, I am sure, would give me an excellent reference, although between you and me there is really not much to do around here except watch Mr Rosenthal re-arrange the dishwasher, cook for the children, supervise the household and create Mrs Rosenthal's post-theatre suppers. Mrs

Rosenthal's job in the household seems largely to consist of speaking for hours on the telephone to minor theatrical celebrities and littering the house with objects she has received at prizegiving ceremonies, which do nothing but sit there and gather dust.

Very little entertaining goes on here and when they do have a dinner party, quite frankly, very little thought goes into it and the guest list is largely riffraff. Everybody sits anywhere, some of the china does not match, the menu is always salmon, the womenfolk – far from retiring after dinner – often take over the whole procedure and tell ribald jokes containing four-letter words, and, on one occasion, an eight-letter word beginning with A. Their two children are allowed into the room at all times. As I said, I am not one to talk but what has happened to the standards of yesteryear?

As for myself, I am, as you will have gathered, extremely loyal, hardworking and discreet. I would be happy to work for you for the salary I am receiving from the Rosenthals: £19 per week, minus tax and stamp, and a bonus of six bagels at Christmas.

I also have references from Lord and Lady Raymond Cooney of Epping and other theatrical luminaries. I enjoyed working for Lord Cooney but there were too many doors in his house. It all got a bit confusing and, quite frankly, I did nothing but pick up trousers wherever I went.

I am of sound mind and body, apart from a little arthritis in my left ear. I would be bringing my husband, Hubert, with me, but we would only require a couple of rooms and a bathroom (we favour high ceilings, cornices and integral fireplaces – although we have nothing against gas coal log effect fires) and perhaps a separate area for my husband to change his prosthesis.

Might I say that I have enjoyed your work in
the past on the television and always admired your
wearing of the cloth.

Please give my best regards to your chauffeur. He
probably will not remember but we had a brief affair
during the War when I was a WAAF stationed in
Batley. I have never passed on his secret.

Yours respectfully,

AMELIA SKILLEN (MRS)

This letter was sent on the 3 December 1992 and when no
word or deed had come back almost a year later, I was
convinced that I had deeply offended the Nimmos and, actually, I was rather afraid of running into them. Then in
December 1993 we received an invitation to dinner Chez
Nimmo and had the ultimate experience of being electronically seated at one of their immaculate dinner parties. It
was, I must admit, rather heavenly with wonderful food,
flowers, wine and conversation. All sublimely well-directed
by invisible, maybe electronic, strings. During the course of
the evening, Derek mentioned my letter and it was brought
out and crowed over by his guests. I was delighted and
relieved. 'I thought you were too annoyed by it to reply,' I
told him.

'Good Heavens, no,' laughed Derek. 'I couldn't think of
anything to top it, and I'm still waiting for inspiration...'

The next day, our thank-you letter went as follows:

Dear Lord and Lady Nimmeaux,

After I heard about the delights of your magnificent
table from my employers, Mr and Mrs Rosenthal, I
have decided to withdraw my application for domestic employment. I do not think I could match the
standard which has been reported to me.

However, I understand that neither Mr nor Mrs Rosenthal have yet thanked you for your munificence, which is typical of their lack of breeding, so it remains for me in their stead to thank you for a totally perfect evening.

Apparently they look forward to returning the compliment as soon as Mrs Rosenthal has bought a plastic tablecloth.

Yours sincerely,

AMELIA SKILLEN (MRS) AND SPOUSE

I wonder why any pre-planned joke is called a practical joke? I suppose it just means actual, or involving a physical item, as practical props on stage mean using a real object instead of just a mock-up. I shall look it up. I've looked it up. It's a joke with actions ... or, in my case, libellous actions.

The verbal jokes have been thin on the ground lately. Political correctness has put paid to most minority jokes, and without someone 'inferior' to laugh at there's little chance of laughter at all. Imagine this one and supply the incorrectness yourself. There's an Englishman, a Scotsman and another man eating their sandwiches on the building site. The Englishman complains, 'Bloody beef again! Every day, beef, beef, beef! If I get another beef sandwich tomorrow, I'm going to throw myself off the top of that crane!'

The Scotsman concurs, 'Me too! Ham again! Ham, ham, ham! Everyday the same. One more ham sandwich and, tomorrow, I'm gonna join ye on that crane and jump!'

'Cheese again,' groans the third man. 'Cheese yesterday, cheese the day before. Nothing but sodding cheese. If I get cheese tomorrow in my sandwich – I'm jacking it in as well, off that crane!'

The following day, all three men opened their snap tins, found, respectively, beef, ham and cheese in them and jumped to their deaths from the top of the crane. (Don't you just love the credibility factor here?)

At the funeral the three wives were commiserating with each other. 'I had no idea he didn't want beef in his sandwich,' says the English wife. 'I could have given him salmon or egg mayonnaise if only he'd said ...'

'I know,' weeps the Scottish widow. 'I only gave him ham because I thought he loved it, I had tuna and tongue and all sorts ...'

'The same with me exactly,' moans the third man's widow. 'He could have had anything! And the thing that makes it even worse is that he made his own sandwiches!'

One of the cleverest stories came via George Baker. It concerns a Professor of Logic at Cambridge University on a brief visit to his childhood roots in the East End of London. Walking down a narrow street and peering up at the street signs, he hears a gruff, strangled Cockney sound and feels a heavy hand on his shoulders.

'Bowers, innit? Phil Bowers, innit, eh? Ent you Phil Bowers from the Old 'All School in Fry'sgate?'

Professor Bowers, for it was he, took a step back and examined the red, coarsened man before him. 'Yes. That's correct. Professor Bowers, and who might you be?'

'S'me! Jimmy Stover, innit – used to sit behind you in 1946, copy yer 'omework! Gawd strewth, you was an 'ell of a swat! What yer doing wiv y'self now, then?'

'Well, I'm a Professor of Logic at Cambridge University, actually.'

'*Are* yew really? *Are* yew really? Well, stone me, ent that somethin'. Tsk-tsk-tsk. Professor of Logic, eh?' He took off his cap and scratched his head. 'Wass Logic, then?'

The Professor glanced first at his watch and then at the heavens and said, 'Well, er, James, Logic is – well, look here, I'm going to assume that you have a couple of goldfish at home.'

'Yeah, thassright, Flossie and Mossie. Gottem in a bowl on the telly, how d'you know?'

'Very well, James. Then I shall further assume you have a cat who watches these fish.'

'Yeah, thassright, Phil, she can sit there for hours and . . .'

'Very well, and I shall further presume that you have a couple of children who . . .'

'Yeah, thassright, boy 'n a girl, Phoebe an Des . . .'

'So, James. I shall now make the *logical* deduction that you are heterosexual.'

Jimmy was flabbergasted but had no time to comment as Professor Bowers tapped his watch saying 'Must dash, splendid to see you – er, James – some other time,' and disappeared down the road at a lick.

Jimmy Stover made his way to the pub where his mate, Ron, was already two pints ahead.

' 'Ere, Ron. You'll never guess who I just saw in the street. Bowers, Phil Bowers, the swatter, 'member 'im from the Old 'All School?'

Ron's face cracked into a wide beam of recognition. 'Yeah, Bowers! Gawd, 'ee was a clever bugger all right – Whass 'ee doin' neow, eh?'

Jimmy assumed his full height. ' 'E's a Professor of Logic, innee! At Cambridge University.'

Ron shook his head in awe. 'Is 'ee really? Is 'ee *really*?' Then drained his glass and said, warily, 'Whass Logic, then?'

Jimmy was in his element. He put down his glass, wiped his mouth clean of froth and took a lecturing stance. 'Well, Ron,' he began. 'I am gonna assume that you 'ave a goldfish bowl on your telly wiv two goldfish in it.'

'No,' says Ron.

'Well, you're a f. . . . . . poofter, then ain't yer!'

It ain't practical, but it's practically the funniest joke I know.

Sprung Chicken

In my youth I never understood the joke: 'Why did the chicken cross the road? To get to the other side.' It was far too sophisticated a concept. The one which made me crow was: 'Why did the chicken cross the road? To see the Duchess lay a foundation stone.' Still, you could generally generate a decent laugh or two with a chicken story, a chicken allusion or a chicken imitation.

Chickens are oddballs. It's an accepted fact that if chickens had big brown eyes and long lashes, then Animal Rights Liberators would be placarding battery farms and throwing eggs at Dudley Moore on a regular basis. Chickens somehow don't have the innate appeal of veal calves: they are infinitely more expendable, less individual, more spikey, more scratchy, less characterful – look, let's face it, as far as good PR goes, they are in need of an image consultant. 'Mum, can I have a hen for my birthday?' is not the cry of your normal primary school kid and 'Let's go and feed the fowl' is pretty low down the pecking order on your average outing in the park.

So it was with some surprise that I surveyed the title of one of the children's books I was to read on tape: *Hilda, The Hen Who Wouldn't Give Up* by Jill Tomlinson. I know Jill as a good children's writer responsible for one of my finest hours as 'Plop, the Owl', on the cassette version of *The Owl Who Was Afraid of the Dark*. No, I'm not being arrogant, nor facetious. As 'Plop', I peaked. Simple as that. Everything since has been steadily downhill. Owls were familiar territory to me and baby owls with husky voices, a hoot.

But a hen. A stubborn hen, who sought various means to

75

travel five miles to another farm to view her auntie's new chicks, then became broody for chicks of her own. Round the house I wandered, clucking under my breath and trying to feel feathered. Should Hilda be a 'kentry gurl' hen with a soft Gloucestershire burr, or a sturdy northern lass with nice round Yorkshire vowels so similar to my own? My preoccupation did not go unnoticed at home and snide comments began to emanate from him indoors.

'I hope it won't *ruffle your feathers* if I ask you where my green jacket is?' and 'Do you still want to meet at the theatre or does it go *against the grain*?' At one point, a *peck* on the cheek was requested and references made to being no *spring chicken*! But when it was suggested that I remove my glasses to take the weight off my beak, I'm afraid I snapped, and more or less told him to cluck-off!

One lunchtime, I regaled Lynda Bellingham with my dilemma. 'So,' I told her, 'Hilda sits on her eggs to make them hatch into chicks but the farmer's wife keeps taking them away.'

'Where was the cock?' asked Lynda.

I assured her there were no 'cocks' in *Hilda, The Hen Who Wouldn't Give Up*, but she, a farmer's daughter, persisted.

'No cocks, no fertilization.' I felt as I had felt when I discovered you didn't get babies through eating Stork margarine. 'Well, what do you think God created cocks for?' she said.

It was an interesting question at my time of life. 'To wake you up in the morning?' I ventured.

The next morning in the studio went reasonably well and I didn't fall foul of too many interpretation problems. Hilda emerged as a regular member of the village of Ambridge and the producer seemed chuffed enough. I went to work that evening with my pride intact, feeling I'd managed to pullet out of the bag, as t'were.

Later that night, on my return home, Jack was in the kitchen. 'How did it go, love? The recording?'

'Oh. OK. I think. Yeah, all right really. I think I managed to be birdlike without being too . . .'

Here I broke off at the sight of my husband, a mature man in the summer wine section of his days, circling the kitchen with a basket under his arm, scattering imaginary grain hither and thither on the kitchen floor. 'Peckish at all, love?'

I'm not one to harbour a grudge. Not for me the long brooding silence, the clipped retort and the crisp closing of partition doors. Certainly not. I'm only too well aware of the value of a sense of humour to a long-standing relationship, the ability to laugh at oneself, yes, to see the yolk, if you like, in a mature marriage. 'Never go to sleep on a quarrel' said someone – Louisa May Alcott? Claire Rayner? Idi Amin? Whoever. And we didn't. No fear.

But the following day I phoned the East Finchley Party and Fancy Dress Shop to inquire after the cost of hiring a complete hen's costume. Gravely, the assistant informed me that it would be £18 but unfortunately they had no hens in stock. My disappointment must have been palpable because just as I was about to hang up, she called out, 'I don't suppose by any chance you'd be interested in a chicken?'

It was a yellow-feathered balaclava with blue eyes, an orange beak and a voluminous yellow fluffy body with cosy mittens and black tights. I was somewhat surprised that *feet* were not included at that price, but a new pair of yellow rubber gloves seemed to do the trick nicely. I was stuffing cushions down the body when my son arrived home from school. 'Hi Mod,' he intoned, deadpan. 'I see you're dressed up as a hen. What's for dinner?'

Dave, the gardener, was hoeing round the stone urn in the front garden. I hopped up on to a small brick wall by the porch and waited for him to hoe in my direction. He was listening raptly to Gloria Hunniford and didn't turn round until my feet, in their rubber fingers, were iced to the brick-work. Finally, he looked round and said, 'Oh yeah?' a whisper of a smile forcing his roll-up to one side, 'What's this then, Maureen? You goin' to a fancy dress party or what?'

I considered telling him what I was doing and why, but by now I was a frozen chicken. 'Yeah, that's right, David. It's a hen party.' He went ho-ho-ho-ing back to his hoeing.

Jacquie, my secretary, was helpless with laughter by now as I sat down in the living-room to await Jack's return. I was rather affronted by her amusement. It has always been the way that once I put on a costume, however ridiculous, I feel completely and utterly at home. I spread myself out on the sofa, my colourful rubber feet akimbo up on the coffee table, my chin on my chest and two hardboiled eggs and a small dish of pumpkin seeds by my side.

The door slammed and his hello sounded cheery enough. 'Everyone all right?' he called. Stifled noises from the study and the kitchen were the only response he got. 'Where's Mum?' he asked Adam, who obviously swerved into another room muttering 'Living-room' in strangled tones. 'Why is everyone smirking? What's happened? Why is the ...' he entered the room and the rest I leave to your fertile imagination. Suffice to say that his glasses went AWOL, his body collapsed, his knees jack-knifed to his chin, his breath came in hoarse rasps followed by violent, painful brays. Finally, painfully, he put up both hands and said 'All right. You win.'

If I'd had fluffy ears, it would have been music to them.

2

Actor on the Job

Lost in Yonkers

Lost in Yonkers was Neil Simon's thirty-ninth Broadway hit. Set during the Second World War, it's the story of Jay and Arty, two teenaged boys forced by the death of their mother and the debts of their father, Eddie, to spend ten inhospitable months at the Yonkers home and candy store of their granite-hard German-American grandmother and her repressed, childlike daughter, Bella.

An impeccable play, it won Neil Simon a Pulitzer Prize and Tony Awards for three of the stars of the Broadway production, Irene Worth, Mercedes Ruehl and Kevin Spacey. Producer Duncan Weldon saw it on Broadway, loved it and told me to get out there fast because Bella was the part of a lifetime.

I got out there. It was. I saw it on Broadway and it was as good as it had been on the pages which I dampened every time I read them. It had to be the part of *my* lifetime.

Mercedes Ruehl, the fine actress you may have seen in *The Fisher King* was a triumph as Bella, an awkward, frustrated sweet thirty-eight-year-old child who seizes the arrival of her two teenage nephews to make a personal bid for freedom. In the scene when she finally tells her mother how she has let men, strangers, abuse her over the years because she was so desperate to be touched and held – by anyone – whole rows of seats shook with the audience's attempt to express its emotion.

Irene Worth, as her mother, was a malevolent gnome with a painful skeetering limp and the eye of a lizard. Even in her most emotional moment, her back rigid with the effort of restraint, she was immutable, never allowing us, the audience, to pity her. So we did, of course. It was a shattering evening. Moving but unsentimental.

Kevin Spacey played Uncle Louie, the steely 'bag-man' with the softest heart in Yonkers. Kevin was mad, bad and enchanting to know and I had the pleasure of lunching with him at the Russian Tea Rooms. At that time, he was set to repeat his role in London and also to direct the show. I wore careful make-up, no glasses and a white wool Escada coatdress with brass buttons, purchased for me, by proxy, by Julia McKenzie at some 'knock-down-'ave-we-gone-raving-mad-we're-fools-to-ourselves-at-these-prices-we're-paying-you!' factory outlet, and as he rose to greet me his first words were, 'Why, you're beautiful!'

Somehow, I knew then that he would never direct the London show.

After seeing the show we met thirteen-year-old Benny Grant who played Arty, one of Bella's nephews, and who would join us in London, and Mercedes Ruehl, who was enthusiastic, encouraging and unspoiled. 'You are going to have such a ball, playing this part,' she promised me, 'and you'll never tire of her.' From her mouth to God's ears.

What is important to me is the near physical excitement I get from the text of the play I want to do. I read it in a sitting, then I sit there wallowing in what I've been reading. I know how to say the lines, I can hear the pauses. Seeing the show confirmed this feeling – although I now feel that I would have served the play better had I not seen the American production first. Why? Because if, at heart, you are a sponge, as I am, then the voice tone of a performance will stay in your heart. In the case of Bella, Ruehl used a slightly thick, underwater sound, almost as though she was slightly deaf. There had been a girl, when I was young, with a similar note in her voice ... almost a masculine sound, veering out of control when she became excited in the way that small boys do. Girls tend to quiver into shrill anger, but boys get angry in their effort to communicate their anguish.

Later, I heard that voice again when I visited, with her parents' permission, Ruth, a weekly boarder at the Ravenswood Home for the Mentally Disabled. Ruth was in her thirties and welcomed me with shyness, took my hand, then showed me her room and her possessions with all the candour, charm and exuberance of a ten-year-old. She had that same timbre in her voice, which I now began to recognize.

In other words, I would probably have arrived, alone, at the same sound had I not seen Mercedes's exceptional Bella in *Yonkers*, but since I *had* seen it, there was no way I could prove that, even to myself.

One day, an actress I knew called to ask if I was doing *Yonkers* and, when I confirmed it, asked, 'Do you have any idea who they are seeing for Bella?' Obviously she, like many, assumed that I would be playing Momma. I felt both apologetic and defiant when I told her that for once in my life I'd be ageing downwards!

Rosemary Harris was to play Bella's mother in our production. Working with Rosemary is like playing great tennis – not that I've ever played great tennis (the joke goes: 'What do you call an Englishman who gets into the second week at Wimbledon? – Umpire!') – but I imagine that's how it must be. It wasn't easy for her, having played Grandma in New York for six months, getting used to having *new* children to destroy, but if she felt it, she seldom showed it.

There was one occasion, in rehearsals, when she thought my Bella was behaving a little more 'sassily' than she would have dared to. (For me to be submissive is as natural as it is for Ruby Wax to be reticent. 'Dumb insolence' was the phrase I remember being bandied about at my primary school.) On this day, Rosie took it into her head to frighten me and, my God, she did, wheeling around spontaneously, she seemed to fly across the room towards me, cane in hand, the world thirty-second limping champion, with a face like an entire German Panzer division.

I was genuinely alarmed. I thought she was going to hit me. I flinched, backed away and took her point.

After four challenging weeks in a Waterloo rehearsal room, we were ready for off. Gradually we outgrew the space we'd been afforded. The day came when producers Duncan Weldon and Peter Wilkins and sundry others, arrived to see if the pig they ordered turned out to be in a poke – perhaps not the best analogy for a play by Neil Simon.

It's an odd stage, this pre-stage one. We were still safe in our space, with tapes on the floor to represent doors, and makeshift furniture. Our set was by Santo Loquesta, who did the New York show. He does all the interiors for Woody Allen's films, too, so he's a bit of a star to all of us and it was a relief when he was nice and normal and funny and wanted it to be right for *this* production, not just faithful to the original.

I was incredibly drained – and that was *before* we set off for Guildford. I knew I was letting Bella's emotional turmoil dictate mine. A fatal mistake and one which I have repeated for, oooh, about twenty-seven years, man and boy. Rosemary was inexhaustible. I don't think in nine months I ever saw her yawn. Or get sick. Or get a cold sore or a headache, or any of my stable specialities.

Benny Grant (alias Sylvio Luciano), playing Arty, was recreating his Broadway role. A seasoned pro of thirteen years, he was acute, sensitive, wise beyond his years and carefully watched over by his mother, Theresa, to make sure he never crossed the line set by his Italian-American background.

Theresa could cook. And how. On weekends she would often invite the cast over to their small rented apartment for Italian food which seemed to spill out of her tiny kitchen like a culinary waterfall. Benny was, of course, word perfect, truthful, concentrated and is the possessor of natural comedy timing. He is such a lovely boy – poised between an obsessive love of model cars, oversize T-shirts and joke-shop gags and a nurturing interest in model girls in undersized T-shirts. He could break your heart with a smile or crack you up with a

funny face and I suppose he's doing just that to some adoring
preppy in California.

When Benny left for home, we gave him a ballad to remember us by:

> He was small and he was Latin
> When he winged in from Manhattan,
> He was neat and cute and dark and kinda noisy.
> When his Jumbo Jet touched down, it brought joy
>   to London Town
> And Emptiness to Hackensack, New Joisey.
>
> With Mama Luciano and case of oregano
> They hit the north and south Provincial towning.
> He had to stand and fall, with the awesome Ross
>   McCall,
> A fate that's only slightly worse than drowning.
>
> The Strand was even merrier, when our little bull
>   terrier
> Stood up tall and called his 'Grandma', 'meanie'.
> The critics raved and roared, 'By God, this kid has
>   scored,
> Let's buy the lad a silver Lamborghini!'
>
> Dear Silvio, we'll miss you so,
> A kind heart always conquers,
> When you go back, you'll leave a gap
> As big and wide as Yonkers.

Matt McGuire, who, because of Equity rules on children
had to play certain nights for Benny, was an American kid
living over here with his parents. He was very cute, very funny
and a completely different but equally valid 'Arty' – less
disciplined, more childlike. It was very interesting to see how
the relationship between the brothers changed when Matt
played the role. Also his mother made the most sensational

company cheese cakes. God, if either of my children had acted, what would I have brought in for the casts, I wondered? Chicken soup? Rice pudding? Migraleve?

Later in the run, Eric Kushnick, Benny's New York under-study, small, dark and handsome, brought a different sol-emnity and maturity to the part, which again shifted the balance in an interesting way.

The older brother, Jay, was played by Ross McCall, a seasoned player of sixteen and natural Artful Dodger, who had played a leading role in *Les Miserables* and, frankly, missed the 'pzazz' side of musical theatre.

I became very addicted to my four boys and missed them a lot when the show was over.

Rolf Saxon played the boys' father, Eddie. Beautifully. He featured in the first scene and the last scene, and the time between drove him mad *before* we got on the road – by the end of nine months he was frothing like a pint of Newcastle Brown – but still playing the part beautifully. People never realize how the construction of a part affects your enjoyment of it. Derek Nimmo, playing the Rev Humphrey in *See How They Run* didn't appear until Act II. He would swan in from his sensational social life at 'Beginners' (five minutes before Curtain Up), don a clerical collar and then go to work, by which I mean virtually clean up, laughwise.

To set up a play in Act I and then sit upstairs until the final pages is enervating. How do you keep up your energies? Crochet? Dumb bells? Have a friend round?

Janette Legge, playing Eddie's other sister, Gert, had a different problem and a different solution. She had one scene only, but her nephews have talked about her all the way through the play and almost everyone has impersonated her. Gert was so frightened Mama would hear her talking in her sleep that she began to talk on the in-breath, not the out. It's terribly funny, but not easy to do. She speaks normally for the first half of the sentence, then somewhere in the middle she talks by sucking in her breath, so the words go to a higher pitch: 'Louie, can't you sit for a few minutes until Bella tells

'Mothers by daughters' or 'Why don't I look like *anyone*?' Kay and Julia McKenzie, me and Zelma.

Check-out girls: Amy and me in completely natural pose. (*Colin Poole*)

The camera gets the sexy look, the wall gets the nose. (*Steve Poole/Daily Mail*)

Lean-Two. Me and my bonkers *Yonkers* boys, Benny Grant and Ross McCall. (*Ian Turner*)

Bella blubs on brother (Rolf Saxon), while boys declare, 'She's just a little "closed for repairs", that's all'. (*Ivan Kyncl*)

Momma (Rosemary Harris) prepares to give Bella some stick, while sister (Janette Legge) holds her breath. (*Ivan Kyncl*)

Who's that snake-hipped guy with the Maureen Lipman lookalike? 'Elvis' and me in Vegas, 1994. (*Paul Harris*)

Would you buy a used bathing hut from these women? Mom and me beside the sea at Southwold. (*Radio Times*)

Woman spitting out enormous Polo mint whilst dancing with Mick Jagger's brother at the *Up the Junction* première in 1969!

I'm afraid the 'one lump' is me – sitting out the samba at the Waldorf Tea Dance. (*Fight for Sight*)

Five Guys Claimed Mo.

Idealistic and Realistic: before and after pics of *The Sisters Rosensweig* rehearsals. (*Alastair Muir*)

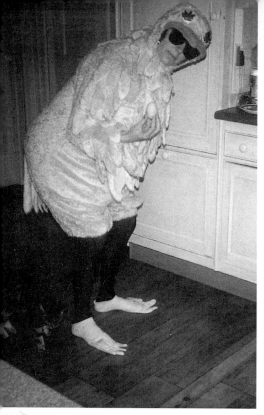

'Hilda the hen who wouldn't give up' and Jack the husband who did! (*Jacquie Granditer*)

MegaTaurus in *Agony Again* – and you wondered why they became extinct? (*Mark Bourdillon*)

Cat on Heat – Pushkin the household tabby, aged nineteen, on the radiator shelf. (*Sally Smith*)

United hooligans in Marbella – Jack and me on Cup Final day, 1994.

Clockwise from top left: Venice Observed (thank God the lighthouse had a phone!); 'Petra-fied' (peeping through the rose-red rocks of the old Jordanian city); 'If it was good enough for Mr Jones ...' (Actor Simon and son Timothy, Amy and me in Central Park); Lynn and me at the Little White Drive-in Chapel in Las Vegas; the first two mobile customers of the day.

us what it is ... (she sucks in) ... she wants to talk to us about?' Occasionally Janette would convulse us, and herself, by, as she put it, 'running out of suck'.

Janette was in her final year of a six-part Humanities Course with the Open University and spent every moment off stage cramming for a degree which she sat and passed during our run at the Strand Theatre. What I love about this is that she *did it*, alone and entirely by self-discipline. As opposed to my, 'During this run I'm going to master French conversation!' knowing there's more chance of mastering French ruddy polishing! Or, 'I'm really going to get fit once this play's over!' For this read, I'm going to pay £300 for the privilege of one swim a week, slowing down to one swim a month till my membership runs out and my perm stops drying out!

Actually, last week I went for a sedate length or two followed by a comfy sweat in the sauna. I was alone in there, practising breathing through the nose without burning your membranes, when Victoria Wood came in. She sat in silence. I sat in silence. I'd appeared in her show and with her on radio but it passed the point where you can start a conversation and I knew, of old, how shy she can be. Finally, I said, 'What a surprise to see you! How are you?' and she said 'Fine'. Then we both sat there till the heat and embarrassment grew as oppressive as a committee meeting of the *Guardian*'s Wimmin's Page, and she got up and left. And they wonder what comediennes say to one another when they meet!

Back to *Yonkers*, where another heated non-exchange took place. Ron Berglas, playing Uncle Louie, and I had a relationship which could have been forged in *Much Ado About Nothing*. Beattie and Benedick, that was us. A love/hate relationship which climaxed one night on stage with the nearest I've ever come to fisticuffs. Ridiculous in retrospect but it revolved around the two boys making off stage noise. Two sharp profiles, large egos and short fuses erupted. The following night he arrived in a crash helmet and I wish now I'd had more humour about it. His Uncle Louie was fast and furious and his heart is, like Louie's, entirely in the right place. It's just you can't *always* remember this when you're trying to stick a stake through it.

The director was David Taylor, a tall, bearded bear of a man who combines a gentle, unflappable exterior with a courteous and intelligent interior, making him one of my top five good directors. To describe his abilities I must resort to negatives. He doesn't use twenty-five words when two would do. He doesn't listen to the sound of his own eloquence. He doesn't grind personal axes on the fragile scalps of actors. What's more, he is well organized and gives detailed notes. Furthermore, he sticks with the show when the reviewers are long gone ... and further furthermore, I like his company and he likes mine. Apart from all that, he's a pain in the ass!

The tour of *Yonkers* was six weeks around England and, during it, I wrote an intermittent journal:

Lost and Bonkers

Last week Guildford, this week Bradford, next week ... Gloria Hunniford ... Who knows? One thing I *do* know is, one more late-night chicken Madras with bahji and stuffed nan in the only restaurants that will take a starving post-performanced actor, and I'm trading my Star of David for a Star of Bengal and painting a red spot over my frown lines.

The play is Neil Simon's *Lost in Yonkers* and it's no coincidence that I've been lost in every ring road of several major cities in England during its pre-London tour. We rehearsed for four weeks in Waterloo, London and I found my way there each day with remarkable ease. Not so my daughter, who came on the tube to have lunch with me one day and, arriving half-an-hour late, said, 'I came out the wrong entrance of the tube.'

'So?' I barked. 'The station's only 200 yards from the rehearsal rooms.'

'Yes,' she replied blithely, 'but it took the taxi driver a while to find it.'

Lost for words . . .

We opened in Guildford, the 'pull-in-your- stock-broker belt', to an audience about as ethnically clean as the one you might get in Balmoral, but Neil Simon's family saga brought tears of laughter and sadness to their steely blue eyes. I was lucky to be in it.

Lucky to be playing poor, silly, optimistic Bella, but luckier still to make it to Guildford each night from Muswell Hill when the great whimsical God of roadmenders in Whitehall had decreed that both the North Circular and the A40 could be arbitrarily closed to all motorized vehicles at any given time. It took two hours twenty minutes each day to drive the thirty miles there, and an hour and a quarter to drive home. So why didn't I take the train? After two weeks of snarling stickiness I asked myself the same question and the answer I gave myself is the reason I'm sitting in Compartment J at 8.50 pm on a Sunday night in October, newsprint all over my palms, struggling to open a mildewed British Rail raisin and oatmeal flapjack, on a packed Intercity Flyaway, straight through from Hull, two hours behind schedule sodding train on my one day off before opening in Richmond, Surrey, a few weary hours from now.

Our 'Senior Steward speakin'' has given us several eloquent singsong explanations for our stationary position involvin' overhead electric cables and signallin'. Biggleswade has been mentioned. It has been impossible to pee for forty minutes. The buffet has thoughtfully closed. My smudge-print tells me that British Rail have announced massive price increases for the new year. Bring me the head of a BR Chairman on an individual fruit pie. I'm all for rallying the passengers to mutiny. Eisenstein fashion. For standing up on my red and grey diagonally upholstered seat and shouting, 'Altogether now! Everyone shout "I'm as mad as hell and I'm not going to take it any more!"' and, 'Anyone with livestock in their luggage, release it in the driver's compartment!' For commandeering the tannoy system and singing 'We shall not be moved' down the microphone. Fortunately, my children and my husband are with me and have their 'Oh, *please* don't do anything to embarrass us' faces on.

They are with me because, in between Newcastle and Richmond, I've been up to Hull for a family funeral. My beloved aunt, Rita, Labour Councillor, friend, shopaholic, ex-Lady Mayoress and total, uncomplaining heroine, was finally carried off by cancer. Last week, by sheer bloody-minded obstinacy and a refusal to acknowledge the rights of five brain tumours, one chest, one lung and, unbeknown to any of us, approaching liver failure, she made it from Hull to the Alhambra Theatre, Bradford, to see the play. Coiffured and coutured, she dragged herself uncomplainingly up the circle steps to watch Simon's bittersweet portrayal of the human condition. Afterwards, over a baked potato she could hardly lift to her mouth, she personified it. I've promised myself, in tribute to her unique spirit, that I'll never complain again about things that don't matter ... But then, what will I write about?

By the time you read this, *Lost in Yonkers* will have opened. Everywhere we've played so far the critics have raved and the audiences have packed out the theatres, raised the roof and gone out into the streets, amused and moved. I'm willing to bet you

a year's supply of Korean Ginseng and all the leaf
tea on British Rail that the pundits of the West End
will find it full of 'American sentimentality
and schmaltz' and complain about the upbeat
ending.

On the whole, our press has been great – and,
having read through them again, there's a genuine
admiration for both the play and the performances.

I'll be OK. I'll keep my sense of humour and
proportion, I promise. And the public will vote with
their Visa cards and cheque books. If we get through
Biggleswade, Bengali, and the critics, I'll never
complain again. Put it down to Travel Sickness –
Mal de Mo.

Meanwhile, I've savoured autumnal sunsets over
Grassington, and dimpled scones in 'The Wrinkled
Stocking' in Holmfirth. I've devoured the David
Hockneys in Saltaire, shared Chardonnay with Princess Margaret in Surrey and had my roots redone
in Jesmond Road, Newcastle, by a hairdresser who
told me that, for her ninety-second birthday, his
grandmother had asked for a brand new set of sauce-
pans with a twenty-year guarantee.

In Newcastle, we heard that dolphins had been
sighted in the North Sea and Rosemary, who has
more spirit and energy than the rest of the young
cast put together, attempted to hire a wet suit and
charter a small ship to get there and swim with
them. In November.

From Bradford, Rosemary and I spent a marvellous Sunday and Monday in Whitby at the cosy
cottage of Ian Carmichael and his wife, Kate. I
didn't know Ian, although we should have met,
being Hullovians, but Rosie had toured with him
the previous year and they had become friends.

Kate and Ian are a May/September romance,
which makes you believe in God and Cupid as a single

being. Throughout the evening, as we chatted our way through a fine bottle of whisky, Rosie sat on the floor, legs stretched in front of her, unsupported and entirely comfortable. Small wonder she was critically acclaimed as Grandma. She is, I think, made of very strong stuff, if not Grandma's steel, then the strongest of parachute silk. An iron butterfly.

Also, I've visited Primrose Hospice in Birmingham, where hope reigns supreme, so you won't catch *me* complaining about Birmingham's concrete underpass. Home in a week, NOT LOST AND NOT YET BONKERS.

I was right. The London critics were obsessed with the word 'schmaltz'. Although, looking back on the reviews of *Yonkers*, I'm surprised by how enthusiastic they were. Why we only remember the snide ones is a sad fact of the nature of our profession and our professional natures.

One, in the *Sunday Times*, gave me a compliment that was *so* backhanded that the writer must have been a contortionist. 'Such is the personal chemistry emanating from this extraordinary actress that she could probably make Norman Lamont's autumn statement sound like a birthday greeting; and, accordingly, she fills this cardboard role, with its improbable psychological insights, brimful of touching and beguiling warmth. Oh, actors – the things they can do!'

The beguiling warmth I felt at the beginning of reading the paragraph had turned to anthracite by the end. I don't remember the reviewer's name but I almost sent him a script with a note saying, 'Read it! Read it! Cardboard role? All I had to do was turn up and learn my lines!' If only I could tell him/her the pleasure, the security of being in the hands of a real dramatist, after so often piecing together the fragments of minor ones. Oh, critics, the things they cannot see!

As a cast, we had wonderful laughs, on and off stage, cook-ins and birthday parties and we've stayed in touch. As a show, we were a 'nervous hit'. It seems that the best you can get out of a play which has any label of ethnicity about it, is six months. For me, I still believe my first impressions are never wrong. Bella was the best part I've ever had and if that's 'cardboard', I'll take a shipment.

Sunny Stories

I realised it was politically incorrect of me to say so but, it
was just what I didn't need. A job. July I intended to spend
perfecting my Bronx and holidaying with my kids, who, let's
face it, are not going to want to holiday with the fogey for too
many more Julys.

Enter Ken Howard – earnest, erudite, enthusiastic, director
Ken Howard – bringing biographies and bumph and Blyton
by the boxful, with a gleam in his glasses and the certainty
that he could make a drama documentary with animation
given a setting up period of just over three weeks and a budget
that would scarcely keep Barbara Cartland in mascara for a
week. Would I do it? Would I be his Enid? It would only
require ten days' studio and two days' filming. He realized I
was pressed for time because I would begin rehearsing *Yonkers*
in August but he felt certain that once I read what a complex,
difficult and fascinating woman Enid was, I would find the
challenge irresistible.

I thought about it. Three weeks to delve into and discover
what made Enid Blyton the voice and mind of several generations of children, three weeks to find out how she looked,
talked, thought, walked and felt. No archive material but one
and a half minutes of scratchy film and two minutes of her
voice on tape. No time to re-read all the books, to visit her
house, her haunts, her descendants. Two weeks' holiday in
Majorca ruined by reading biography instead of bodice
ripper, Bella's Yonkers' accent yanked out of the Walkman
and Noddy and Big Ears shoved in. No time for costume
fittings, nor to make wigs or padding to cover the ages of

twenty to seventy. No time. Little money. It was everything I didn't need. I looked Ken straight in the glasses, smiled to indicate my gratitude at his offer, shook my head firmly and said, 'Yes. I'll do it.'

To save time I borrowed Beattie's old padding (Bless her, she didn't bat an eyelid) and dug out and dyed one *About Face* wig, whilst the wigmaker resurrected a coarse, wiry ready-made one from his dump bin, for the older Enid. Costumes were period originals from Sheila and Alan Buckland in Barnes, whose small modern house in a suburban crescent is literally lined and tabulated with authentic costumes and accessories from vanished eras. It was done in an afternoon. All it required was one stand up, trying on session. For six hours. Enid's shoes were of the sensible mould. Bunions, I suspect. I would not feel happy until my feet pinched where hers did.

Meanwhile I read. And read. And listened and looked and began to feel a tiny stirring of something symbiotic. She was ambitious, manipulative, opinionated, irrational, clever, charming, witty, didn't suffer fools gladly, workaholic, given to temper tantrums, sudden bursts of affection, enthusiasms and equally sudden withdrawal. Gosh. I wonder why Ken had thought of *me*?

I had, of course, read her ceaselessly as a child. Once I'd opened, devoured and closed *Five Go to Kirrin Island* six or seven times, I was, like most children of my generation, hooked, blinded and sunk as far as any other author was concerned. I simply couldn't wait for the next appearance of good old solid Julian, upright old Dick, if you take my meaning, tousled, rebellious hot-headed George and Timmy the barking mad mutt. Frankly, I could take or leave mumsy, whiney old Anne, but she came with the package and I could at least feel infinitely superior to her in spite of the retrospective realization that her courage in a crisis was roughly 900 per cent more than mine in an everyday skirmish in the school milk queue. The great thing was you didn't have to wait for long. Enid could turn out thirty books a year. She could start a *Five* book on the Monday and write 'Well, that's the smugglers taken care of. What about that chocolate cake and homemade lemonade you've got in your knapsack, old girl?' on the Friday.

Since her own miserably unhappy childhood, Enid Blyton had developed the ability to turn fear and uncertainty into a kaleidoscope of adventures, a running fantasy of Sunny Stories which she could summon at will into her mind. It cancelled out the reality of her parents' loveless marriage, her mother's stubborn pride and her adored father's departure from her life when she was twelve. In many ways Enid's development as a woman ended with this traumatic event. In the same way, her career as a writer began. The child Enid explains in *Sunny Stories* that 'When I went to bed I used to be still and wait for my "thoughts" ... They seemed to come from somewhere else ... not myself. They were about children I knew and children I didn't know.'

Later, explaining her craft, she tells her audience of children, 'I am just as surprised by the adventures as you are. I sit down with my typewriter on my knee and shut my eyes for a few minutes and make my mind blank and then – as clearly as I would see real children – my characters stand before me in my mind's eye, where the story is acted out, almost as if I had a private cinema screen there.' She never re-wrote or revised her work and typed it herself. The first and final draft.

Years later, when researching for my one-woman show *Re: Joyce*, I came across one of Joyce Grenfell's sketches called 'Writer of Children's Books' in which she mercilessly satirized a famous lady writer talking to children in a large store about the writing process. For Joyce, it is quite a hard-hitting piece and she clearly didn't like her subject: 'First of all I go upstairs to my Hidey Hole ... I pin a notice on the door and it says "Gone to Make-Believe Land". This is just my way of saying "Please don't come and bother me because a book is writing itself to me and we mustn't disturb it, must we?"

'No I never re-write and I never read what I have written.

But you children do, millions and millions of you children do
and that is my great joy ... and it is my husband's great joy,
too. He has given up his work to encourage mine. Well, I
think it is time I got back to my Hidey Hole, don't you?'

I learned that she had indeed watched Enid with her tiny
fans in Harrods and had instinctively smelled a rat in the
Wendy House. Enid's two daughters, rather like Joan Craw-
ford's and Nancy Reagan's children, recall two very different
sides of their mother. Gillian Baverstock, the elder daughter,
reveres her mother's memory and remembers mostly the good
times. Imogen Smallwood, the younger daughter, in her sad
memoirs *A Childhood at Green Hedges*, paints a very different
picture of chilling neglect, bordering on cruelty, on her
mother's part.

My own suspicion, based on a biography of Enid by
Barbara Stoney and Imogen's book, was that the truth was
somewhere in between and relative to the characters involved.
There are some actors who only remember good reviews and
there are those of us who do the reverse. Certainly, Gillian
was a much wanted child. Enid's failure to provide her
husband, Hugh Pollock, with a child was a subject of great
sorrow and frustration to her and she underwent pioneering
and painful hormone treatments to enlarge the unusually
under-developed uterus she was found to possess. She was
delighted with her baby daughter but devoted less and less
time to her as her work load increased. There was a mis-
carriage, a boy, before the difficult birth of Imogen, and this
time she made little attempt to form a relationship with the
difficult baby of the wrong sex with which she found herself
saddled. It may just have been a case of the doctor who never
treats his wife, or the psychiatrist who spoils his children, but
Enid certainly seemed to have found it easier to form a bond
with the world's children than with her own.

Similarly, she moralized in her books and articles about the
rights and wrongs, the blacks and whites of life, yet fell
into the arms of surgeon Kenneth Darrell-Waters, whilst her
husband was in the army, and conducted a double life with

him for at least a year before finally engineering a divorce from Hugh and marrying Kenneth. Gillian had been sent to boarding school but Imogen was told in a five-minute interview that she was to have a new daddy. That was all. Hugh, who agreed to be the guilty party in order to retain access to his daughters, was never allowed to see them again, and the girls' names were changed by deed poll to Darrell-Waters.

This was not going to be a character I could take to my heart. It was, however, one with whom I could sympathize and whose late development I could understand.

The filming was strangely arduous. Studio work invariably is, but this more so than usual because the background to each scene was a huge scythe of blue paper – Chromakey – upon which all the animation would be projected at a later stage. I understand this even less than *you* do and *I* spent ten twelve-hour days working against it.

'The blue post on the studio floor is a gate – the cottage is behind you – so walk arm in arm from the tape mark down right, then stop at the post and lean over it, and it will look as though you're leaning on the gate,' said Ken, who had all this stuff in his head, which was a blessing because I had very little in mine but the lines I'd learned at ten o'clock the previous night.

Day after day, costume after costume, against the sea of blue. Sometimes with children from the Anna Scher School, sometimes with fellow actors, sometimes with imaginary dogs, I was cosseted by Ken and poured into younger, older, fatter, thinner Enids by Hazel Pethig, wardrobe, and Shirley Channing-Williams, make-up, almost as though they all knew what they were doing. My face, devoid of make-up for the scene after Enid's second pregnancy, is a virtual daguerreotype of the clapped-out woman that I was.

Malcolm Rennie, with whom I'd recently worked on stage, played my husband Hugh. Fifty years in the business, between us, and neither of us had ever done a screen kiss. Elderly crumpet at last! The high point of the shoot was a day's filming at the original Thatched Cottage in Beaconsfield, where I tried, and didn't entirely succeed, to soak up atmosphere and verisimilitude. I've never been great at all that. Just learn the lines and don't bump into the blue parts, that's my motto.

We worked long and hard into the evening on our last day – Ken and our dear, crusty, painstaking cameraman, Tom Ingle, propping their eyes open with blue matchsticks and me virtually on automatic simmer. Then I went home to Muswell Hill and *Yonkers* and they worked on for three more months with 'Harry', the mysterious electronic computer whose moment of glory had now come, creating all the background animation and cartoon characters for the final creation.

The resulting film, with a cast of thousands including Noddy, Big Ears, Famous Fives, actors, biographer Barbara Stoney, daughters Gillian, playing herself, and Imogen, played hauntingly by Anna Massey, is a full, fair and, I think, fascinating portrait of a woman who was as familiar to a generation of children as their parents or their teachers, but whom nobody really knew at all.

She was often incorrect, but politically so? I think not. She angered a generation of librarians and teachers, not, I think, because she typified upper middle class niceties, but more because of her prolific output which, once tried, became an addiction, thus utterly excluding other authors. Twenty odd years later, in the wake of *Terminator I* to *IV*, it is clear to us that what matters is less what children read than that they read at all.

When I was in Scarborough, *Re: Joycing*, I had a request from my primary school in Hull to open their new library and read to the children from some of my favourite books. It was irresistible.

I had not been inside Wheeler Street School for thirty-eight years. It was, of course, smaller than I remembered and the years had freshened and jollied up the dark tiled walls of my memories. I imagine the tiny toilets had gone too. The ones down which I was convinced the spiders lived and

whose cubicle doors burst open the minute you'd started an
undeflectable pee.

Visiting schools is always joyful and invariably exhausting.
After a mere half hour of the children I was flailing around –
and teachers have a seven-hour day. Plus all the wretched
administrative work so generously thrust upon them by the
National Curriculum. They are, give or take a few miscreants,
heroes to a man or woman, and their status, salary and the
respect due to them cannot be elevated high enough. There
now. It needs to be said and I've said it.

Moreover, when successful people re-visit their old school
to talk about their lives since school, I don't suppose there's
one who wasn't inspired to succeed by some unknown,
unsung (Emlyn Williams aside) educator. Someone who suddenly reached through all the sham and the rebellion and the
gauche poses to the still, receiving centre of that child and
opened a door to a way of life with possibilities.

So here I am, in my nice dress, standing on the stage which
looked so huge and imposing to me when I was under three
foot and I realize it's about a foot high and maybe ten feet
wide by seven across, and I'm gazing out at a funfair of faces.

It is Comic Relief Day and every child is in fancy dress
sitting cross-legged on the floor. They look magnificent.
There are Blobbys and Batmen and clowns and nurses and
shiny headed robots and huge headed dinosaurs who wished
to heck they'd come as cowboys, and I start to talk about
reading after the first tumult has died down. For a while they
listen because that's what they've been told to do. Then I ask
a question and everyone answers at once, and I ask another
and a chorus breaks out, and I panic for a moment because
how will I ever retain order, and the teachers down the sides
in their chairs are wondering whether to help me out or not
... And, suddenly, as has happened so often and in such
timely fashion over the last six years, Joyce Grenfell comes to
my rescue.

'Children! Children!' I call in that pitch so known and so
attended to by those of a certain age – and I clap my hands

together. 'Children! Gather round now, because we are going
to do our lovely *moving to music now.* And Miss Boulting is
going to play her piano,' and I gesture towards the wall of the
Assembly Hall where there is no piano and they all look left
to where I'm pointing and accept there is one. 'And we are
all going to be lovely flowers, growing and dancing in the
grass.' There is a puzzled silence . . . 'Now isn't that nice?'
They are not sure that it is. 'Yes, it *is*, Sidney. It's *very* nice!'
And they start to laugh, and we're away.

It really is magic. Thirty-five years after she conceived the
slightly out-of-control teacher, Joyce's creation is as fresh as
the daisy in the circle suggested by Peggy, the invisible pupil.

You should have *seen* those kids. How they looked around
at George every time he did whatever it is that he does and I
tell him not to. How their eyes followed Sidney out of the
room in disgrace and back in again when he refused to give
me whatever he'd had in his mouth. 'A big button, Sidney?
Well. I'm ashamed of you. Yes I am. A big boy of four, eating
a button off the back of little girls' dresses! Well, I'm very
glad you spat it out. You didn't? Oh. I see – you've, yes, well
. . . Do you *feel* all right, Sidney?'

And when Jemima came back into the circle and I said,
'Oh, Jemima dear, what do we do when we come back from
the littlest room? We pull our knickers *up* again, don't we?' I
thought the roof would fly off. Knickers of every hue were
revealed as they rocked backwards and screeched out their
pleasure. It was a triumph that the lady herself would not have
been able to resist. The staff were almost equally amused,
although they tended to dab their eyes rather than flash their
knickers.

Joyce once asked a roomful of children to tell her what the
word frugal meant. One little chap said it meant 'to save',
and she congratulated him on his knowledge and suggested
the class might all write her little stories that contained the
word frugal. The prize-winning story went as follows:

The princess was inprisoned in the towr and she

shouted 'Frugal me, Frugal me,' and the hansom prince came and he frugalled her and they lived happily every after!

I think even Miss Blyton might have flashed a knicker at that one.

The Jittering Prizes

The award-giving season is officially upon us. That ritual shooting of endangered actors from awkward angles, followed by mutual back-slapping at M'Lord's house over warm wine and tepid fowl. The season lasts from November to, well, November really, and you can tell it's happening by the number of frenzied celebs you see scurrying down Bond Street hauling bags of designer garments borrowed for the occasion and due back the following morning for a *Hello!* shoot.

I was clutching some Chanel crêpe flares for the Variety Club Awards when I ricocheted into Miranda Richardson clutching Calvin Kleins for the Golden Globes. 'Don't forget to leave by midnight,' I warned her, 'or you'll wake up in Dorothy Perkins!'

The BAFTAs are even dafta and they do go on so. Last year they imported a 100-foot catwalk for the express purpose of fore-shortening the approaching presenter.

'We couldn't find your Joyce Grenfell music for the intro, Maureen,' said the musical director. 'So we've settled for something nondescript.'

'Perfect,' I said, setting off down the catwalk in my new excruciating Maud Frizons.

This year I've watched the Oscars in a New York apartment, the Oliviers from a 'hostility room' backstage and the BAFTAs from my newly distressed living room. It's hard to say which was more distressing.

I was in New York when resident English actor, Simon Jones, invited me over to his cosy eclectic apartment for his annual Oscar night party. We were all given Oscar forms to fill in our favourites. There were twenty-one people there and I came twenty-second, largely because I voted for people who did not have the luck to be nominated. Like John Turturro, who gave such a funny, brave and characterful performance in my film of the year, *Quiz Show*, that he was totally over-looked – 'Gumped' at the post. Likewise, Linda Fiorentini in *The Last Seduction* outclassed all four official nominees.

Our party was wonderfully vicious, New York style, about the ladies' gowns. Oscar winner, Dianne Wiest, looked like a coach and four. And David Letterman's teeth! And his patter! It's a new and, I feel, disastrous concept that the host should have wildly witty and entertaining patter. It's an impossible brief amongst a mausoleum filled with professionals in tight stays and borrowed rhinestones. Besides, they can't laugh too much because their surgery might slide. So now we have endless nervous foreplay from the host and the winners are shuffled past on a conveyor belt or edited out on the 'ank' of 'I'd like to thank...'

On the other hand, at the 1994 Olivier Stage Awards one young recipient said, 'I know I shouldn't do this but I really must thank a few people ...' and then proceeded to unroll a list written on a roll of paper which spread from her hand to the footlights. Funny gag. We all laughed – until she pro-ceeded to read every name on the bloody list including her agent's chiropractor and her mother's spider plant.

When Tony Slattery insulted the critics at the Olivier Awards the incident was widely and negatively reported. Michael Coveney was still referring to it in his column as late as May, ten weeks after the event occurred. Two vital aspects of the issue were never, to my knowledge, reported. The first was that Slattery's introductions were *before* the TV recording began. In other words, during the presentation of awards which the Society do not think important enough to be televised – he was addressing the audience in private, rather as if he were giving an after-dinner speech. This is important because every report indicated that his remarks had, in some way, to be removed from a TV programme. Not so. He was addressing those already 'in the know'.

Secondly, when he made the remark that a certain critic was the C word that rhymes with what you bob along in, 'neath 'dreaming spires', it got the biggest laugh of the evening. The place went up. The roof rattled with the sheer cathartic pleasure he gave to so many in no position to say the same. As an actor, it was both a brave and foolhardy move and many suffering souls secretly saluted him. All eyes and ears are on the next West End production starring Mr T Slattery when the quality of mercy shall be strained to its limits.

Most of the 'hosts' of the Olivier Awards had been rung up two days before the event and accepted humbly in the knowledge that Albert Finney had taken off for Ireland and Jennifer Saunders couldn't be fagged. Peter Bowles, rung only the previous evening, was a disturbing shade of green in the hospitality room beforehand. Sir Ian McKellen had been sitting quietly in his sitting-room, digesting a light luncheon, when the call came to don a monkey suit and appear live in front of 2,000 people with no script. It's conclusive proof that all actors are tarts at heart ...

(There's a whore who lives up seventy-four steps on the seventh floor of a block of flats. Her downstairs neighbour sees her trudging upstairs with yet another client at the end of a *very* busy day. 'You all right dear?' asks the neighbour. 'Gawd, what a day!' moans the prostitute. 'I've had forty-nine clients! Forty-nine! I mean! My poor feet!') ... any time, any place, anywhere – except that tarts get paid. Humiliation money. We don't. Our humiliation is both public and penurious. And sometimes we even pay for our frocks.

So why don't we say no? Or 'Nice of you to ask but I'm having a boil lanced in Cirencester that night.' Or 'Yes, if you'll pay me in laundered ingots and seal me up in a lift with Liam Neeson at the aftershow party.' The late Peter Cook was once famously phoned by David Frost and invited to a dinner party to celebrate the engagement of Prince Andrew and Sarah Ferguson. After hearing the A-list of guests, Cook went off to get his diary and returning said with regret, 'Sorry, David, but I'm afraid I'm watching television that night.'

All actors know that these occasions will be similar to the regular nightmare. You know the one: all alone on the Palladium stage; two thousand punters; music, drum roll boom-ting, 'Good evening, it's lovely to be here with you tonight . . .' and absolutely no idea on God's earth what comes next. Perhaps the reason we have it is to stop it happening in real life. Like a steam vent. To stop us, literally and metaphorically, dying on stage.

Last year, the British Comedy Awards gave the Comedy Writers Award to Jack. It was a low-key evening, televised, but only in the London area, and without the benefit of a long-drawn-out meal and low boredom threshold. The high point of the evening came when a sad, tired and seemingly 'out of it' Spike Milligan was called up to receive his Lifetime Achievement Award. The host read out a fan letter to Spike from HRH The Prince of Wales. Suddenly the light went on in Milligan's eyes, the gleam of anarchy illuminated his wispy face, causing him to drop twenty-five years in a single shrug. 'Oh him,' he smirked. 'Grovelling bastard.' The place went up. The laughter refused to die down and, like the most diluted remedy, it turned a sick man into a deadly comic instrument sharp enough to puncture any amount of pomposity. It was a great performance. And nobody would have laughed louder than HRH. We were on our feet applauding his past, his present and, unbelievably, his future.

There is nothing intrinsically wrong with rewarding talented communicators for doing their job well. It's the 'Best' in 'Best Actor' which really constitutes the rot. I could quote you *Lost in Yonkers* notices from two people writing their pieces on the same day after seeing the same performance the night before. 'A' says the characterization is tyrannical, hard, merciless and without a trace of sentimentality. 'B' says the performance is played with a roguish twinkle throughout and no hint of real danger or malice. So, who is right, and which is 'Best'?

Add to this the vagaries of fashion. For two or three years an actor will be an automatic nominee followed by the inevitable, 'Oh, we've seen it all before, thank you', then the dropped-from-favour years leading, inevitably, to the big squashy comeback when the years/drink/near brush with death have taken their toll.

In this way England lost the most fruitful and, I'm sure, amazing years of Maggie Smith. All through her Old Vic years she could do no wrong, then came a little heady commercialism and, suddenly, in the eyes of her erstwhile adorers, she was 'mannered, camp, OTT' and, worse, 'difficult'. Ms Smith didn't wait for martyrdom; instead she packed up her family and headed out for Canada, where under the direction of Robin Phillips, she did her most consummate work, playing all the great classic roles. Thanks to her detractors we missed all of those performances. When Ms Smith returned, she could have stood centre stage and recited selected passages from *Which Greenhouse?* and won a virtual landslide of bronze lumps on armatures.

This is not to denigrate her or anyone else's talent. Quite the reverse. My point is that fine actors don't 'go off' or cease to have talent – although some may abuse their talent, obviously – what 'goes off' is their impact on critics who have, on the whole, a low familiarity threshold.

And the public can be equally fickle. We want our singers to be 'divas' and our actors to be 'hell-raisers' and our stars to be scarred. Gods and Goddesses who somehow fall back to earth when we tire of them or they over-reach themselves. Nothing pleases the amphitheatre more than the demise of the 'over-dog'.

They call it the British sport. We love 'em on the way up; we're proud of 'em when they conquer Hollywood – then there's a brief plateau when the chunter of, 'Oh, not her again!' can just be discerned amongst the proud, possessive acclaim. Then, at some point, *money* will be mentioned rather more than before ... 'In their £1½ million Windsor pile ...', 'In her Christian Lacroix gown and wearing the Plotnik diamond ring he bought for their second anniversary ...', '... believed to have demanded £550,000 for a thirty-second commercial ...' And it's then that the plateau descends sharply to a gorge whilst the assembled public and press fan each other to deeper and deeper layers of malcontent. 'I always *thought* there was something odd about her ... she's just the same in every film, except for the accents ... and who cares a mink muff what she thinks about Bosnia?'

Sorry about this Huge Rant ... speaking of whom ... I've just put the phone down from a certain reporter who wants to know of a Saturday afternoon, my reaction to Ms Hurley's reaction to Mr Grant's version of 'Not Very Pretty Woman'. Before I can stop myself I've remarked that Ms Hurley has happily accepted everything that rubbed off on her from Mr Grant's success. It will be interesting to see if she does the same when what rubs off may be a little less flavoursome. At which point, my oh so sensible and kindly husband walks through the kitchen saying pointedly '... and what's it got to do with you? And, furthermore, what's it got to do with him?' He's right, of course. He always is, dammit!

Perhaps if a public figure survives their worst nightmare, it acts as a kind of aversion therapy. Take Woody Allen. Silent, paranoid, uncommunicative, and in daily therapy for most of his adult life, he is accused of virtual incest and literal child abuse. He survives the case which exonerates him from the abuse but, *Catch 22* like, forbids him access to his daughter ... 'No, you didn't do it, but the fact remains you might!' The outcome in a book by his beloved Dostoevsky would be depression, lethargy, alcoholism, tuberculosis and an offstage gunshot. In reality, Woody Allen continues to work ferociously, writing and film-making, playing clarinet, eating out and produces his most accessible work. Victim as survivor. And more. Suddenly the publicity-shy recluse became Paula Yates in hornrims. In print and in public he explained, he philosophized, he mused – and once he almost smiled. He allowed us to know him, warts and all . . . and almost admitted he would value our approval. His latest film, *Bullets Over Broadway*, unlike eighty per cent of his previous films, is a critical as well as a commercial success.

As far as I'm concerned, there's a nomination missing in all these prizegivings. It's for valour and dedication in the face of peril and it goes to those unsung heroes – The Great British Viewing Public.

By which I don't mean the ones who sit glazed as a Virginia ham through ceremonies which last as long as Lent, or those, apparently of sane mind, who are *Framed, Blind Dated* or accept an invitation to *Noel's House Party* for fifteen minutes of dubious fame.

Neither do I mean those viewers who stay loyal to their favourite sitcom long after any com has gone leaving nothing but a load of sit, nor the ones who accept without protest that their newscaster must have 'F-factor', their radio station pop-classics, their *Play for Today* stretch over three nights and their national sports restricted to those houses with large white plastic zits on the front stucco. 'Good on ya, Mr Murdoch, you're a real sport!'

What have they done which qualifies them for my 'Academy of One' Award? I'll tell you. They've *gone out*. They've swelled cinema queues more than any time since John Logie Baird's mother bought him his first crystal set. They've rejected Four Channels, Sky, Video Hypermarkets, Nintendo, Trivial Pursuits, the new Madagascan take-away on the corner and *The Word* (I'm talking intellectualism here), and they've *gone out*. OUT. Through the front bloody door. Into the loveless streets, over the thousands of sleeping policemen, braving the bombs, and the sudden frosts, even more sudden droughts, and the soaring rates of the baby sitter, and the sheer greed of the towers-away and the clampers, and the loonies on the buses and the terror on the tubes, and the disinterest of the boys in the box office, and the price of the tickets when you *do* get 'em, and the fear that you've chosen the wrong show ('Wasn't it the *other* one that Jack Tinker said was an oasis in a cultural desert?') when every theatre in town sports nonsensical praise in identical prose: 'I laughed till I cried' – W Hazlitt.

Out they've gone, these sweet, old-fashioned radicals in pursuit of art, cinema, opera, theatre, whatever. The chance to slip into someone else's world for a couple of hours. It's a risk. An expensive risk. They know they may even be changed by what they see as opposed to being prejudiced by what they read. These are today's conquistadors. Give 'em vouchers! Give 'em trophies! Give 'em the Freedom of the crumbling City, that's what I say!

A few weeks before we closed, my friends, Stanley and Judith, came to see me in *Lost in Yonkers*. Twice before, on different nights, they'd set out to see the show and turned back because of diversionary or bomb-scare traffic. On this occasion they parked in a quiet 'office' street, at 7.20 pm, on a meter, knowing that meters were defunct after 6.30 pm. At ten past ten, the three of us wended our way back to the car. Though I say it as shouldn't, they'd had a wonderful evening, loved the play, me, everything. They were alive with praise, up to and excluding the moment they realized their car had been towed away.

It was impossible. They were on a meter! In *no one's* disabled, medical or private parking place, blocking no doorway known to man (indeed, every doorway was already blocked with the cardboard homeless, all calling ' 'Ere, Maureen – s'you innit? Come 'ere, Maureen, give us a quid, will ya? My mate's a big fan of yours! Come 'ere, girl!') For whose benefit had a police truck been brought out and a perfectly harmless car been winched up and transported one mile down a wide, empty road into a full car pound?

Well. Camden Council's, actually. Er – bankrupt Camden Council. At the car pound – 'That'll be £100 for towing it away and £30 for the offence' – they alerted us to the fact that this particular street was, unlike the next street along, in Camden, and the meters in Camden specifically stated, albeit in the dark, that they were effective till 8.30 pm. And if you think one penny of that £130 might go towards housing those gentlemen in the doorway then you probably believe Nigel Lawson's fat and Hillary Clinton *always* looked like that.

See what I mean? Valour in the face of apathy and danger. And greed. Two genuine, avid, appreciative, law-abiding theatre-goers were £170 poorer, plus petrol. Will they go to the theatre again this year? Or will they, instead, turn up the gas coal log effect, unfreeze the deep pie pizza, tune in to the Annual Theatre Awards from dusk till midnight and wonder what the winning plays must have looked like in real life?

A Sense of Direction

Unlike many of my contemporaries, it's never been an ambition of mine to direct. There's a joke about Mother Theresa being interviewed, whilst passing through California, by a reporter from a Hollywood newspaper. 'You have done so many good deeds for mankind in your extraordinary life, Mother Theresa,' gushes the reporter. 'Is there any one thing that you feel you haven't had the chance to do, before you meet your Maker?'

'Well, yes, there is actually, my dear,' replies the saintly old woman. 'The one thing I would most like to do is to *direct*.'

Something of a 'pro's' joke, but it illustrates, I think, how clichéd the desire to direct has become. Every actor, every writer, every commercial copywriter, every school drama teacher expresses the same ambition – everyone but one, that is. Me.

Still, one fateful day in 1993 the director in residence of the Lyceum Theatre in Edinburgh rang my agent and suggested I would be the perfect person to direct Neil Simon's *The Sunshine Boys*. 'I think you should do it,' said Anne, my agent. 'It will be a challenge.' I didn't realize at the time how right she was. It was a challenge all right. To my sanity. At the time I just heard a voice in my ear saying, 'Why not? Who knows Simon's work better than I? Who's had twenty-seven years of watching directors watching her watch them?'

In another ear, another voice said, 'Who put the "t" in tactless? Who never notices if a show is lit, even if it's just with a single bulb? Who thinks she can handle a technical

112

run when she doesn't understand why a plane stays in the air?'

So I did my usual. Shook my head and said 'yes', and from that moment on, sleep became something I once read about in Shakespeare.

'Why are you putting yourself through this?' said a loving friend.

'Because I don't know if I can do it and I need the danger,' was my reply.

'You want danger?' he inquired. 'Stay home and eat beef.'

The weeks went by as weeks must and I spent many an evening hunched over French's acting edition of the play, scribbling notes on the subtext, the wants and motivations of every line of every character. I interviewed and hired a designer and discussed my ideas for the sets. Ideas I didn't know I had until said designer sat there before me waiting for them. He didn't laugh, bless him, and I realized proudly that he didn't laugh because I hadn't said anything ludicrous. I was nearing my half-century not out, and I still couldn't believe in my own intelligence, still felt that every turn would leave me in danger of being found out as an impostor, a charlatan.

Then I hired a lighting designer. 'Julia,' I bleated down the phone to my actor/and now director friend, Julia McKenzie. 'The lighting man's on his way over, what the hell do I say to him?' To her credit, she didn't laugh. How could she have done? The first time *she* directed (the play *Stepping Out*) had she not rung me in a state of paranoia, saying that her left arm had gone completely paralysed and she'd lost the use of her thumb?

'Just ask his advice,' she advised. 'Nobody minds being consulted on their expertise. In fact they bloody love it.'

Casting was fascinating, not least because Edinburgh is long on distance and £300 a week is short on incentive. You'd be amazed by the number of sixty-five-year-old men who said no to playing seventy. Vanity, vanity, all insanity. 'But I was forty-two when I played Beattie!' I cried. 'And that was in front of a camera!'

'Yes, but you got well paid for it,' came the response.

A friend, Geoff Morrow, said, 'Would you like me to talk to Jerry Lewis?'

'Er ... yes ... wow ... are you serious? *The* Jerry Lewis? Being directed by *me*? Er ... no.'

The single greatest talent a director can have is casting ability. Without it you can have the sensitivity of Ingmar Bergman, the intelligence of Peter Brook and the wardrobe of Zeffirelli and you're still dead meat. This is closely followed by the need for an honours degree in psychotherapy. *Group* psychotherapy. That, plus a pen with a light on it to take notes in the dark, a vat of antacid tablets and you're off and running.

Loneliness? Can we talk here about loneliness? No matter how much you understand actors, love actors, respect actors, *are* an actor – when you are the director, you lunch alone. Actors have stories and anecdotes and little self-deprecating yarns which under fellow-actor circumstances would make you bark like a seal, rub your legs together like a cricket and generally decompose with eagerness to get your tale in next.

As a director, however, your sense of humour is in your briefcase with your notes for the stage manager from this morning's run, your need to telephone the theatre carpenter 400 miles away to put the legs back on the desk you've recently asked him to lower and your need to get on to Dress Circle Records to find you an outdated tract from an unnamed 78 you once heard in your sleep.

As the opening night drew near, my notebook took on the likeness of an electro-cardiogram as day after day I filled it with the same notes. It wasn't that the actors wouldn't do them, it was that by this stage they *couldn't* do them. The vision in my head had to be compromised. I had to let it go. Even Joan of Arc had time off to chase the odd rabbit or mend her chainmail. Short of having John Kennedy Jnr on 'call waiting' while you're holding on to get through to the

Hotpoint man, there is nothing more frustrating than watching passively from the dress circle whilst the actors struggle with late sound cues and dodgy doorknobs. You are a midwife at a Caesarean section.

My friend Lynn had travelled with me as an assistant and helpmate and late at night in my Edinburgh eyrie, she would pour oil in my troubled bath, feed me oatcakes and Earl Grey and fill up my hot water bottle. Some nights I clutched it so tight I woke with water blisters all over my thighs. They didn't even impinge on my pain threshold.

Well. We opened. It wasn't perfect but it wasn't bad either. The reviews said it was 'dazzling' and the public donned their parkas and flocked in to see it.

Jimmy Logan was authentic and dynamic in the role of Willie Clack and Robert Cartland had a stolid dignity which made their scenes together have real history. Jimmy's background as a vaudevillian made him perfect casting and his natural belligerence made life on stage dangerous, to say the least. Howard Samuels, playing his nephew, Ben, was a gifted saint who picked up clothes, pace and cues with equal alacrity.

There is little more thrilling than throwing out an idea to an actor and seeing the intelligence behind his eyes as he makes it his own. This is the power buzz of directing. No wonder the old joke goes: Sir Peter Hall is at the Gates of Heaven. The Angel bids him enter but he is adamant. He won't come in if Trevor Nunn is there. The Angel assures him he's not there, he's in the other place. Still, Sir Peter demurs, he won't come in because he's *sure* Trevor Nunn is in there. The Angel reassures him again and again. 'I'm an Angel, Sir Peter, surely you don't believe an Angel would lie to you?'

Finally Sir Peter acquiesces and goes through the gates to the inner sanctuary. He stands before a white palace of luminous beauty, hears heavenly choirs and sees flights of angels surrounding the palace. Suddenly a golden limousine draws up and out steps a small, dark, long-haired man with a goatee beard. Sir Peter is apoplectic. 'But ... but ... but ...'

he splutters. 'You lied! You told me Trevor Nunn wasn't here!'

The Angel smiles and raises his arms in all innocence. 'That's not Trevor Nunn, my poor friend,' he assures the trembling man. 'That's God. He just *thinks* he's Trevor Nunn.'

After an emotional first night and a calmer second one, Lynn and I kissed selected thespians goodbye, bought some smoked venison and tartan marmalade and caught the shuttle home. This is perhaps the director's greatest perk. The fact that 7.30 each evening you can sit by your own hearth, feeling a glow that is nothing at all to do with the smokeless fuel. 'They're all "on",' says the glow. And then it adds, 'And *I'm* not. Yipeeee!' Some directors, like Alan Strachan and David Taylor, stick around, come in with notes, pop round for tea and rallying. Others, like Michael Blakemore, disappear off to the next triumph, leaving behind but a wisp of smoke and a calling card and are rarely glimpsed till the last night wake. I guess I've just confessed the kind I'd be . . .

Unlike acting, the reviews which followed were almost an unnecessary aside to the work itself:

> 'In a decisively triumphant directorial debut, her production gleams with shrewd psychological observation and sharp comic detail.'

> 'Lipman says her ambition is to "boil the perfect egg". She is a perfectionist and, even if she thinks that this show is not perfect, it will do until the real thing comes along. Don't hold your breath because this one has got the lot.'

Now I have a cold sore on my lip the size of Wales. It's just reached the interesting crusty stage which looks like I should be wearing a pointy black hat and cackling a lot. This means it's getting better. It's especially fetching when smothered in Zovirax and can be seen on a starlit night in several counties.

I am told these things erupt when one is run down. Hah! Flattened describes me more accurately. Will I direct again? Just ask me.

3

Actor at Sea

Not All It's Cracked up to Be

If the Fairy Godmother of travel asked me for my dearest long-distance wish, I would ask to be transported to one of the great small hotels of the world. It would be family-run, laid back, classic in food and feel, and obscenely discreet. So it will come as no surprise to those of you who are old enough to know that fairies only come in liquid form that I went, instead, to Las Vegas. It goes without saying that this fairy story has a Grimm ending.

Las Vegas, I adored. My summing up was that Las Vegas is a refreshingly *honest* sort of place. It greets you with a 900-watt neon smile and says, 'Hi! I'm here to take all your money. Yes, sir, all of it. But while I'm robbing you, I'll be entertaining you with wunnerful food, wunnerful service, circus, spectacle, magic and a potted history of civilization (as no civilized person ever knew it), theme parks, shows and all of it marginally cheaper than staying at home.'

I stayed in the Luxor Palace with my travelling companion, Lynn Shindler. Lynn hails from California and has settled in Muswell Hill – from the sublime to the gor' blimey – and we go back, and now forth, a long way. The hotel was a black glass pyramid (of 2,500 rooms, 8,000 staff and the world's largest atrium), which boasts a life-sized sphinx in fibreglass at the entrance and two talking camels in the lobby. Inside there flows the Nile river and if you are feeling nihilistic you can take the cruise around the 'Manhattan Buffet', the Imax cinema, or the 'Nile Deli'. The inclinator, a lift which moves, naturally, sideways up the pyramid (leaving most of your Nile Deli brunch in your ankles) deposited Lynn and I on the twenty-eighth floor. If your inclination is then to look down, you realize that the pyramid is completely hollow and you are looking down on thousands of feet of conditioned air. The small and somewhat movable wall between you and it makes one wonder when the first guy to lose thirty grand in the Keno Room ('Gambling for people who've lost the will to live') will take the bungee jump of a lifetime, sans bungee, and land on a crooner in a loin cloth and 'Mantan' who happens to be singing 'Ptolemy. Why not take Ptolemy?'

On the 'Strip' I witnessed a drive-in wedding. The couple drive up to the chapel window and stick their heads out of the car and Charlotte, the lady pastor, wearing – no, *balancing* – the complete works of Max Factor on her face, leans out the window and pronounces them man and wife. 'To go'. It was a gas. I cried. But then I always cry at drive-in weddings.

I also saw a show called *The Winds of the Gods* which explained away a few centuries of history in a sonic American voice-over complete with zebras, a baby elephant, a pure white camel and a chariot race which sent sand scurrying up into my Bacardi and Coke. The next day I visited Caesar's Palace shopping mall – The Forum – a perfect representation of the Via Veneto. Indoors. There are talking statues of the Bacchae and friends on the hour, and the 'sky' turns from cloudless blue to twinkling purple as the day progresses. I actually heard myself say, 'Hey, let's eat *outside*.'

I nearly OD'd with excitement when I saw George Burns billed to play Caesar's Palace, but this was advance notice of his ninety-eight advancing years old appearance. Instead, I saw one Al Jarreau, who makes musical instrument noises with his mouth. I made a few with mine whilst watching him. My compensation was a night out in 'Glitter Gulch' with a gold-suited Elvis impersonator who sang 'Love Me Tender' to me on the bonnet of his pink Cadillac and addressed me, alarmingly, as 'Ma'am'. When he left I didn't know whether to kiss him or knight him.

Now, my gambling skills are about as developed as my white-water rafting. I had a lesson in craps – yes, I know, you wouldn't have thought I needed one, *thank* you – but I just kept yelling 'SIX!' and chucking the dice off the table.

The one place they don't want you in Vegas is in your room. Shame, really, because I rather liked mine. It had steeply sloping windows, a jacuzzi, and hieroglyphics on the wardrobe. Cleaning the sloping windows is a bit of a problem – they have to employ spidermen who risk life and limb 2,000 feet up, presumably suctioned to the glass with a little state-of-the-art bucket and a magnetic wash leather. God forbid, though, you should want a hairdryer in your room. 'A hairdryer?' barked the *karncierrge*, who would have been less offended if I'd asked for a dildo, 'Well, I guess so . . . if you return it within the hour and we receipt you for it.' Because, you see, you can't *gamble* with wet hair. Well, no, you probably can. After all, there is a sign in one hotel which says 'Gamble While You Sleep'.

I got a taste of the headiness of the 'high roller' when my slot machine began pouring out quarters by the gross, when all I'd done was to feed it a dollar note. The noise was deafening, and most of that was me, cackling with glee at the idea of beating the house. 'The machine's conked out,' I hissed at Lynn. 'Quick. Watch!' I fed it another dollar and 'Ping, ding, pong, clatter, clatter' out poured the quarters. I now had a tubful and was transmogrifying before Lynn's eyes into the Wicked Witch of the West. 'Lynn! Lynn! Watch this!' I put another dollar in and out it spewed for the third time. People were beginning to look around, half-encouraging, half-envious. I was beside myself . . . 'Ha! Ha! Ha! You *and* your little dawg, Toto! Ha! Ha! Ha . . .!'

Lynn, the unflappable, studied me gravely and said, 'Er, you're putting in *twenty*-dollar notes. The only thing the machine is doing is giving you change.'

The only thing that stopped me from throwing myself into the atrium was the weight of the $60 worth of quarters in my jeans.

We followed the yellow brick road past Dorothy and the Wicked Witch and the Cowardly Lion in the MGM Hotel themed *Wizard of Oz* Park, we gawped at the animal parade at the Circus World Park and asked directions from passing gladiators in the Roman Shopping Mall. One bronzed young woman with a black bob and her own asp wanted to be remembered to her mum in Horsham. And everywhere we went the backdrop noise was that of falling money.

When we left for Los Angeles we stood in the airport lounge feeding our last dimes and quarters into the banks of slot machines, turning out our pockets for the last pickings. Suddenly Lynn, ever my conscientious minder, said, 'Gee, I hope the flight time was 7.30 not 7.15. I guess I should check ... Oh, my God! Quick, run! Run!'

She set off at a cartoon speed fully expecting me to follow, but it was like a scene from our morning runs around Highgate Woods: Lynn – who won't mind me telling you is a little older than me – running effortlessly without panting or stopping for breath once, me, wheezing, gasping and stopping every ten yards for anything ranging from cramp, stitch, fallen arches or a twig in my path.

Within seconds I'd lost her in the airport corridors. I'd come to a T-junction and she was neither left nor right. I would have tossed a dime if I still had one. Instead, I hared off right and right again, as she, no doubt, returned from the left and hared off back to the last place she'd seen me. This took some time. We missed the plane. Lynn was distraught, feeling that she'd somehow flunked her end of term exam. Me? I'm used to chaos, it runs off my back like a duck. We phoned Rita and Johnny Lynn who were meeting us at Los Angeles airport and found to our relief that their son, Edward, was flying in later too from Stamford University, so we could be picked up together. Lynn could then catch a later connection to her parents' home in Santa Barbara and we were back on schedule.

In thirty minutes we were on the next plane out. To sleep off one-and-a-half hours of Vegas disco dancing (roughly one hour twenty-five minutes more than I'd done in the last decade), gambling, jet lag and overexcitement – perchance to dream by a luxurious Bel Air swimming pool.

Oh yes? And my stepmother's a vampire.

Jonathan and Rita Lynn are old friends of ours. Our children grew up together and we sat in each other's studio audience for his creation, *Yes, Minister*, and my *Agony*. We acted together in *The Knowledge* and created Kev and Maggie in *Outside Edge*. Rita, now a distinguished psychotherapist and Johnny, now a successful film director (*My Cousin Vinny*, *Nuns on the Run*) live in Beverly Hills and love it. I knew that Hollywood could be a haemorrhoid on the anal fissure of America but felt sure that, amongst good friends, in lovely surroundings, with sun dried tomatoes nestling in a bed of something bitter, even *I* would relax and unwind.

Their house, old by Hollywood standards, is quite stunning, exquisitely antiqued and their latest acquisition was a Pyrenean Mountain puppy. His name was Ernest, he was six weeks old and not a great deal smaller than me. One day he would be a guard dog. Right now, one word from anybody and he did precisely what he wanted. The J-cloths and disinfectant were much in evidence.

I was tired as we ate our delicious homemade chicken soup, but more than that, I was embarrassed by the oncoming migraine which was marching inexorably up the back of my neck. 'Oh, please God,' I bartered. 'I'll have it when I get home. I promise. Not when I'm a guest ... it's so *boring*.' Well. You can't whack a sincere prayer. An hour later I'm crunched up in my bed with my head under my arm and my teeth in a reef knot.

The following day I waged a war against the pain by having the best massage I've ever had, given by a paper-thin girl with hands like power drills and thus I improved enough to keep my engagement at a Sunday matinée of *Sunset Boulevard*. Glenn Close was masterly. Like a black widow spider. Beautiful, terrifying, vulnerable and seductive. Several hairs stood up on the back of my newly massaged neck and remained so for some time till I felt like a gooseberry.

Out for dinner that night in the glorious outdoors and home for a longstanding appointment in the Land of Nod. (This is an expression I frequently and rather archaicly use. One morning in Muswell Hill I came downstairs and announced, in the high-pitched, piercing tone of a seven-year-old choirboy with no hope of *ever* possessing descending testicles, 'Heerrow eberyone ... OI'VE BEEN IN THE LAND OF NO-O-O-OD!' Jack glanced up momentarily and said, 'And this is Tom the plumber and he's under the sink fixing the new water purifier.' Tom was more than laid back and from his laid out position merely mumbled, 'Morning, Maureen,' but I felt just a touch mortified in his presence ever since.)

Meanwhile, back in Beverly Hills, disaster struck Nod at roughly 4.20 am *precisely* and I was precipitated out of my bed by what lack of experience told me was an earthquake measuring 6.8 on the Richter Scale.

How to describe the indescribable? The ground rolls. Like a ship. Pictures and mirrors thud to the floor. The burglar alarm started to scream, the music centre suddenly played *Don Giovanni*, dogs bayed all over the city – but not our Ernest, who slept unsoundly on regardless, as did Edward, who's nineteen and would sleep through 'The Clash Live in Edward's Bedroom'.

And what of me? Oh, cool as a chilli, that was me! Not knowing any earthquake rules, i.e. stand under a door lintel, I got under the bed – and straight out again. I cake-walked down the corridor to Johnny and Rita's room and, with the boldness of a Brit in a crisis, coughed discreetly and murmured, 'Er ... hello ...'

Not surprisingly, no one answered, so I ricocheted back. My next masterly thought was, 'I must find my knickers.' You know, clean knickers when the doctor comes? One problem. Can't find glasses to find knickers. Next thought: 'Must pee.' Lurch to toilet but, mid-stream, think 'What if I'm found dead and buried on toilet by future generations?' so attempt with difficulty to stop the process which takes much mind over waste matter. All this in fifty-eight seconds of a huge 6.8 tremor. It felt like a decade.

By now the house was awake. Rita came calmly towards me saying, 'Now don't panic. This is the Big One.' An oxymoron which rendered me incontinent again since I assumed she meant that San Diego not LA was about to become the Western coastline of America. I did not, I realized, wish to be buried at Wounded Knee or any other part of the US anatomy. I wanted to go home. Now. To Jack. In the Hills of Muswell as opposed to Beverly. Visions of D W Griffiths filled my mind ... troughs the size of Norway appeared in roads. My shoulders rose up above my head till I looked like Plug in the Bash Street Kids. 'Now,' continued Rita, 'it's over, but there will be lots of afterquakes for the rest of the day.' This was not totally reassuring and my neck started to thud in rhythm with the music centre which was now giving us Mahler's Ninth. The radio power returned and the local seismologists telling us the extent of the damage were wildly overexcited and should have been put to bed with a warm drink.

As Johnny and Rita went round the house picking up fallen artefacts, I stood there quaking and suddenly ravenous. 'Anyone mind if I eat these bananas?' I asked. They didn't, of course and tea was brewed and we sat around comforting Ernest, who, placid as a late September wasp, didn't *need* any comfort. As for me, I was just a touch hungrier than I was before the bananas. 'Anyone want a boiled egg?' I asked to a ring of glazed faces. 'And soldiers?'

Nobody did, it seemed. Not even Ernest. Yoghurt followed and four doorstep slices of bread and jam and I felt better. They, of course, felt sick just looking at me so I thought I'd best forgo the yearning which then came over me for rice pudding – with skin.

At 5.00 am I phoned Jack in London with news of my apparent survival. His TV was working, unlike ours, so he reported on the scenes of destruction and chaos in LA. I started writing to friends – postcards from the edge: 'Dear

Lizzy, we're just having our fourteenth afterquake and I'm having an egg.' At one point, in the garden, a five-pointer shook me off my chair and propelled me back into the kitchen squealing, 'There was an afterquake just now out there!'

'Yes,' said Rita, patiently. 'We felt it in here actually.'

There was a night-time curfew, so we watched Clint in *In the Line of Fire* and he quite took my mind off my mortality. Still, that night I slept fully clothed, jeans, sweater, bra, socks *and knickers*, with my glasses in my shoes and my passport under the pillow. At 7.00 am, a 5.3 tremor shook me out of bed and in the two-and-a-quarter minutes before the next one, a 5.8, I'd packed my suitcase.

They were *not* diminishing. I, on the other hand, was. The radio said that the sets of *Murphy Brown* and *Murder She Wrote* had been damaged and an irreplaceable statue of a Roman Pugilist in the Getty Museum had a chip on its shoulder. Hadn't we all? A man phoned in to say he'd lost every glass in his huge collection, save one which was engraved '1971 Commemorative Earthquake Glass'. Walter Matthau's house collapsed one week after he cancelled his quake insurance. Ernest turned out to be profoundly deaf and left for sign language school in Colorado (*Children Of A Lesser Dog*?) and M Lipman, wife, mother and sometimes entertainer, fled to the airport three hours before her flight home. In a natural disaster, I'm naturally disastrous. Anyway, my name's not Andreas, and it's not my Fault.

I flew from the loving Lynns in LA, to lovely Lynn in Santa Barbara, where her parents, Steven and Freda, have built an ocean-front house with stunning vistas of the sea. Steve is an astrogeophysicist – so that gave me plenty to talk about – no, he's a delightfully easy man who runs six miles on the beach each day and he and Freda, who has exactly the same gentle, good-humoured warmth as her daughter, welcomed me like another daughter.

I stood at my bedroom window watching seals grooming themselves on the rocks and dolphins on their way to schools and the tension drained out of me like sprout water through a colander.

Santa Barbara is an old Spanish town with an early mission house, a court-house built in ceramic tiles, a quaint run down harbour and a laid back *mañana* quality. From the mission you look down on orange and lemon groves and by the harbour we watched happy hippyish rollerbladers flying psychedelic kites and whole families on bicycles with fringed canopies. It was a traveller's balm and within days my nerves, formerly on the outside of my body, had been sucked neatly back inside.

Still, you know what they say, 'Be it ever so humble ... whatsit, I mean, any place I hang my hat is ... thingy – thingy – on the range, where the deer and the antelope play ... the old folks at doubrey after all, show me the way to go – whatyamacallit? – yeah, you've guessed it – and there's no place like it, apparently.

Suffolk Catered

The BBC *Holiday* programme have this tendency to ring up and say, 'Feel like a weekend away with a camera crew for company?' and I have developed an alarming inability to refuse. It's when they say, 'Where do you fancy going?' and flutter a map of the world in front of me that I go blank. It's rather like those questions that go, 'What makes you laugh?' or 'What's your most embarrassing moment?' Your mind goes completely blank and, as Joyce Grenfell once said, 'The only thing I can think of is my own rear view, in trousers.'

So, under the aegis of 'better the devil you know', I suggested Southwold.

I'd visited this quaint and low-lying seaside spot in Suffolk twice before, the first time for a weekend break with my husband when the kids were small, and it proved perfect for rock-pooling and wave-chasing and sand-sifting in a way reminiscent more of *Five on Kirrin Island* than the 'Gelati Moi-Tutti-Frutti Lollipop let's all do the Birdie Dance' type Continental holidays we'd previously given them. The second visit was to play *Re: Joyce!* at the tiny Southwold Summer Theatre run so professionally by Jill Freud from a charming Church Hall. It is perfect Grenfell country and one could almost believe, looking down at rows of brightly painted, individually named beach huts that time had stopped and Joyce might well pop her head around one and hoot, 'I say! What a simply spiffing day!'

It occurred to me then that my ideal travelling companion would be my mother. She would adore the whole business of filming and a nice break away together would be good for us.

I did try to explain to Mum that she would be *on* screen, up there with me, 'fronting' the show, sort of thing, but I could tell in the preceding phone calls that she was persisting in regarding the whole thing merely as three days' unexpected 'skiving off'. Originally, I'd planned to go with my daughter, but Amy grasped the BBC principle immediately and baulked, 'Appear in front of the camera? *Me?* With *you?* I'd never hold my head up in the Union bar again!'

No, fair's fair. I'd rather be told it like it is. I'm not proud. Not these days, anyway.

So, relatively speaking, my mother was next on the list and, bless her sporting heart, she didn't take too long to make up her mind. The conversation went: 'Hi, Mum, I don't suppose you'd like to come with . . . ?'

'Yes, I'd love to. Where?'

So, up on the bus from Hull she came down with a 'shocking cold' and the worst backache since simians went from four legs to two and somehow, mysteriously, as the chauffeured car drew up and our luggage made its way into the boot, she became as fit as a flea and positively bristling with energy and *joie de vivre*, unlike her daughter who was characteristically wheyfaced and irritable.

On our first venture out of the Swan Hotel, microphoned up and with a cameraman backing down the street before us, we encountered a similar camera team backing towards him. The director was someone I knew and her squad were covering a genius schoolteacher nearby. Small wonder that a formidable tweed-clad lady rounded on me saying, 'I wish to high heaven you people would stop publicizing this town by telling the world how *unspoilt* we are! I mean, there's nowhere to *park* on weekends now!' Ah, such is civilization.

Well, sorry, ma'am, but unspoilt you are, and though we haven't come on a spoiling mission, I have, in my task as a roving recommender, to report that the air was clean (always excepting the Sizewell signs marring one's approach), the natives friendly and the pace sedate. The town is lively with binoculared visitors, bustling with bistros and, after twenty-four hours, I felt better than I had in weeks.

I do love Southwold. It's often painted as the town that time forgot but its memory has lingered on with me. An unchanging harbour the colours not of Hockney but of Turner, a proudly named ferry consisting of old Bob in his row boat, a sedate market-place and a Norman church big enough for most of Suffolk to worship in.

'So you like it here?' I prompted Mum as we walked, microphones down our bras and cameramen backing down the street before us, towards the sea front.

'Ooh, it's fabulous,' she beamed. 'What a wonderful spot. Who'd have thought it? I mean, I've never even heard of it before ... And isn't it *clean*!' (Mum's greatest accolade, a sort of Egon Lipman, highly polished, five stars.) 'You could eat off the streets. And isn't the Swan marvellous! It's like a five-star hotel, there's *nothing* you could want for. I mean, it's so refined and ... well, I couldn't fault the place really, it's beautiful.'

'It is,' I nodded then, probingly, for the viewers, 'so would you come here with a friend for a weekend?'

She looked at me as though I'd suggested throwing a Bar-mitzvah in the Vatican. '*Me*? Come here? Nooooo! What would I *do*? I'd be bored stiff!'

My eyes were jitterbugging warnings to her. I felt like a lighthouse. But Mum was blissfully unaware that this was perhaps not the way to 'present' to camera and, well – who knows? – perhaps her approach was a healthy one. Certainly it might make for funnier viewing. I can't imagine Judith Chalmers, wishing she *wasn't* here in quite Zelma's fashion.

'Cut!' said Jon, the director.

Later, Jon had arranged to shoot the Town Cryer welcoming us into Southwold in traditional fashion. In full regalia and Cap'n Birdseye facial fuzz, he rang his bell, 'Oyez'd' thrice, unrolled his scroll and, in a barnstorming baritone which made Brian Blessed sound like Blossom Dearie, boomed, 'We are proud to welcome Miss Maureen Lipman and her mother, *Zemla*, to Southwold.'

Mother and daughter fell off their bench, Jon called 'Cut!' once more and pointed out politely that although Zelma *was* an unusual name, it would probably be better to say it, since Zemla sounded like a tiger cub in Whipsnade or something you rub on your bunions.

Later that day, we took Bob's ferry over to the delightful and slightly rivalrous village of Walberswick and wandered around the tiny village green. Jon suggested we walk down the slope, chatting, and go into the impressive village craft shop. Whilst they were setting up the camera, Zelma and I looked around the shop for possible gifts. When the shot was set up, Gary, the Production Assistant, called us and we set off from the slope to walk back to the shop.

'Shall you *go* to Clement Freud's wife's house for dinner, then?' Mum threw in as a somewhat cryptic opening gambit to those eight million or so viewers who didn't know that Jill Freud lived nearby and I'd stopped by earlier to say hello.

'Oh *look*, Mum!' I said over-emphatically by way of response, 'There's a lovely craft shop here, let's see what's inside.'

Mum stopped in both our tracks and gave me 'the look' again. 'What do you mean?' she challenged, disbelievingly. 'We've just *been* in there – there was nothing you wanted.'

'Cut!'

The three days fled past. We ate well, the sun shone, I bought a watercolour of bluebells in one of the many local galleries, we laughed a lot, no one more than the person who caused the laughter, and we came home refreshed and replete.

On the quayside I bought fresh-today fish from an extra-ordinarily chic fishmonger, to butter up my husband. I seemed to buy at least forty quids' London's worth of fish for £18. You could've knocked me down with a wet turbot. Perhaps *that's* why they call it the town that time forgot.

It is a perfect base for exploring nature, wonderful birding, exquisite light for painting, frightfully cultural and did you know that *really* fresh fish doesn't smell at all fishy? I even pointed out a windsurfer struggling to maintain his balance on the sea.

'That's not a *man*,' said Mum.

'Yes it is,' I retorted.

'Don't be ridiculous,' she countered. 'What's he hanging on to then?'

I followed her gaze which was firmly fixed on a hovering seagull a hundred feet up. 'Grim death, Mum. With his beak.'

The crew and 'Zemla' said emotional farewells. Gary was off to Greece the next day. 'Oh, are you going cruising?' said Mum blithely and gazed in astonishment when, not for the first time, the lads' beer went all over the table. 'Tell them what I said in the Greek restaurant, Maureen,' she giggled . . . 'You know, when I asked for the fellatio and chips!'

Of course, it's dangerous to say that to a writer, even if she's your daughter, because she almost certainly didn't mean me to tell you lot. Oh, and don't bother writing in for the address of the restaurant – it was a 'special' . . . and it certainly sounds like one.

Start Spreading the Noos

It doesn't take much incentive to get me to New York. A weekend off, a friend's baby shower, a sudden depletion of Paul Mitchell Fast Freeze Hair Spray – anything really. So a phone call from the BBC *Holiday* programme producer, Angela Wallis, saying, 'Anywhere you'd like to go for a few days, Maureen?' led to fourteen seconds' silence before I suggested a shopping weekend in Manhattan.

They gave me *carte blanche* for most of the world but most of the world doesn't thrill me like New York and to be paid for shopping is to be twice blessed.

To be honest, I never buy much on specific shopping trips. I buy en route to somewhere else or to cheer myself up. Department stores, with the exception of John Lewis and Dickens and Jones, frighten me. I'm not joking. I can do untold damage in a shop which measures twelve foot by sixteen and contains user-friendly assistants, but put me in a turn-of-the-century, six-storey building, with a ground floor teeming with taupe eyeshadow, liposomes and glossy women with small, evil-smelling aerosols and I'm out the other door before you can say Peter Robinson.

Still, to peep, perchance to preen – aye, and there's the grub! It couldn't be missed. And Sally, my assistant at the theatre would accompany me and make sure, as Lynn had done in Las Vegas, that the plane I boarded was the one mentioned on my ticket and not the one which would transport me to the People's Republic of China, steerage class. Sally would accompany me to the strangely unfamiliar Renaissance Hotel in Times Square – *in* it, mind, not off it,

135

or abutting it, or adjacent to it, or, best of all, six blocks east
of it, but *in* it, and Sally would remind me, when I was about
to spend five hundred dollars on a pair of baby blue alpaca
mittens that there were drama students starving in Wilmslow,
and would field the filthy look I gave her when she said it.
And Sally would carry the Rescue Remedy. And Sally could
have her long, black hair cut in a chunky New York style at
last. Say no more. We were already spiritually gone.

We spent the hour before flight revelling in the Virgin Club
Room. Deep leather armchairs, every paper and periodical
imaginable, hairdressing, massage, aromatherapy, con-
servatory viewing room with earphones and thousands of
CDs, all you can drink and a virtual peanut farm. The odd
bed and I'd have booked in for the week.

The hotel was, well, let's just say it was handy for the shops.
Yes, you could have bought a couple of dozen whips, a lurex
thong and a vibrator shaped like the Empire State just by
leaning out of the window. Angela Wallis and the two-man
crew had already been there doing a 'recce' (reconnaissance –
film jargon you know, luvvie) and I was to start, bright and
bleary, the following morning with the high-powered (for that
read turbo-charged) personal shopper, Elaine, in Bergdorf
Goodman's store.

Elaine was of enormous stature in everything but height.
It was arranged that she would be fitting a personal client,
Barbara, a lawyer, with her seasonal wardrobe.

Shopping was a serious business, fitted into the hour
between the gym and the office, no doubt, and Elaine knew
Barbara's taste better than Barbara did herself. Several hundreds of thousands of greenbacks would pass, courtesy of
plastic and patter, in to the Bergdorf Goodman coffers before
the given hour was over. It sure takes the 'sh' out of shopping
and supplies the 'ping'.

There's a lovely girl called Carolyn Robertson, I've discovered, who performs the same service at Dickens and Jones
in London and I've since ventured into one of their private
cubicles to try on clothes for *Agony Again*. It was a kind of

aversion therapy for me, not just because of the cups of tea, the digestives and the allowing us to have about three or four hundred items in the room, but almost certainly because, at the end of the day – and here I mean literally, not in the Desmond Lynam sense – someone else paid for all the clothes. Actually, as I discovered from Elaine, the service is free, so, in other words, Elaine and Caroline are fairy do-goods who turn six floors, two elevators and an atrium into that little tiny boutique I mentioned earlier, with the one friendly but non-pushy assistant.

I always feel that living in London, or even New York, operates on rather the same principle. It's vast. Every conceivable distraction imaginable is there, should you want it, which of course, you don't. Instead you settle into Hampstead, or Barnes, or Queens or Greenwich Village (the latter only if you like to wear leather, silver studs and a moustache – and the men dress interestingly too) and you turn it into *your* village. You get to know the barber and the grocer and your kids say 'hello' to the street sweeper and the dry cleaner asks after your budgie and the librarian saves you the latest Carol Shields and you wait for *Muriel's Wedding* to come to your local cinema and so on and so forth. You're in Ambridge, with yellow cabs. Where was I? Oh, yes, sorry, Bergdorfs in my twelve-year-old camel coat bought from a long-closed boutique (16' × 12') which specialized in Irish fashions (it's true, I swear – you doubt me, try shopping in Dublin, the fashion is amazing). Anyway, everyone admired my coat and, since the film was shown on *Holiday*, has continued to admire my coat, so I shall keep it for another twelve years and watch it come back in again.

After the 'poisonal' shopping I was filmed wearing two hideous bracelets which were made of semi-precious stones, cost $24,000 each and looked like spray-painted tractor wheels. Then we moved on to the new trendy store, smaller, more modern, different atrium – palm trees if I'm not mistaken, and a deli-restaurant – and from there to the fabulous new branch of the bookshop, Barnes and Noble, which has most of the qualities of the Virgin Clubroom without the red logo. Easy chairs, tables, coffee shop, people sprawled on the floor writing their thesis till closing time at 11 pm. Apparently it's a great pick-up joint and it was a pick-me-up for Sal and I to perch above it all, having a cappuccino and a prune Danish and watch the pickings. Below us were three fabulously attractive men, black, beautiful and sartorially endowed, poring over a large illustrated book for fifty minutes or so, turning pages and conversing in low murmurs. They were rapt. I was rapt. Finally, the book was wrapped and I read the title. It was *Origami at a Snip*. That's Noo York!

People say 'That's Noo York' a lot in New York. It means 'Take us as you find us', 'Take the rough with the smooth' and 'If you don't like it, piss off'.

In some yellow cabs, there is a grid between customer and driver. For his protection, not yours. I asked our driver for a receipt – we were on our way to see three one-act plays off Broadway – and I needed to retain all my receipts for the BBC. I always assume a nasal American accent for New York cabs, because without it they simply cannot understand a word I'm saying. Sally found this hilarious, as well she might. 'I wanna go to Broadway and Nointh, OK?' I'd snarl and, *ooworf* we'd go. If you say, 'Can you take me to, er, the corner of Broadway, please, where it meets Ninth Avenue?' on the other hand, you get one response only, 'Gnuh?' or 'Vnuh?' if your driver is Russian, which is more often the case.

'I needa receipt pleeze,' I nasally holler at the driver, who responds with a click of his meter to the 'ooworf' position and a surly, 'Too late. I toined it worf already,' (except it was in a black patois that I am unable to recreate with this pen. Incidentally, this pen has just revealed to me the words 'Jewish Care' on its side, and now I don't know whether to write more precisely and painstakingly as instructed, or whether to just put it down and have an early night.)

So here I am saying, '. . . but I need the receipt – no receipt, no money,' when the guy hurls open the passenger door, whirls around to reveal the meanest face since the Beastie

Boys and screams at the top of his lungs, 'Geddout of the fucking car of I'll throw you out – asshole!'

We got out of the car, with me saying, Britishly, 'I'm taking your number, you horrible man, and you will be reported.' I didn't get it, of course, and he would have been fined $500 immediately if I had, so always take the number before you pay. Don't you just love the words 'You horrible man' though? Yeah – I really showed *him*! Too true. He'll think twice before meddling with the likes of me again.

It reminds me of the incident which happened in bed the other night – now settle down, will you, this is me, remember – when Jack, in the epicentre of a nightmare, half-woke and threw his arm out to envelop me for comfort. Unfortunately he miscalculated and hit me across the head. What did I do? Well, I have it from the horse's mouth that I sat bolt upright and said, 'You hit me on the head – you *bad* man!' I'm a frightening woman when I'm roused. Swear like a swearing-in clerk all day long but in my sleep I'm as chaste as a hare at a fox hunt.

Interestingly, I hope, at the Sony Radio Awards when I had the pleasure of Mr Terry Waite's company at lunch, I asked him whether he still dreamed of his captivity, and he replied in the negative. 'Although when I was imprisoned,' he added, 'my dreams were all wonderful. Dreams of freedom, open spaces, beaches, woodlands, glorious vistas. And funny? Sometimes I woke up laughing. I was always a great believer in Jung and the unconscious and that confirmed it for me.' He continued, 'I think my dreams protected me.'

There speaks a man with a clear conscience, I thought.

So there we are, Sally and I, in the Variety Arts Theatre on 110 Third Avenue at 13th watching a David Mamet (boring and predictable), an Elaine May (Linda Lavin, the actress who received a Tony Award for her part in Neil Simon's *Broadway Bound*, was dazzling) and a Woody Allen (evilly funny) entitled *Death Defying Acts* and directed by Michael Blakemore. It's incredible to be in this tiny, off-Broadway theatre and see fabulous Broadway names, having paid $45 mind. It's now punitively expensive to mount a straight play on the Broadway stage, the overheads and running costs being much more than can be recouped from the ticket prices, even though the latter are astronomical. So the great writers have moved off the high street into the suburbs. Neil Simon's last play, his fortieth, was his first ever to play outside Broadway. And while it toddled along at off-off Broadway theatre (tickets $40!), the theatre *on* Broadway named after the maestro, The Neil Simon, stood empty.

So. Here we are. The show's over and we're hungry, but the area around 13th is too dodgy for restaurant hunting, so I scour the playbill (programme) and come across the jazz restaurant 'Iridium' on W44th and 63rd St across from the Lincoln Center. Gingerly we hail a cab and have an uneventful journey to what looks like a darkened corner café, as opposed to the 'Symphony of taste, sight and sound!' advertised under the 'Jazz Club and Restaurant' section.

Still, a door was open and we found a waiter who directed us downstairs to a low-lit lobby where a gorgeous black girl welcomed us with an unbelievable sentence, 'Gahd! It's Maureen Lipman, isn't it?' Well, you could have brained me with a Teflon skillet! She turned out to be English – she'd left England eight years earlier and had been an *Agony* fan – she could only have been about six at the time!

So we got the treatment: best table, best service and, best news of the evening, 'We're not sure, but we think Wynton Marsalis is going to be in tonight.' Marsalis, as I'm sure you know, is a brilliant jazz trumpeter. Over-excitement was such that we could scarcely swallow our New American Cuisine baked red mullet. (We did. It was delicious). We watched the most wonderful jazz quintet with a fine black singer with a voice like a tenor sax and a stunning bass player in African gear, for the first set and then, after the food, we were moved to an even better, stageside table and we watched the second set – heads on the swivel for Wynton.

Then the singer announced his good friend Cassandra

Wilson, the Grammy Award-winning singer, was in the house. She climbed on stage and sang full of grace and so musical that she and the sax player just melted into one seamless syrup of sound. *Then* the young jazz singer sang something simple to his Mom and Dad and his Grandparents in from somewhere far away and finally he announced Marsalis.

Sal and I were all but ready to pass out – and Sal had never heard of him till I told her who he was. I wish I could tell you that he played the roof right off the club but unfortunately he'd come without his horn. Still we met him and simpered a lot and told him we'd be at his next English concert wherever it may be. Since then, of course, we've had his marvellous series of TV Master Classes and watched him accompany Kathleen Battle in classic mode and I'm hooked.

The following day it was an early start in SoHo where my kind of shop, undersized and eclectic, resides. We filmed in a shop which specializes in bones and skulls. It was called Evolution but I saw it more as The Remains of the Day! There was a whole case of human skulls. Funny, isn't it, we all have two eyes, a nose and a mouth and no two people look the same. Except the 7,000 who look exactly like me, of course: 'Come 'ere, come 'ere, Maureen! I want you to meet my wife. Now, go on, go on, tell me, is she your living double or not? Eh? Eh? Go on, I'm asking you!' I look at the four-foot nose, pebble glasses and clamouring teeth before me, swallow gamely and confess the *amazing* similarity.

There were preserved starfish, sea-horses and a delicate array of turtles; there was a giraffe's skull which amazed me with its size. Of course we see the head at the end of an enormous muscular neck, so it looks tiny. Pinheaded. No prizes for guessing why I identified so strongly with the dis-membered object.

The assistant, whilst packing up the dead zoo which would, later, mystify my family (and cause Gloria Hunniford con-siderable shock on her birthday, when I presented her, on *Pebble Mill*, live, with a boxed sea-horse vertebrae), suggested we eat across the street at a charming and friendly bistro. It was at this point, as we pulled ourselves away from boxes of sharks' teeth and eel ribs, that Dudley, the soundman, realized that his entire box of sound equipment had been stolen from inside the shop and under his nose. Well, dat's Noo York!

Chastened, we trooped into the restaurant opposite and ordered our various lunches. Cameraman John had bought African daisies for all the ladies and we gave them to the 'charming and friendly' waiter to take care of. An hour and fifteen minutes later, when some meals had arrived, some hadn't, some were cooked, some raw, all delivered with the off-offhand manner of a Harley Street gynaecologist and the grace of Jo Brand, we stood up to leave, trading insults and striking inedible items off the bill. Finally, we asked for our flowers. Need I tell you, they had mysteriously disappeared. Now, dat isn't *always* Noo York, but, oh boy, one could be forgiven for thinking it's getting that way.

Having said that, my New York friend, Shirley, and two travel agent friends, have just been nastily mugged by a gang of five outside a house in Notting Hill Gate, so maybe I should just shut the hell up, as the waiter suggested I did in the – er – what's the word I'm looking for? – er – restaurant.

In the afternoon we filmed a sequence in the Metropolitan Museum which took a couple of hours and left me a hundred dollars poorer. The idea was for me to stand in front of a Tiffany stained-glass window, a twelve-foot landscape of pink hills and wistaria, and express a desire to hold it in my mind for ever. You must understand that there is a basic idea for these features and then one just improvises.

Cut then to the Museum Shop where I'm holding a $70 replica of the Tiffany window, about twelve inches instead of twelve feet, and beaming, '. . . and the great thing is, you can not only look at it – you can *BUY* it! *Yes*! I'd like this packaged please!' I added to the assistant, who, playing the part to the hilt, packaged it, took my credit card, ran it through the machine, and the bloody thing is now standing on my sofa table 3,000 miles from its natural home. *When Art Becomes*

Reality: A How Not *to Do It Manual* by M Lipman.

This exercise in Method acting was followed by the swift purchase of Nefertiti's necklace, the Duchess of Windsor's earrings and, thank God, the Head of Customs and Excise, Valerie Strachan, was a prefect at Newland High School in Hull, and her employees *can't* read me like a book. Nobody else on the crew seemed to have my problem with leaving somewhere empty-handed. Memo to me: your mother said 'Never *arrive* empty-handed', not the other way round!

We did F A O Shwartz, the mega-floor kids toyshop, where I reconnoitred with the world's most exceptional child, Mr Timothy Lewis Jones, son of dad, Simon, and mom, Nancy, and Timmy got to do his first line on BBC TV and to learn the hardest lesson for people like his dad and me: that however good your performance may be, it can still end up on the cutting-room floor. Our scene revolved around the discovery of the new 'Ken' – as in 'Barbie and Ken' – doll, who is called 'Shaving Ken'. Yes, folks, bearded Ken can shave. With just one application of some God-awful foam, your child can remove Ken's stubble and by re-applying some other potion, he can make Ken hirsute all over again. Nice, eh? Bring your child up to have no single grain of imagination whatsoever! When I think of my kids weaving complex fantasies out of six plastic pegs and a ball of twine – well, perhaps it was three *Star Wars* men and a Lego block, but the principle remains.

Recently I flew from Edinburgh and witnessed a ten-year-old boy, an unaccompanied minor, making his first air flight. The stewardess showed him the sights and he looked out of the window for a few seconds as we took off. Then he took out his Nintendo, started peering into the screen in that twitchy-engrossed way they do, and beep-beeped his way all the way to touchdown. It was quite depressing. A sort of exclusive possession. Oh Lord, preserve our progeny from Shaving Ken and nincompoop Nintendo. And I know I'm a dinosaur and will doubtless end my days in Jurassic Park trying to fathom out Sir Richard Attenborough's accent.

Dining with dear friends, Don and Eleanor Taffner, we

bemoaned the schedule for *Holiday* which made me unable to visit Secorcus, a vast tacky outlet in New Jersey where, according to Eleanor, you can pick up Calvin Klein jeans for $10. Don is a TV tycoon with strong connections with the London-based Theatre of Comedy and he and his wife have probably the most prized collection of Charles Rennie Mackintosh furniture and artefacts in the world. Their house and office are lived-in but breathtaking shrines to the man and to see the immense boardroom table, surrounded by 'those chairs' with their tall symmetrical deco backs is impressive enough. More so to note that in a corner of the room is a duplicate table and chairs in perfect miniature for their young grandchildren's meetings. I'm keeping everything crossed that Shaving Ken never puts in an appearance.

Don is avuncular, bespectacled and disarmingly cheery and looks like he might well be in Bilko's inner circle. Eleanor looks like I'd like to look in ten years' time but won't. She is beautiful, courtesy of entirely her own face, and elegant but with an eye for the fun in fashion. I would be quite unsurprised to see Eleanor in a Missoni two-piece and earrings which light up. Her hands are a lyric poem which taper and curve entirely unconscious of their illustrative effect on her conversation. It was Eleanor who first took Julia McKenzie and I to Orchard Street and Delancey Street to purchase fake bags and watches for all our friends and it was to Orchard and Delancey that the team repaired the next day to sample pickles from the barrel at Sam's Pickle Store. If you haven't seen the film *Crossing Delancey*, go get the video. It's the ultimate working woman's romantic fantasy.

From there we cruised the stores with an Eastside guide, buying watches which failed to fasten on return (Jack kept his 'Cartier' on for at least twelve minutes before sneaking the Timex back on), and I bought a ridiculous white fake fur which I couldn't pack and knew I would never wear. Outside, there was a near fight in the street as a Russian maniac with an English wife threatened to smash in our faces for filming as we walked past his tatty stall.

The incident was ugly and propelled us into Katz's famous delicatessen – now even more famous since Meg Ryan's fabulous 'faking it' scene in *When Harry Met Sally*. Ever since director Angela Wallis had suggested we film in Katz's, I'd been harbouring a plan to repeat the orgasmic scene *in situ*, then cut to the cause of my excitement, a corned beef sandwich. Which in Katz's and, in fairness, in most New York delis, is too obscenely sized, packed with salt beef (as we call it), to actually get your mouth around – unless you're related in some way to Mick Jagger.

Now, in a crowded restaurant on market day on the Eastside, you only want to make a complete tit of yourself *once* at most. Needless to say, the first time we shot it, there was a considerable outburst of laughter from all around and New Yorkers were spitting out rye bread and roll-mops a considerable distance. But something was wrong. I could feel it in my ancient waters. A glance through the camera showed what it was, through the miracle of the instant playback. The corned beef sandwich was in shot throughout the orgasm – a sentence I never thought I'd write, and I'm sure one that you never thought you'd read – so the cut away to what was causing my enthusiasm didn't work.

So, red-faced and apologetic, we ordered another Pyrenees-style sandwich, and went for it again. This time it was funny. In fact it was so funny that when the *Holiday* programme came out, they showed the New York trip in the second half of the show, and the orgasm scene as a trailer.

'I mean, do you show the bloody murderer as a trailer when you are doing a "whodunnit",' I moaned down the phone the next day. 'Well, we needed a hook to keep them watching the second half,' I was told. This is the era of the short attention span.

On our last day, Sally and I lunched with Wendy Wasserstein, author of *The Sisters Rosensweig*, the play I had just finished doing in London, in the Baroque-arched splendour of Grand Central Station's Oyster Bar, where my red snapper and Sally's oysters remained plate bound, not because they were anything other than perfect but because we never stopped giggling for long enough to get fork to mouth. We were helpless. The maître d' was thrilled, he said, to see such happy ladies, although I suspect the noise level was what had sent him over to our table in the first place.

I was telling Wendy, amongst other things, about the new series, *Agony Again*, and, at that point, our wires crossed. 'I've left my husband and I've taken a young black lover,' I said, expecting an expression of impressed glee to cross her face. Instead she just blinked and tried to rearrange her features and failed. Wendy's face is a homestead of curves and curls; in fact her face and mine would make a great Red Queen and Black Queen on a pack of cards.

'Oh,' she said bravely, 'and how's Jack, er, taken it?'

Telling Wendy about the last eventful weeks of *Sisters* took several bottles of Sauvignon. Then we moved quickly in and out of Greenwich Village, which is considerably nastier than it must have been when Comden and Green based *Wonderful Town* on its Bohemian streets. We then did the top of the Empire State where I spent ten minutes fighting with a set of powerful binoculars which had swallowed my dollar, then refused to reveal anything but a blank sky. Fortunately, Sally returned from one of the other viewing platforms in time to stop me complaining to the management and quietly lifted the caps from the end of the lenses.

What a sensational sight it is. Unique. And mesmerizing: dominated by skyscrapers against water, glass reflecting chrome and rust and dust turning industrial brickwork into art history. No wonder it has inspired so many lyric writers to their finest expressions of love in rhyme. And in the centre, Central Park, looking like chargrilled broccoli on a New American Cuisine platter. We took a walk around there, in bright sunny weather, the only human beings without single rollers beneath their feet, and I Ogden Nash'd into camera those immortal lines:

De spring is sprung, de grass is riz,
I wonder where de boidies is.
De little boids is on de wing.
Ain't dat absoid – de little wings is on de boid.

The whole place is absoid, frankly, East Soid, West Soid,
State Soid and soid by soid. Mad as a bathmat, all of it.
Wonder why I feel so at home there?

Our last lunch was in the Russian Tea Rooms with friend,
David Taylor and *Lost in Yonkers* director and New York
Rosensweig producer, Lenny Soloway, and a vat of bortsch
and sour cream. Lenny was producing *Rosensweig* on tour in
the States and when I told him just some of my tellable
stories, he reminded me that the touring Sara and Gorgeous
had ended up giving each other vicious pinches on stage and
that the original cast in New York were not exactly lunching
on a regular basis. I reckoned I'd probably got no worse than
I deserved.

Show business, though, took a backseat to the new
Bedroom & Bathroom Superstore and David, Sally and I
spent the pre-flight hours wandering around its many floored
domesticity. Punch-drunk I came out respectably with a small
venetian blind cleaner (useless 'cos I didn't buy the special
accompanying spray) and a perspex matzos holder (which
Carmela, our housekeeper, decided was a tray for holding
Windowlene). David gave me a present too, *The Silver Palate
Cook Book*. I tell you, it's the only cook book which doesn't
make me recipe blind. So I conclude by giving you *The Silver
Palate Cook Book* recipe for Chicken Dijonnaise which any
fool can cook – well, this one has. It's so good, you could eat
it!

1 chicken, $2\frac{1}{2}$ to 3 pounds, quartered
$\frac{1}{3}$rd cup mustard (half Dijon-style and half coarse Pommery-
style mustard)
Freshly ground black pepper, to taste
$\frac{1}{3}$rd cup vermouth or dry white wine

$\frac{1}{2}$ cup crème fraîche or double cream
Salt, to taste

1 Coat the chicken with the mustard and set in a bowl, covered, to marinate at room temperature for two hours.
2 Preheat oven to 350°F.
3 Arrange chicken, skin side up, in a flameproof baking dish. Scrape out any mustard remaining in the bowl and spread it evenly over the chicken. Season lightly with pepper and pour the vermouth or wine around the chicken.
4 Set dish on the centre rack of the oven and bake, basting occasionally, for thirty to forty minutes, or until chicken is done. You may have to bake the dark meat sections for another five to ten minutes.
5 Scrape the mustard off the chicken and back into the baking dish. Transfer the chicken pieces to a serving platter, cover, and keep warm.
6 Skim as much fat as possible from the cooking juices and set the baking dish over medium heat. Bring to the boil, whisk in the crème fraîche or double cream and lower heat. Simmer the sauce for five to ten minutes, or until it is reduced by about one-third. Season lightly with salt and pepper. Taste, correct seasoning, and spoon sauce over the chicken. Serve hot or at room temperature.
  Serves 2–4. Sod all left to go in freezer.
7 Eat in the comfortable, chipped splendour of your own kitchen, with a nice glass of privatized water, leave washing up to congeal till tomorrow and retire to own bed. Do *not* take corned beef sandwich.

4

Actor in Trouble

Memories Are Made of – Er –

Well. They are going. The cells. The little irreplaceable ones that perish in the brain, never to be replenished. Going. Going . . . With a rapidity that had me devouring with indecent haste an interesting article on memory then, four minutes later, forgetting what it had advised . . . Gone.

I work in chaos. My desk, as I survey it from my vantage point, looks like a still life from Hieronymus Bosch. Telephone wedged on unread comedy script from anxious writer. Radio lying on three unused glass paperweights, empty cassette case, empty tea mug, small wooden doll's house chair, cylindrical rape alarm reading 'Emits 30 + shrills' in five languages (which foreigner, I ask you, is going to assault me in my own study?). Ahead of me, there's an oblong maroon box which reads 'More Balls Than Most' and contains implements to teach me 'The Joy of Juggling'. It's been there for a year. Have I juggled? Have I balls!

All of which serendipity, plus two-dozen assorted Christmas cards, a half-consumed packet of Lockets, a foot-high pile of scripts and a video tape inexplicably labelled Richard Stilgoe, inspire me to the task of creativity which lies before me.

My husband, the proper writer, has a clean desk. Just a silver blotter, a fountain pen and eight assorted chewing gums. Of course, his word processor is on my dining table but my point remains the same. *Real* writers have tidy minds. We 'dabblers' live like pigs, which is why we are so often *sty*mied for words.

Words which keep vanishing. Like serendipity for example.

Complete short-circuit on that one. Had to stop, go downstairs, eat huge quantities of rice and make a phone call,
before 'serendipity' popped into the mind. And it's not even
the word I want. The word I want is long and begins with
M*, but every time I get close to it, I can only think of
Mesopotamia. If I'd had a Thesaurus to hand, of course, I
could have looked it up under serendipity and saved myself
the indigestion.

Sometimes I ring someone up and by the time they've
answered I have no idea whom I've called. 'Hi!' I burble. 'It's
Maureen. How are you ... All?' in the hope that their reply
will yield a clue to whom I've rung. And why.

Then there are the books I find I've read before, but not
until I'm one hundred and eighty pages in. The countries I
claim never to have visited until the man with whom I co-habit
reminds me of the week we spent there. On Honeymoon. The
faces at parties who lunge towards me saying 'Great to see
you again, how are Amy and Adam? Gosh, they must be
twenty-one and nineteen by now and how's the cat's dia-
betes?' when I've never clapped eyes on them in my entire
life and don't even know what *sex* they are. It's a bit of a joke
really.

Which leads me, pedantically, to the memory joke told to
me by Barry Cryer. A man rings his friend to enthuse wildly
about a restaurant he'd visited the previous night.

'It was fabulous,' he exclaims. 'The food, the ambience,
the service – faultless ... the best ...'

'Really?' says his friend. 'And what was it called?'

'It was called ...' he hesitates, 'the ... er, the ... er ...
Hang on a tic ... the, oh, God ... the ... er. Wait a minute!
What's the name of that long green thing with thorns on the
sides and a pink flower?'

'Rose?' suggests the friend.

'That's it!' he shouts. 'Rose! That's it.' Then shouts, 'Rose!
What was the name of that restaurant we went to last
night?'

My phone just rang actually. It was my friend, Jennifer, the reflexologist. From Manchester. I told her I was musing on memory and she said 'Ginko'.

'Ginko,' I repeated, largely because I've never said it before and may never say it again. 'What's Ginko?'

'The new miracle memory elixir,' she informed me.

'Does it really work?' I asked her.

'I don't know,' she replied. 'I've got a book all about it but I keep forgetting to read it.' Then she added, 'I *must* buy a bookmark.' Oh yes. *That'll* help. We're only in our forties for Pete's sake. What's it going to be like when we qualify for our bus passes? I'll have forgotten what a bus *is*.

Somehow I manage to remember my lines though, said she hastily, remembering that producers' wives have been known to read the odd book. Different part of the brain, I suppose. The part which isn't irreparably losing thousands of brain cells per minute. And jokes. I remember jokes. In batches. M for memory.

'There's just one thing I can't stand,' I said recently at a gathering. Every eye in the room swivelled towards me, reflecting interest, concern, curiosity and more than a touch of anticipation – except that by now I had no idea why they were looking at me, what had been the first part of the sentence or who was the current President of the United States of America. Mind you, the last one is excusable since most Americans have no idea either. I love the story of Clinton, in despair, seeking advice at the statue of Thomas Jefferson. 'Ahm in a hole, suh, an ah cain't get myself out of it. No one lahks me, or mah wife or mah policies, suh, und ah don't know what to do for the best, suh.'

A low voice from the statue rumbles, 'Go to the Constitution!' But Bill figures it's too darn late for that, so he goes and puts his problem to the statue of Theodore Roosevelt, and a mighty voice rumbles, 'Go to the people!'

But, once more, Bill feels he needs some miracle that will transform his luck, so he goes to the statue of Abraham Lincoln and he bows his head and mumbles the same liturgy of despair and hopelessness. 'What can ah do, suh?' he cries.

The statue of Abe Lincoln rumbles, 'Go to the theatre!'

And finally, a little something for the weekend – old ones, new ones, sad ones, blue ones, remembered ones, forgotten ones ... Here is a forgotten one ... Er ... Um ... hang on a sec ... it's on the tip of my whatsit ...

A couple consult their doctor about their failing memories. He advises them to repeat the cogent word in each sentence over and over to re-pattern the brain. That evening she asks what he wants for dinner and he replies, 'I'll have some steak.'

'Steak,' she mutters on her way to the kitchen. 'Steak, steak, steak.'

'And what sort of potatoes?' she throws back at him.

'Er, I'd like some chips, please.'

'Chips,' she reiterates. 'Chips, chips, chips.'

'And for vegetables?' she asks.

'I think I'd like peas.'

'Peas, peas, peas, peas, peas,' she says.

Half an hour later she calls him to the table and puts his dinner down in front of him. 'There you are,' she says. 'Just what you wanted. Eggs, bacon and tomatoes.'

He stares at her. Puts down his knife and fork and says, 'Where's the *toast*?'

* *M for Miscellany! Pass the Ginko...*

Spine-tingling Success

Doctor:	I have some bad news and some worse news.
Patient:	Give me the bad news first.
Doctor:	You have 24 hours to live.
Patient:	And the worse news?
Doctor:	I forgot to ring you yesterday.

In this chapter I intend to cover Recovery and Recuperation and, for want of another alliterative topic, I shall begin with *Re: Joyce!* which I performed for the Manchester City of Drama to 2,000 people in the Royal Opera House in March 1994. It could have been, I believed, my last performance and I gave it 'my all, and then some'. Short of clinging to the curtains at the finale, blowing kisses to the usherettes and gracefully expiring on the apron, I don't think I could have done more.

Afterwards, somewhat flushed with success and suppressed tidings, I had the unenviable task of telling my student daughter that her performing seal of a mother was about to be clubbed. More precisely, operated on for the removal of a neurofibroma deeply embedded in her spine. My daughter took it, as I knew she would, on the chin. The said chin was loose and wobbly, but otherwise she accepted it like a man, which is more than the man sitting on my bed did. He had a look in his eyes like a two-times loser at Crufts.

The alternative, I explained to Amy, would be paralysis. The 'nodule', which was spotted by my neurologist (or, St Jeffrey, as I now think of him), quickly became a 'tumour' in

155

the mouth of his brilliant but brisk colleague, the neuro-
surgeon, Mr Afshar.

I had been at the BBC reading a prize-winning short story
for radio and afterwards drove straight to Dr Jeffrey Gawler
for neck x-rays and consultation. He told me the nodule was
in my spinal cord. A neurofibroma. It was wrapped around
all sorts of things and it had to be removed right away.
Depending on how attached it was to nerve endings, my right
arm could be affected. He was 99 per cent sure it was not
malignant. He couldn't believe I did not show any side-effects
like pins and needles or loss of feeling in any of my limbs.

Mr Afshar came in. He called the neurofibroma a tumour
and reiterated that it would be unusual for it to be malignant.
I was worried about whether to have it done immediately or
after the upcoming Manchester *Re: Joyce!*. Dr Gawler said it
should be immediate. Mr Afshar said ten days wouldn't make
any difference. He was going away for a few days the following
week. So it was then or never. I walked back to the car and
rang Jack, just as I'd meant not to, and blurted it all out and
wept. The radio played Beethoven's Violin Concerto all the
way home. It was a comfort. Jack made me tea and sympathy
and we cancelled much of the next week's engagements. In
the loo the *American Bath Book* opened to, 'The time to repair
the roof is when the sun is shining'.

Re: Joyce! was poignant for those of us in the know, which
amounted to five out of 2,000, and for the others, I guess it
was one of our best ever. Sometimes Joyce just flies in,
Poppins-like, and does the show for me.

The next day an operation relieved me of most of the deeply
attached 'todule', which had probably been with me for
twenty years, distorting my spinal cord and pressing on an
artery to the brain. I wondered how far I could have gone
without it. How gorgeous I could have *looked* without it. What
a great scuba diver I would have been without it.

Seriously, it was a lesson in how easily a chronic complaint
like migraine can be fobbed off for years. Even *I* didn't really
believe me. It's the old triple bluff. You're a working mother,

you're an actress – listen, you've a headache! Take a pill, take therapy, take a break, take my bill. So in all these years of consultations and their alternatives, I've had my feet kneaded, my torso needled, my cranium manipulated, my mind hypnotized, my eyeballs drugged up to – all I hadn't had was common or garden x-ray.

So on the same day that the London *Evening Standard* chose to print 'Me and My Health' (in which I'm quoted as saying 'I'm probably the healthiest person you've ever interviewed'), my intrepid neuro-surgeon was slicing and digging and sucking and stitching for the best part of six hours. Doesn't time fly when you're anaesthetized?

I shall skip over the intensive care bit because you may be eating your muesli and regular throwing up, and down, from all ends with a recently sliced neck is nobody's idea of a good laugh. Except maybe Carlton TV's. We are, it is written, a stiff-necked people and, boy, am I stereotypical.

For the next ten days I watched the Thames flow oh-so-sweetly past my window, wept copiously for no apparent reason, and thanked my Maker for making Dolores, the sort of Irish nurse you could lay on an open wound. Sloping-bosomed and apple-cheeked, she came into her own on finding me mid-blub after learning the 'todule' was benign. 'There now,' she murmured soothingly. 'Don't you feel a whole lot better when you hear it straight from the doctor's ears?'

My husband slept the whole night after the operation in a chair and opened his eyes each hour when they came to shine a light in mine, my kids were impeccable and my mother perched on the bed and told me excitedly that 'a tall tin of red salmon in Sainsbury's is now £1.59.' I felt twice blessed. 'That's amazing,' I replied. There was a lot of love in the exchange.

During my hospitalization, one visitor was Michael Codron, who was to produce *The Sisters Rosensweig*. It had been a full day if I'm to believe my journal:

Monday today so a lot has happened and I'm tireder
and lower, without knowing why.

Sunday was too many visitors, I think. Sandra
and Buddy, then Mom, Jack bearing deli stuff from
Hampstead, Christine Goldshmidt looking won-
derful and bearing a translucent blue fossil, then
Valerie and Ruby, then Bryan and Edith and finally
Michael Codron and Mark Raiment.

I mean, can you believe this? Tuesday I have the archae-
ological dig into the central nervous system; Tuesday night
they shine a miner's lamp into my eyes every hour; Wednesday
I throw up; Thursday I swallow pain killers and hospital food;
Friday I learn the news that the tumour, if left, would have
lead to a tetraplegic future, and see first visitors, Lizzy and
Lynn, who call with gifts and date cookies and I doze through
their love and friendship till the physio arrives; Saturday
Denis and Astrid and then Julia McKenzie and I sleep a lot.

Then Sunday I entertain twelve visitors in shifts and write
'I feel tired for no apparent reason'!

Michael suggested I would be happier if I played
Gorgeous, not Sara, in *The Sisters Rosensweig*. At
this point his optimism is staggering. He only has to
look at me to realize that 'Gorgon' would be better
casting but he's absolutely serious. 'You won't have
to carry the show in the same way, shoulder as much
responsibility, and it's a far less emotional stretch –
think about it.'

It wasn't easy to think about anything. The nadir came when
a nurse came to take my stitches out. After a short bout of
clipping, she said in clipped tones, 'Oh dear ... there's a bit
of spinal fluid leaking out ... hold on, I'll be right back ...'
and she disappeared for fifteen minutes.

Now I don't know what the term 'leaking spinal fluid'
means to you but to me it meant a few many syllabled words

like meningitis, haemorrhage and, ultimately, rigor mortis. That fifteen minutes was the longest waiting period of my life. When she returned with Mr Afshar to stitch me up again, I was rigid with fear and shivering uncontrollably. 'C-c-c-can you pass me some Kleenex?' I managed to stutter ... and her next sentence should be engraved on her heart: 'One moment please. I'm helping doctor at present. When I've finished, I'll pass you what you want.'

I would march from London to Mississippi in support of higher pay for nurses. I would picket Stephen Dorrell's picket fence with a placard of the chaos his predecessor caused Casualty in London. I would give every nurse in the country a bonus, a rise and, if possible, the Freedom of the City and a flock of black-faced sheep to drive over Tower Bridge – but I wouldn't cross the road to save this particular 'angel' from a colony of fire ants. There you are. It's out. Malevolence. Childish, but I feel better for it.

In the same mischievous mode, I answered a 'How are you?' call from Julia with the sentence, 'I'm fine, love, really ... pain down to a minimum, just had a decent piece of salmon trout, weather's looking up, I'm gazing out on the Thames flowing sweetly past, the doctor says I can go home on Wednesday and "So-and-So's" just got *terrible* notices – I'm fine.' It was exceedingly un-Christian and I thought McKenzie would never stop laughing.

Once home I set about recuperating, which basically meant trying to find a decent chair to support my back in a house which was a haven for furniture with sick-building syndrome. What hadn't been hand-minced by the cat had collapsed under its own aegis and I was reduced to sitting on a straight-backed kitchen chair propped up with duvets. It was strangely comfortable and seemed to cry out for soft-boiled eggs, soldiers and sago pudding.

All was right with the world. So long as you didn't turn on the news. Or the TV. At all. TV has been the biggest turn-off since Bienvenida Thingy. God bless Dennis Potter for saying everything I've thought, but thought incoherently, about what's happened on our screens. One more gross sitcom, peopled by casts of grotesque morons, one more testicular- and menstrually-obsessed comic, one more formula-ridden and written corpse and robbers show, and I'm going to have my licence revoked. Thank God for Classic FM, Home Videos, and the best 'best friends' a whinging woman with more rings round her neck than a Masai tribeswoman could wish for, to cling on to and make sodden.

As patients go, I had none. Patience that is. I wanted to be not only up and about but *higher* up and more *visibly* about than before. And I couldn't. It just took one well-meaning stranger to come up to me in the street and tell me how thin I looked for the dam to break all over again. 'Look, you don't even know me,' I bleated. 'I wouldn't dream of commenting on *your* personal appearance. Sod off.' Four weeks after the op and still in my styrofoam collar, I had to meet an American agent who was only here for one day. I spent hours on my face and my hair, but kept ducking out of her eyeline, feeling ugly and unemployable. 'I felt so awful,' I said to my mother afterwards in the kitchen. 'I didn't want her to see me.'

'Don't be so silly,' she reassured me. 'You won't *always* look like that.' Life has a way of going on, hasn't it?

The one day I *had* to pull myself together was the day Jack went up to Buck House to get his New Year's CBE. We discovered his distinct lack of morning suit and top hat a few days before and since I buy his clothes for him, or at best, with him, I had to be slowly perambulated and driven to Golders Green in my collar, like one of those nodding dogs in the back of an old Morris Oxford. It was exhausting but triumphant and I had to be put to bed for the rest of the day. Two days later my friend Lizzy slid a pale blue Ronit Zilkha suit over my wobbly head. 'I'll take it!' I burbled as the skirt slithered over my hips (all shopping should be accomplished this way) and the following day combined spinal monitoring at Bart's with a lightning limp to Selfridges with Julia McKenzie for the hat. This took twelve minutes flat and was perfect.

All we needed now was two inches and some binding on Adam's trousers (he'd obliged us by lying down growing whilst I was lying down shrinking), a job lot of crumpled linen for Amy and an entire pot of mortician's wax for me, and we were all set.

I could hear a band playing in the Minstrels' Gallery behind me but I couldn't turn my head to see it. Too vain to wear the neck collar, I sat tremulously in the ballroom whilst four Beefeaters marched solemnly on to the podium to the accompaniment of 'Strangers in the Night'. Then, after six or seven men and women, whose names began with O, P or Q, in walked our Mr R, jauntily out of step, to the tune of 'I'm in Love With a Wonderful Guy'. The whole thing was fabulous and unforgettable and our stiff necks were entirely to do with pride.

No matter that the *Daily Mail* called me Beattie nor that the *Jewish Chronicle* gave Jack an MBE and a daughter called Lucy, we were still ecstatic. I could have complained but, hell, who needs the headache? It's called prioritizing and maybe, after forty-seven years, I'm finally getting it right.

Then, quite suddenly, I remembered one migraineous day, when Zelma and I drove to Shepherd's Bush to drop our close relative, Ms Amy, at the medium's. The medium was a New Zealand lady, over for the odd consultation, and Amy was anxious to know how she would best cope with being torn from her home and family and banished to the frozen wastes of a Lancashire campus. When I say anxious, I mean anxious in the sense of 'I'm going to chain myself to the cat and sing protest songs, rather than leave home.' I was driving her to the medium in Shepherd's Bush because it was obviously my fault she felt this way. I'd either made it too pleasant here, so there was nothing to rebel against, or I'd made her too dependent on us to feel anything but fear at the thought of going. Either way, I was a miserable failure and boring. And migraineous to boot.

An hour or so later we called back for her. She answered the door herself, looking rather chipper, I thought. 'She wants you to come in, Mod. There's a spirit guide and he thinks your migraines are to do with your teeth!'

'Me?' I hissed. 'What's all this got to do with *me*?' Nevertheless, I sat down and had my head felt and in due course spent £500 at the orthodontist on a dental bite plate in which I occasionally sleep to render myself *totally* irresistible. 'I cah – I go' dith thig id by gnowth', being the standard reply to 'Give us a kiss then, love'. Well, 'Not tonight, darling, I've got a headache', would hardly be unusual in our house, would it?

On the journey home, Amy clutched the tape she had recorded of her 'reading' and told us as much as she could remember of what was said.

'She said Daddy's going to get a tremendous honour soon,' she remembered. 'But I told her he'd already had one, from the Royal Television Society, but she said, no, it hadn't happened yet. Then she wrote down the letters CBE, on a piece of paper.'

We all sat thinking of reasons why the coal board should wish to honour Jack for a while, then we forgot it. This was in November. In January he was awarded the CBE. Ooooooh! Makes you think, doesn't it? I reckon she was an above average medium.

So, Commander Jack and I decided a holiday was in order and flew off in May to Marbella with swimming costumes, Chinese herbs and a spare neckbrace. The hotel, the Incosol, used to be a very posh health spa; it's now a very empty one, the whole thing resembling the inside of a multi-tunnelled, closed-for-repairs, swimming pool complex. We left for the cosy informality of Los Monteros Hotel after a day or two and never regretted it.

On the day of the Manchester United Cup Final, the Australian Manager of Los Monteros arranged a large screen in the lounge, Jack and I bought red polo shirts and headbands to wear with our white shorts and ankle socks and a Brits Abroad afternoon, complete with wine and sandwiches, was arranged by the frangipani-covered terrace. We were ecstatic, jingoistic, ritualistic and over the Eldoradan moon when the lads in red did us proud. Kevin Keegan was staying in the same hotel, but I couldn't help noticing he had better things to do on a sultry spring afternoon by a Spanish sea. I guess he was on holiday and didn't want to be a busman.

We came back, as we always come back, with Jack – who hovers in the shade – a deep mahogany brown, and me – who lies motionless on a lounger doused in oil – a brightish beige but for a beaky scarlet protuberance in the middle of my mush. 'Hello, Maureen,' chortled a Birmingham wag as we waited for a cab at Heathrow. 'You meeting him from holiday then? You look like you could use one yourself!'

Once back, as May flowed predictably into June, I settled into *The Lipman Test* which, since it appeared only on Radio 4, could happily contain me and my large styrofoam neckbrace and quietly prepared myself for rehearsals of *The Sisters Rosensweig* to begin in July. I still felt as though I was carrying a small Barbary ape on my shoulders and my energy swayed erratically from up to under, but with the help of Tony Porter's magic reflexology on my feet, every day, in every way, I got better and better.

I wonder if you are wondering about the migraines? Have they gone for ever, you are asking? If only life were like *Dr Finlay's Casebook*. All Tannachbrae, tea cosy and miracles. 'Fraid not. Still, are we downhearted? Er – well, once or twice a month we are, but we cope. We cope and take all the drugs we can and avoid all the dodgy foods and try to lead a stress-free life and if you believe that, you'll believe Persil washes whiter and Bill Clinton didn't inhale. Let me elaborate.

Last Friday, for example, I went to BBC Radio to record a ten-minute life study of Joyce Grenfell. I'd written too much and neglected to time it and the production team hadn't collated the record excerpts, so the whole exercise was time consuming. Afterwards, I lunched at the Langham Hotel with ex-BBC producer, John Fisher, to discuss a possible series, then met Jane Asher and a photographer for an article in her new magazine, interestingly called, er, *Jane Asher's Cookery and Craft Magazine.*

I like Jane a lot. She is funny, practical, genuine and dashed attractive. With edge. She's also bloody clever and a good actress and it's high time she had a 'Lumley', if you take my meaning. We once appeared on the same page of a teen mag in 1969, and I've kept the picture ever since, scarcely able to believe I ever could have looked so dewy.

We were due to work together on a series by the writer, Lesley Bruce, and met for lunch with producer, Colin Shindler, to discuss it. During the course of several courses, I mentioned the fun I'd had buying up fake designer watches in New York. 'It's such a slap in the face for all those ghastly Rolex wearers,' I glowed, flaunting my fake Chanel and burbling on about people with Moschino on their belts and Louis Vuitton scrawled over their handbags.

'Like me, you mean?' grinned Jane, waving her Rolex-clad wrist around loudly. I hope I had the grace to blush, or at least to gush, but I'm not altogether sure.

Minutes later, revenge was beautifully extracted when the series, which was about a perfume dynasty, was being discussed. 'It's like those awful people who wear Tea Rose,' said Jane, scathingly, only to see me wave my wrist sheepishly under her nose, crowing, 'Like *me*, you mean!' We laughed a lot. We would have laughed more but sadly the series bit the dust.

She still has her Rolex and I still smell just as appallingly and this day's venture was to photograph Jane presenting me with a cake representing a carton of Tea Rose perfume and a delicate porcelain cup. Very nice too. Fruit cake. My favourite.

I'd forgotten my make-up and was dressed to maim, in a Madras checked smock and a rather tired old body – not mine, it was blue and stretchy, well mine could still answer to that description I suppose, but you know what I mean. I borrowed Jane's powder and lipstick and her Carmen rollers and we posed and posed.

Then Jack arrived for a furniture-buying expedition we'd been putting off for months. He was so excited at finding a parking space outside Broadcasting House that he forgot to put any money in the meter, a fact he realized some twenty minutes later. He raced out of the hotel to find he'd been given a parking ticket, then raced back to hurry me up, having first stuck a pound in the meter to avoid further trouble.

By the time he'd run the fifty yards to pick me up and we'd said goodbye and left the hotel, the traffic warden had observed that the meter had been fed and phoned the clamping van. As we limped, stumbled and puffed back to the car, we saw they had clamped us and were about to drive off.

We started out reasonably enough but the dour warden just kept writing his notes and repeating his mantra which apparently involved him not making the rules. It seemed Jack should have removed the ticket before putting money in the meter. 'But how was I supposed to know *that*?' shouted Jack, getting redder and hotter and more distended with rage as the minutes went by, till I began to worry about his survival prospects.

'Okay. Look,' I reasoned, shrilly. 'You've already fined him – it's ludicrous to then clamp him on top of that, when all he did was . . .'

'I don't make the rules, Madam.'

'But you sodding carry them out and it's sheer sodding greed – privatized greed – when . . .'

'You should have taken the ticket.'

'But he didn't *know* he should have taken the ticket!' By now I'm leaping up and down like John Cleese and my voice is attracting bats.

'Calm down, Maureen!' shouts Jack, apoplectically.

'I *am* bloody calm. It's *you* who's hysterical!' I yelled. I return to the warden. 'Look at him! If he gets *ill* it will be *your fault*! Do you understand? YOUR FAULT!' By now I'm hopping and my arms are over my head and people are beginning to snigger.

We finally sorted it out by paying by credit card on a borrowed phone – yes, they won't allow you to use theirs – and we were ceremoniously unclamped and, shaking with rage and injustice, we were allowed to leave. In fact, I was so livid that when I got to the furniture store I bought the most expensive piece of furniture in the shop. There, that showed him!

From there we hurtled to Robson Books to look at the book cover photo, which had been cut off in the wrong place and to take a message from our son that Lizzy the hairdresser from *Agony Again* was waiting at home in Muswell Hill to colour my hair. It was now night and since there was the beginning of light drizzle, the traffic was at a total standstill.

An hour later I got my hair coloured. It caught my mood and went maroon and we had to frighten it brown again with strong shampoo.

I went to bed and awoke with the killer migraine from hell. It lasted three days. Can anybody think what might have triggered it? So now it's beta-blockers, reflexology, acupuncture and, possibly, a head transplant. Oh, and for fellow sufferers, I've moved the 'charging' phone from beside my bed. It may be psychological but I feel better for it.

The man in the fresh pasta shop, Mauro's, says an old gypsy cure is to boil milk with peppercorns. I told my daughter and she said, 'Do you have to drink it?' It's the kind of logic that only missed one generation.

Meanwhile, if anyone has a new miracle cure involving Jeff Bridges and a desert island, I'm aching to hear it.

Doctor:	I have some bad news and some good news.
Patient:	Tell me the bad news.
Doctor:	You have two weeks to live.
Patient:	What's the good news?
Doctor:	See the man in the bed opposite?
Patient:	Yes.
Doctor:	He wants to buy your slippers.

Doctored

It's official. After years of being a hypochondriac, I'm now a doctor. I've got my own stethoscope, an off-white jacket, an off-hand manner, and I'm in practice, hoping to get it right before the first opening. Thanks due to the powers that be at Hull University for the honour of Doctorate of Literature. True, it's only my words that heal, but words are powerful instruments.

Also, it means my mother can now say 'My daughter, the Doctor' instead of 'My daughter, the well paid telephonist'. There is a long list of doctors in my CV. My first starring role at fourteen was as Doctor Faustus at an all-girls school. I've played several doctors since on television and my last stage role was that of 'Dr' Gorgeous Teitelbaum in *The Sisters Rosensweig*. The dialogue runs: 'How did you get to be a doctor?' Gorgeous: 'You heard of Doc Martens? Well, I'm Doc Gorgeous.'

I also have a medicine cabinet the size of an Edwardian wardrobe.

To be honest, I have not just one but three medicine cabinets, which should tell you a great deal about my particular brand of hypochondria. The one in the conjugal bathroom is the sleazy one, although you'd never guess as much from its neat inlaid mahogany exterior and quaint old Victorian key. Sadly, since it is situated immediately above the quaint old Victorian lavatory, every time it's opened – particularly in haste in the wee small hours – the key falls directly into the lavatory along with a tube or two of chilblain cream and a packet of sponge ear plugs. I keep meaning to do

167

something about it ... I've kept meaning to do something about it since it was first put up there eleven and a half years ago.

This is the Bermuda Triangle of bathroom cabinets in that it takes in a good deal more than it ever gives out. There are medicines in there that probably treated some victims of the Crimean War. I am not proud of this and I have recently removed the beta-blockers which appear to have been prescribed for my piano accompanist, Denis King, the Entrotabs from the Portuguese villa holiday in 1987 and the packet of Lillets snuggling optimistically behind the Optrex bottle of a woman who had a hysterectomy in 1992.

What remains is a chronicle of my myriad chronic complaints and my husband's stolid reliance on Mycil Foot Powder. Nurofen, Migraleve, Midrid, Ponstad Cathergot and Voltarol are on standby for my various levels of migraine. If you catch it before it catches you then the former will do the job with a cup of strong black coffee. If it gets settled in nicely and you are rolling around the Tumbletwist bathmat with your head in the wastebin, then it's the Voltarol suppositories you must turn to. Well, turn *round* to really. One of my favourite old chestnut jokes is the man who is prescribed medicine in a *pharmacie* in France, in the usual insertable French form, and comes back two weeks later saying 'For all the good these did me, I might as well have shoved them up my arse!'

Holistically, my cabinet is also well served by Arnica tablets and cream for bruises, Rescue Remedy for everything else and Agnus Caster, which sounds like a Hollywood character actress from the fifties but claims to aid digestion. There is magnesium and kelp, zinc, folic acid and even Aconite – 'for fear of oncoming events'. Quite frankly, there is every reason on earth for me to feel as effervescent as a french-fry in a pan of nut oil. But do I? At the last count I was taking Vitamin C for immunity, coral calcium for longevity, ginseng and Royal Jelly for elasticity and by the eighth show on a Saturday night

I still have to be wheeled home like a straw Guy Fawkes in a Silver Cross Pram.

Meanwhile, there is also the family bathroom cabinet which contains a finger stall, a packet of lint, some Ralgex spray and a tin of 'Fiery Jack', long since banished for its propensity to stay on the hands long after the painful spot has been rubbed and other spots have been inadvertently cuddled. Downstairs in the utility room is a genuine medicine cupboard, white and shiny with a green cross on the front, the Silver Cloud of medicine cupboards. It is virtually full of Lemsips and Elastoplasts, the sign of a healthy household, I feel, and once the remaining child has gone off to university, I shall fill it with Sanatogen and never open it again.

Why three medicine cabinets, you ask? I can't think of one answer. All I know is that the medicines I need when the night-goblins wake me are all stuffed in my bedside cupboard along with reams of dental floss, velcro rollers, a plastic mouthguard, a foam neck collar and a Virgin Airline mask (would *you* fly with an airline named after someone who doesn't go all the way?).

So there's not much I don't know about doctoring. Hell, I'm almost a consultant. My air of gravitas was already in place on the day we travelled to Hull for the ceremony.

I was unexpectedly excited and moved by the splendid dignity of the ceremony in Hull's historic City Hall and wore my robes with tender pride. I was especially touched by the six hundred students who mounted the podium to collect their degrees, in a hundred degrees of heat and two hundred varying degrees of self-effacing slouch, rendered irresistible by their uniformly alarming orthopaedic footwear.

Not for them the hopeful optimism of youth, when youth merely stands for lack of opportunity. My heart lurched for them, and for all our children, most of them saddled with an iniquitous student loan and the prospect of facing unemployment *and* debt. What, I mused, is this self-serving Conservative government actually conserving other than misery?

During my address I considered the similarities between

actors and doctors. We both work long unsociable hours and require endless patients/ce, work in theatres, study parts, and in a while claim, not humbly, to have made someone feel a little better. Oh, and my initials are MD.

'This doctorate will give me a much-needed air of respectability often denied to members of my profession,' I told them. 'Too often we are associated with "resting", the casting couch, voice-overs for Chicken McNuggets and too many appearances on *Blankety Blank*. I'm sure you've heard the joke – why does an actor never look out of the window in the morning? Because it gives him something to do in the afternoon.'

I concluded with the thought:

'If I've earned this Honorary Award, I hope it's not, as the *Guardian*'s Francis Wheen would have it, for my services to BT, but for writing a few things which made people laugh and cheered them through rough times, operations and, according to one recent letter, Germans taking their hotel rooms on the Costa del Sol. For acting in one hundred and twenty odd plays (some very odd) in twenty-seven years and for not forgetting that you can take the girl out of Hull but you can't take Hull out of the girl.

'I've lived in London for six years longer than I lived in Hull but I'm more shaped by being a northerner than by any other influence. I live near enough to the M1 that should the going get tough, this softie could get going and I'm constantly cheered by the number of students I meet who tell me they've had the best times of their life here in Hull.

'I would also like to congratulate all my fellow Honorary Graduands here today and to promise I will do my best to act in the most interesting plays, to write the funniest and most truthful columns and to fly the flag of my home town (twinned logically, as it is, with Sierra Leone) and to fight the fight for peace, freedom and care in and out of the community to the very best of my capacity as an honorary "luvvie".'

It was a momentous occasion followed by much jolly retrospective chat into the night. The following morning we set out bright and early and drove the two hundred miles back to London because, that very afternoon, I was due at a wedding in Cambridgeshire. Yes, I know, this is not the way to rest and recuperate, but you must by now have picked up on my lifelong habit of shaking my head and saying yes.

Which is why I found myself at four o'clock that same hot, sticky Saturday at Liverpool Street Station, wending my way to a wedding which I was sworn to attend in spite of road fatigue and inflamed intercostal muscles which woke me stabbingly in the wee small hours for a panic of the 'Oh my God – cardiac arrest!' variety. (Physician, heal myself.)

From Liverpool Street Station I travelled through delightful rural Elysium to Audley End, where I was to be met by someone's son. Unfortunately, someone's son had been quaffing the wedding champagne from about the same time in the morning that I was pressing the stethoscope Jack bought me as a little joke hysterically to my chest. There were no taxis at Audley End and I was alone, but very prettily dressed, in a large, hot, airless car park.

Just as I was about to phone home and wimpishly whimper 'You were right, I shouldn't have come', a large white but battered Mercedes van approached and out leaned a strong-faced, cropped grey-haired lady of three score and ten-ish who sort of barked, 'Are you all right? Where are you heading?'

'Er, Hellion Bumpstead actually. (I don't make these things up. They happen!) It's a wedding. Do you know where I can get a taxi?'

'Well if there isn't one here, there won't be one,' she said cryptically. 'Hop in. I'll take you to Saffron Walden. You'll get one there.'

Now, I don't usually 'hop in' to vans driven by strangers who promise to drive you to towns the whereabouts or county-abouts of which you have no idea, but over the years I've developed a built-in-shit-detector about people and it rarely lets me down. I hopped in.

'You're not a kidnapper are you?' I burbled inanely. (Can you imagine a *stupider* question?)

'Do I look like one?' she replied briskly. 'No. I'm a healer.'

I was impressed. 'Gosh! You're the fourth healer I've bumped into in six weeks.'

'Hmmmm,' she replied. 'You must need healing.'

Saffron Walden appeared. And disappeared. 'Erm ... weren't you going to drop me at ... ?'

'It's all right, you can phone from my place. I'm just down the road.' She must have caught my slight air of concern (i.e. I'm gonna end up headless in a clearing, or, worse, topless on a Taiwan bar), because she also mentioned that she did reflexology.

'Oh, I've been having brilliant reflexology,' I told her.

'Who with?' she asked me and on being told Anthony Porter, added, 'Tony Porter? He's the absolute best. Taught me everything I know.'

I let my breath out naturally for the first time for ages, only to suck it in violently as Karel, as I later learned was her name, swung the van swiftly to the right saying, 'Here we are. Now, don't be alarmed. I live in the cemetery.'

Flatly I repeated her last three words. 'In the cemetery.'

'Yes. "Peace Lodge". It's a haven of peace and tranquillity. I've been here for thirty years.'

She pulled up outside a small Gothic lodge, fenced off from her horizontal neighbours, surrounded by wildly eccentric flora and fauna. Huge flowers grew out of horse troughs, sinks and other unusual appliances. A sunshelter appeared to be made of plastic bags over a velvet sofa – it was a set designed by Erté, for a play about Bloomsbury, starring Patricia Hayes. Inside was even more eclectic with a magnificent display of glass bottles and papers, books and medicines and piles and piles of everything. I loved it but was still vaguely fearful of sitting down in case I woke up in a poppy field in Oz. Not so.

We chatted and drank tea and, when she asked my name for the taxi firm, she raised an eyebrow and said, 'You're not *the* Lipman, are you?' When I replied that I was, she harumphed, 'Oh, that'll explain why you're so well dressed. Oh well. *That's* something to tell my daughter in Bolivia!'

The taxi man, once he'd got over the shock of being asked to pick up a live passenger from the cemetery, would be a while, so at Karel's request I took off my party shoes and gave her my feet to hold in her hands for ten minutes. It was very peaceful. Then I thanked her, kissed her goodbye and left.

In retrospect it was bizarre. What do I mean in retrospect? It was bizarre *then*. I mean I was in Yorkshire at 9 o'clock in the morning and at 9.10 at night, I was sitting in a Saffron Walden cemetery with my feet in the capable hands of a total stranger. And I *still* had a ruddy wedding to go to. All that was missing was Hugh Grant. Still, we all know where he was!

The taxi driver laughed so much he went way past Hellion Bumpstead and I spent the entire wedding party telling and retelling my journey. The young people rested their Doc Martens on the fragrant lawn and quite my favourite moment was hearing the beautifully silk-gowned bride berating a guest with, 'Oh, come on! It's my wedding day, don't be such an arsehole!'

My husband took it all with weary resignation: 'How is it,' he sighed, 'that when *I* go out, I just go out and come in again ... You go out and all manner of things *happen* to you. Do you *have* to always jump in feet first?'

Are There Any Massages?

My house was being decorated so I decided I needed a spot of renovation myself. With four days to spare before the onset of *Agony Again*, I fled to Grayshott Hall – my nearest and dearest health farm. Behind me, at home, I left Roy, the decorator, marooned in my bedroom with maroon paint and conflicting instructions.

'Put the wallpaper above and below the dado then, will you? But when you've got it up, take it down if it looks too much and I'll think again on Monday.' His face was a study. Which is what needs decorating really, come to think. As does the small toilet situated near the guest room, where my husband and I are sharing one twin bed. It's not that there aren't two twin beds, it's just that my feet get so cold on the journey from the small toilet to the bed and his body is like a griddle, but it's no use my getting into *his* bed because then, when I get into mine, it'll be sub-zero, so he has to get into mine and I've no sooner got my feet luke, than he's fast asleep and sounding like four bison and a phone pest.

So, what with the noise and the temperature, my dreams have become hallucinatory. Ruffians knocking me down the stairs of a number 27 bus. Cabinet Ministers breaking the door down whilst I'm in the loo. Elderly aunts beckoning me in ghostly fashion to gasp out the inaudible. I tell you, for the last week or two, I've been that *busy* in my sleep that I've woken up knackered beyond the call of beauty.

In other words, the house is upside down and I'm Taurean and need my security. Also I'm about to start a new TV series and I'm Maurean and riddled with insecurity. Somewhere upstairs my son is swotting for his A Levels and making no fuss at all. (White-faced and heavy-eyed, but actually enjoying his Greek and Latin and, sort of, liking his English. The family loo is full of Wordsworth. I'm sure he'd be thrilled. I've been cooking meals of greater and greater exoticism and complexity just so that he'll take longer eating them and then at least I'll *see* him.)

Where I should be, is in Manchester, where my daughter is performing in a play called *The Cage Birds*. She's told me, in a huffy sort of voice, that it doesn't matter if we don't come up for this one – she's only playing a *canary* – but I'm riddled with the kind of conflicting emotions which drive you into driving, for two hours on a hot Bank Holiday weekend, straight into an hour's traffic jam over the 'Hog's Back' on the A3 to Grayshott Hall Health Farm.

'You've got the most terrible back,' puffed Linda, the holistic masseuse as she grappled with it, me and a bottle of oil. I'd stipulated two things at the start of the massage. No New-Age music and no aromatherapy. She was perfectly amenable, though vaguely huffy at the idea that she would entertain such music. 'It's not New-Age,' she assured me. 'It's Enya.'

I'm afraid I couldn't suppress a small scream. 'Can I pay extra for No Enya?' At the end of an hour and a half I was doing my obligatory weeping with gratitude routine. When she ran her hands over my stomach I felt as if I was being hoovered. The woman had hands which performed psychic operations. I could have kissed her. Instead I crawled back upstairs promising to drink a litre of water and go to bed. I floated, I felt tingly all over, even around my lips.

Once upstairs, in my beautiful blue and yellow room with leaded light windows, gazing out on rolling green lawns and banks of fluffy mauve rhododendrons, I did what any sensible, kneaded, relaxed woman would do. I ran through my worries. The new TV sitcom was an old one really – *Agony* – which I first played fifteen years ago. I had given myself four days to get plumped up and bonny. In fact, on my way down in the car, I practised an exercise from the

Daily Mail which showed gullible morons like myself how to get a fuller face.

Now, I know most people would kill for a thinner face, but all my life I've been reading novels featuring thin-faced villains and I want some of what Roseanne had sucked out! Open-faced, apple-cheeked, bonny and blithe – a few centimetres on either side, just so that elderly women don't come up to me in the light diet room and tutt, 'You're so *thin*. What are you doing *here*?' Maggie Smith is also in the light diet room. She's thin too, but no one goes up and tutts at her. Including me, though I'd love to, but I'm shy.

As I was saying before I interrupted myself, the *Daily Mail* exercise: Pull down the lip over the top teeth, roll back the corners of the mouth. Place two fingers on the upper lip and slowly pull them away to a count of thirty-five whilst visualizing your face filling out.

I want you to picture me, stuck on the A3, face in a rictus-like grimace with two fingers stuck up in the air twelve inches from my face, looking like Ken Dodd in tattyfallarin mode. I turn to my left and a young black man in the next car is staring at me in disbelief. I try to straighten my face and pretend to rub a spot off the windscreen with the rigid digits but I can already see him mouthing the words 'Are you all right, Beattie?' through his window.

So I'm worrying about my face. And I'm worrying about finishing this book, and I'm worrying about a career decision which has to be made by tomorrow. And I haven't found any material for the new sofas I haven't yet ordered and I shouldn't have left the boys home alone and would *The Cage Birds* be the crisis which turns my daughter from a friend to a fiend?

It was at this juncture that the tingling lip revealed itself to be a full-blown cold sore. It popped out from its undercover status and took on that swollen silicone look so beloved of supermodels and the odd cast member of *Coronation Street*. I'm filming on Tuesday! I'm kissing an actor on Thursday. I *never* get kissed on screen and now I'm going to kiss some poor guy – and the next day the poor bugger's going to look like I look now!

By now I'm rigid again. All Linda's loving ministrations have gone out the leaded window, pausing only to drool over the Designer's Guild drapes. I phone home to dispense my good cheer around the house but think better of it. Instead I pick up my book to take my mind off my troubles.

A mere five hours later I drop into a deep and dreamless sleep, counting not sheep but my blessings and seven dreamy hours later I woke up, still blessed. I walk, I swim, I exercise, I attend a meeting on visualization. I'm better. Lumpy-lipped Lipman I may be, but I'm the luckiest girl on earth and it's time I knew it and thanked God for it.

Want to know the name of this novel cure? It costs about a milimetric per cent of a health farm, a holiday, a meal out at any calorie conscious hostelry of your choice. It cost £6.95 actually and it's called *An Evil Cradling* by Brian Keenan. In case you've forgotten, he's the Irishman who was incarcerated in Beirut by mindless zealots for five and a half years. It's about violence and injustice and survival and madness and man's inhumanity to man. Most of all, it's about love. I'm going home tomorrow to my boys and my bedroom – with flab on my thighs, hope in my heart and a face that may be thin but is glad it's been a round.

PS at the meeting on visualization, an earnest Californian blonde told us how she'd been broke, hungry and depressed until she'd discovered how 'to visualize'. She told us how her dog had been dying of cancer until she had visualized him healthy. She advised us to return the following evening for our first training session. Some of us did, to find a note on the door, saying, 'Sorry, session cancelled due to illness.'

Raising my Glasses...

I am a woman who has always been prepared to make a spectacle case of herself. Since the days before National Health glasses were associated with lazy eyes, lazy pupils and Elastoplast, rather than young men in baggy linen and floppy quiffs, I have sported maybe thirty or forty assorted pairs of glasses and have a proud and pinkish indentation on my not inconsiderable nose to prove it.

Occasionally, it must be admitted, I have begun a sleazy, adulterous relationship with a contact lens container, but, in the end, loyalty has prevailed and I have skulked, penitently red-eyed, back to the glasses case sulking in my dressing-table drawer.

I'm short-sighted, astigmatic and as daft as a brush, so the lenses always ended up in the wrong eye, inside out or else I returned furiously to the practitioner and found I had someone else's lenses in. Coupled with which, the sight of myself – bare faced in a mirror, under the overhead fluorescent lighting of the M & S Food Hall – was a moment of real terror, unparalleled by the Delivery Room. People who habitually wear glasses have a funny look when they take them off. Their eyes look hunted. Slightly puffed up and vulnerable and, of course, if you're short-sighted, you haven't seen yourself at a distance *without* glasses since the Old Queen died. It's a fearful shock to the central nervous system and the certain cause of cartons of Taramasalata and Hummus and individual Salmon and Courgette Kebabs hitting the deck with a worrying frequency in the hallowed halls of St Michael –

178

and try taking those back and asking for a credit note!

I had three pairs of hideous – by my standards I hasten to add – glasses for Beattie, after the producers realized that they added years to my age, and in the series *About Face*, three out of the six characters I played wore glasses, ranging from half-moon rimless for the batty animal rights liberationist to matching frame to every outfit for Deirdre, the career woman on the up. I love character glasses. I feel safe behind them and unworried by the rigours of lamps on lines. I once ran on stage in my blue-tinted hippy, gold-framed rectangular ones, only to see the audience for the first time in my life. This would have been fine except the play was a sixteenth-century Jacobean one, and I was wearing a farthingale and neck ruff to accompany them.

I have a pair that are not that dissimilar from the ones I wore on that fateful evening, gold-rimmed, small, but rounded. They say on them, Paul Stig Design, and they come with a variety of frame covers in different colours, rather like a Swatch. I rarely wear the frame covers but I love having the gimmick. I'm delighted the fashion for huge spectacles has passed on because on a face as small as mine they tended to make me look like an inverted pair of garden shears.

I'm also intrigued by the High Street Opticians turning into the glamour shop of the nineties, replacing the Moroccan Wall Hanging shops of the sixties, the Habitats of the seventies and the Nexts of the eighties. Opticians' windows used to favour a couple of rows of spectacles, a merry laughing four-eyed family group and a snap-shut glasses case. Nowadays you'll see the head of Zeus in life-size proportions, draped in Thai silk with a picnic hamper from Fortnum's spilling out its classical repertoire of fine goods on to a surface of gleaming perspex. The music of Saint-Saëns will be playing sweetly through the open doors and the only way you'll know it's an opticians is by the number of people walking straight into the clear glass doorposts.

I'm getting long-sighted, of course. Isn't that fun? Bifocals beckon. My eyes feel seriously stuck together in the mornings and I have to swab them down like we used to swab our tortoise, Zuckerman, after a long winter in the bike shed. Almost everything, from a baby in a blue babygro to an old Fred and Ginger film on Saturday afternoon telly makes me cry these days and no mascara invented by man or Maybelline can stop the rivulets. My glasses are my friends, comforting, covering, protective, dirty and dependable – and once I'm done with my current ones I don't put them out to glass, they go in a special drawer with all my old friends to show my huge appreciation for services rendered, over the increasingly bleary years.

This year I've attempted a new idea in lenses which gives you one lens for short sight and another for long sight. Then the brain, apparently, does the business of adjusting. That's how the blurb goes anyway.

In my case, my brain decided it was April Fool's Day all year round. When I tried to read, the print fox-trotted, and when I looked into the middle distance, I fell over. Back to the drawing board, I'm afraid – if I could see it. I'd love to have the laser operation and just wake up with normal sight. As the man said, 'Show me a guy with 20/20 vision and I'll show you a gentile!' It wouldn't work though. Something would slip. The laser wouldn't lase. I'd wake up in the middle and my tears would wash away the surgeon ...

Listen, I'll just have to improve my groping – why not? I look at my desk and there's a pair for going downstairs in, there's the smart Raybans for venturing out of the door in, there's the very chic, non-prescription sunglasses to go over the corrective lenses which I'd given up on, there's the cheap and not very cheerful prescription sunglasses for quick trips up to the pool when I daren't risk losing my best ones, and there's the querulous gold-rimmed ones, hanging on the end of my nose, for the increasing long sight. Putting one pair of specs on to look for another is no longer amusing to my family as they wait all dressed up in the hall, for me to race around the house barking and swearing. The day I give in and allow the word bifocal to enter my vocabulary, is the day I'll also stop dying my roots, having my teeth capped and cantilevering my boobs. It'll be a courageous moment and fortunately I shall be too dead to see it. 'Glasses to glasses and bust to bust...'

5

Carry on Actor on the Job

The Sisters Rosensweig

In 1993 scarcely a week went by without someone calling to tell me about a new play in New York by Wendy Wasserstein called *The Sisters Rosensweig*. 'It's got your name on it,' said my agent. 'You must do it,' said friends. 'Kill for it,' said friends of friends. Others said, 'Don't do another American comedy. They don't appreciate them over here – you've seen that.' And they invariably added, 'Don't on any account, do another American *Jewish* play here – they'll crucify you.'

They were right, of course. I knew they were right. Of course. Post *Agony*. Post *Beattie*. Post *Yonkers*. Of course. (Post scriptum ... doing wrong can be mighty exhilarating and I will never regret it, even though the production was on and off more times than Liz Taylor's confetti account.) Came the day, producer Michael Codron said, 'Shall we do it? I will if you will.' I was already booked on Virgin with my daughter, my muse and my amusement, by my side.

The play tells the story of three sisters – all very different in nature – who meet up in London, where the eldest one, Sara, a banker celebrating her fifty-fourth birthday, now lives. Dr Gorgeous, the middle sister, is the 'funsy', suburban Jewish housewife and mother who also has a career as a radio agony aunt, and Pfeni is a roving journalist, unable to settle down either with or without her rather dubious boyfriend Geoffrey. The action takes place over three days and is in turn comic, romantic and moving about the problems of assimilation and identity.

I had been introduced to Wendy Wasserstein's work years earlier by producer Peter Witt and when I finally met her in

New York, it was like coming home. After the show, Wendy took Amy and me backstage to meet Madeleine Kahn and Jane Alexander, respectively Gorgeous Teitelbaum and Sara Rosensweig. At the time, all my sensibilities and sympathies were with the part of Sara, the sister played by Ms Alexander with strength, charm and humour. I told her so, and she thanked me with a distracted air. Ms Kahn's performance had been a tour de farce – at once funny and desperate, she worked the audience like a seasoned star of the Catskills 'Bortsch Belt' without resorting to caricature, although teetering dangerously near the line. There was no way I could have done what she did that night, vocally and physically, as the shopaholic Dr Gorgeous who dispenses homely radio advice whilst her own home life is in shards. Hunched and brittle in her fake Chanel suits, Alice- banded 'big' hair and Nancy Reagan legs, she stole not only the show, but the furniture, the wings and most of the auditorium. It wasn't theft, it was grand larceny.

When I tried to compliment her, she was polite but distant and hurried off to the phone. I later learned that this was the evening of the Tony Awards and the cast were anxiously – for this read paranoically – awaiting the calls to tell them of their nominations. In an ideal world, Ms Alexander would have been listed for Best Actress and Ms Kahn for Best Supporting Actress, but given Ms Kahn's audacious style, the critics' propensity towards camp and her own determination, they were both nominated for the same category.

None of this swayed me from my love affair with the part of Sara Rosensweig. A brilliant woman, celebrating her recovery from cancer, three times divorced, seamlessly assimilated into society, atheist, mother – her seventeen-year-old daughter is about to take flight – and, though she seldom admits it, she is terribly lonely.

Into her life, by chance or divine design, comes Merv Kant, a Bronx furrier who is everything she has spent her life running away from and to whom she is irresistibly drawn. It's a love story first and a romantic comedy second, and the thawing of Sara Rosensweig is at the heart of the play. At the end of Act I, Jane Alexander, after driving her lover away, unwraps her last birthday present and, from her childhood, quietly sings:

> Oh, my name is Moishe Pippick
> And I come from Palestine,
> I live on bread and honey
> And on Maneschevitz wine.
> Oh, my mother makes the best
> Gefilte fish in all the land.
> And I'm the only Yiddish girl
> In MacNamara's band.

There was a tugging, empathetic moment shared by that melting pot audience before applause rang out. It was very moving. Very sad.

By the time the rehearsals for the London production came round in August 1994, I was not playing the part that I had originally fallen for, but the showy but technically difficult Dr Gorgeous. Janet Suzman was very good casting for Sara, excelling, as she does, at playing intellectual characters and strong women. Lynda Bellingham cast as Pfeni, is Church of England but, married to an Italian, she is, in terms of warmth, chutzpah and cooking as a form of breathing, an honorary ethnic. Besides, go separate an Italian Mamma from a Yiddishe Momma!

Michael Codron was very keen for Larry Lamb to play Merv, the furrier, and Brian Protheroe seemed an excellent choice for Pfeni's bisexual boyfriend, Geoffrey, a part which had been 'graced' in New York by a performance which would have made Julian Clary look butch. With Hellena Schmied as Sara's daughter, James Arlon and Robert East, we were a small but perfectly formed cast.

We had decided to wait six months for the director, Michael Blakemore, who had faxed his approval and delight in the script from Australia, where he was filming *Country Life*. I'd

worked with Michael five times previously: in a stunning
National Theatre production of *The Front Page*, as a witch in
his *Macbeth* with Anthony Hopkins, a maid in his historic
Long Day's Journey Into Night with Laurence Olivier, in the
memorable key role of Second Randy Woman in *Tyger*, a
musical based on the life of William Blake (*Tyger* is now as
extinct as the one with the sabre teeth) and as Miss Prossy in
his production of Shaw's *Candida* with Deborah Kerr. We
saw eye to eye. He was known as an actor's director and,
being Australian, he had no axe to grind about American
writing and no prejudice about the value of comedy.

Lynda Bellingham and I live as back to back in Muswell
Hill as two actresses could possibly get. I could stand on my
garden wall and throw dumplings into her azaleas. We had
worked together on Neil Simon's *Chapter 2* and we love each
other to pieces. So much so, that we never see each other.
No, it's not what you think. She has small children and a
husband with a restaurant to run. Her life makes mine look
placid. As the first days turned into weeks and the weeks
turned into months, the bloom left our faces to be replaced
by hollow-eyed hysteria and the car journeys became a professional pick-me-up, laugh-in, cry-out and anti-depressant.

But I'm jumping ahead. Here are some diary notes I made
at the time:

> Day One: readthrough in Maida Vale Church Hall.
> Readthroughs are purgatory and should be banned
> by law. They are useless to everyone but the phar-
> macist who supplies the muscle relaxants. The air
> is heavy with paranoia – the moment of truth pro-
> longed through discussions of the set, the routes
> taken to Maida Vale and the mercenary nature of
> the council's parking squad. Finally, it can be pro-
> longed no longer. Now is the moment they are going
> to find out how miscast we are. We cough, shuffle
> and read. I'm mindlessly nervous throughout the

readthrough, my hands and legs are shaking uncontrollably and my teeth are chattering.

Later Janet Suzman tells me I showed no sign of nerves whatsoever. Now *that's* acting. It's four years since Janet did a play and five-and-a-half since Lynda trod a board and I'm still recuperating from major surgery.

Author Wendy Wasserstein has flown over from the States. I'm as worried for her as I am for myself. She's watched at least three casts of *The Sisters Rosensweig*, three actresses playing my part. My insecurity is tangible. I'm playing 'Dr Gorgeous'. If my character was called 'Fairly Attractive in the Right Light', would my knees be knocking this way?

We struggle through. It's not a good reading but to our amazement none of us is handed a red card. Michael Codron's face is set in concrete as he leaves.

Day Two: we break down first scenes and warily pad around the tape-marked indications of the set, our heads in our scripts.

The next three weeks lurch past. Some days are invigorating, some enervating. I go home tired but worked – it feels good to be exercising the old familiar muscles. I worry about the set, which has two sofas coming together in a V and a coffee table in front. I always feel as if I'm legless behind them. Michael Blakemore assures me that the auditorium is raked so you'll see 'all of us' but I'm never happy until my feet are. The sisters have no familial feel as yet – that won't come until we've all been *really* legless together.

When I did suggest that the three of us abandoned the rehearsal battlefield for the pub, we got on pretty well – three strong women, all balancing home, kids and careers. It was our approaches to the work which were utterly different, and our confrontational styles. I suppose Lynda and I tend to plunge in from the start with funny business and snappy ideas, whereas Janet works more like a director, watchfully rejecting rather than risking anything new. It was Michael Blakemore's job to guide us all to a point where we peak at the same time. It's not an easy job. Sometimes he looked like a man who would frankly rather be in the garden tending to his beloved wormery – but his patience held up extraordinarily well. There were moments of fun and creativity, but often rehearsals were like walking on day-old chicks. Lynda and I would turn the problems over and over in the car on the way home then, next morning, pick up exactly where we left off the night before.

My sleeping pattern began its familiar Morse code and I was up and down more frequently than Radio One's ratings. You could have sliced the air with a cheese parer when, in week four, we finally moved from the rehearsal room to the theatre – a journey which always reminds me of leaving the security of the Maternity Ward for the uncharted chaos of your own home with a week-old baby.

We were to open at the Greenwich Theatre and every day Lynda and I would attempt to hold our breath through the almost tangible pollution of the Blackwall Tunnel but give in three-quarters of the way through and gulp lungsful of it. We were thrilled to find that the Greenwich parking system was every bit as mercenary as its Maida Vale counterpart. Lynda, Hellena and I were in one tattered and overstacked dressing-room, giving each other back massages, pep talks and Rescue Remedy. Lynda would bury herself in eleven or twelve glossy magazines – there's nothing that woman doesn't know about Claudia Schiffer's bedtime routine. Failing that, she would talk to both children on her mobile phone, negotiating bedtimes and pouring healing words on domestic warfare. Hellena would write love letters to her American boyfriend and I would lie on the floor pretending to meditate, but actually mentally writing confrontational speeches and proclaiming them silently. Finally the management took pity on me and imported a folding beach chair so that I could hyperventilate without ruining my clothes.

The Greenwich stage was small and Lez Brotherston's set was ingenious to the eye but treacherous, as is so often the case, to the people who had to negotiate it. Not unnaturally, it looked and felt almost nothing like the rehearsal room mock-up. The staircase was the theatrical version of the north face of the Eiger to those of us who had to climb up and descend it frequently and in five-inch heels.

The technical and dress rehearsals juddered by over two days and our first real audience arrived the following night. There were fantastic flowers at the stage door from dear wellwishers who couldn't be expected to know that the nearest thing I had to a vase was a sawn-off Evian bottle and a plastic bucket. The audience amazed us by giving us our first real laughs – paralysing us into glassy-eyed panic and serial mis-timing. The heat was ferocious in that air-conditionless box and the entire house waved their programmes to fend of asphyxiation, making it look like a secretaries' nail-drying convention. However, they liked the play. They laughed. They listened and, although we knew it was early days, after a versatile drop of Sauvignon we all felt vaguely comforted.

Back to my diary:

The Third Preview: Saturday afternoon and the temperature is the same as that in Tiberius where my daughter is hacking banana leaves on a kibbutz. Wish *I* was. By Act II, in leotard, Lycra shorts, tights, leg warmers, silk shirt and woollen suit and a wig, I feel like a circuit judge in closed chambers. Five minutes before the second show and my second litre of water, we are asked to evacuate the theatre. Audience and actors pile into Greenwich Park as the police cordon off the streets. We are fully made up but in various stages of fancy dress. Some of the audience ask for autographs. The local pub offers us a bottle of wine. The spirit of the blitz begins to surface, as do the rumours. The rifest is that the police have found a bomb on the roof.

A thunderstorm has failed to clear the air and has dampened the grass. But not the spirit. After a quick referendum around the cast, I tell the punters that we'll start the play on a nearby hillock in Greenwich Park and we'll see how we go on. Cheering and cheerily they follow us, rather like the Inn of the Sixth Happiness, across the turf and, with a few hasty stage directions from Fiona, the stage manager, and sound cues given by actors 'resting' between trees, we begin Act I.

It's fab. It's a lesson in what should go on between actor and audience as Lynda and Hellena tell the story, simply and clearly. No props. No chairs. No lighting. Just a really cracking good yarn. Wendy Wasserstein, sitting front stalls on a grassy knoll, later dubbs it 'incredibly moving'. Fortunately or unfortunately, the theatre is given the all-clear and we have to tell the rapt audience to move back into the velvet sauna. The real thing is a bit of an anti-climax, but we do it and finish to tumultuous applause. Of course, if Joan Littlewood had been there, she'd have made us continue in the park. And she'd have been right.

Our six weeks at Greenwich were sizzling in both con-notations. Still, Michael Codron was panicky as to whether full houses at the 400-seater fringe theatre meant unlimited audiences in the West End. The reviews had been a mixed batch, with not enough cream in the mixture and too many eggs. The performances were acknowledged, as was the direc-tion, but on the whole they fell over themselves to patronize the play. The American reviews used words like, 'The most touching scene in *The Sisters Rosensweig* comes when the eldest of the three sisters, the fifty-four-year-old Sara, who goes by one of the names she acquired through marriage, the bland, WASPish Goode, comes to terms with her given name, the ever-so-Jewish Rosensweig. The scene itself is quite a great contrast to the uproarious witty tone of most of Wendy Wasserstein's play.'

The English critics took a more jaundiced view. '*The Sisters Rosensweig* is an entertaining piece and brings a fine cast to Greenwich, but I cannot have been alone in looking at the solemn WASP faces round me and wondering what an American comedy so centrally about Jewishness was doing in Greenwich in the first place,' said Benedict Nightingale, mildly, compared to some.

I thought of the producer of an interview the three of us had done on radio. She was in her early thirties, fair, attractive and very English and, after seeing the show, she said, 'I'm not fifty-four, I'm not Jewish, I'm not American and I'm not a banker ... but I *am* Sara Rosensweig.' I thought of the nights *after* the First Night when faces both WASP and ethnic split with some of the most deafening and rolling laughter I've ever heard in a theatre in my life and, most of all, I thought that such a comment would never be made of any other minority subject. In other words, would *Dancing at Lughnasa* have been 'so centrally about Irishness that one wondered what it was doing in little old provincial Greenwich'? Or, indeed, what *Boesman and Lena* or, yes, *The Three Sisters*, with their innate Baltic bent would have to interest those discerning WASP Greenwich folk? A nice maritime drama perhaps. How fractionalized must we be in this diminishing globe?

I thought of all of these issues and more and more felt the need to bring this delicious crowd pleaser into a home where West End bums were more important than WASP faces. Michael hummed and haaed, not wanting to risk the capital at a time when a show without music was as rare as a producer without qualms. Then, in the final weeks at Greenwich, the Old Vic came to our rescue with a generous offer and we were in. 'Happy New Year,' I wrote to Michael Codron, 'The Chinese Year of the Transfer – I believe.'

When I say we were in ... The Old Vic is the best theatre in the world, with the greatest history and an auditorium of divine proportions, but ... The walk-past trade – the number of theatregoers who happen to be passing by looking for action – is slightly less than East Finchley Crematorium. In the days of my three-year stint in Sir Laurence Olivier's repertory company, it didn't matter because it was ninety per cent subscription booking, but now, with ticket booths and blockbuster musicals, and, we were told, little or no money for advertising, how would a small comedy playing to 450-seats a night, bearing mixed notices, fare in a 1,100-seater house on the wrong side of the river?

'Dearest Wenderella,' I wrote to Ms Wasserstein on 7 October in a thank you note for a company basket of fruit that was bigger than she was, 'An update from Waterloo Road. My dear, we are a monstrous hit, well up on last week's advance at £57,000 advance (the best for a straight play in London) – isn't it *sweet*? The audiences are having such a good time. All the business is due to word of mouth – the critics were not invited to the first night and the only PR I've done this week is a staggering request to write a Christmas Carol for Sainsbury's Christmas magazine! That'll bring 'em in! I'm working on *Away with John Major*. We are a tentative hit though and the play is working better than ever. Thank you on behalf of the Sisters Gorgeous for another totally OTT basket of fruit. The fresh dates are delicious and undoubtedly they're the only dates any of us will get this year! PS: Loved the *New York Times* piece about our 'Theatre in the Park' version of *Rosensweig*. Tonight I met a man after the show who had been walking his dog through the park that night and had happened upon our impromptu pageant. He said it's the only time his dog had ever sat still for twenty minutes. I should add that his dog was a Yorkshire Terrier with three legs!'

'Dearest Mo,' replied our esteemed playwright. 'I am so happy about the success at the Old Vic. There's nothing as delicious as overcoming critics. Moreover it's proof that plays

with gefilte fish jokes and Chanel suits work. I am just
delighted.'

I also wrote to David and Ed Mirvish, who own the Old
Vic and are based in Canada,

'Dear David and Ed,

It's quite wonderful to be back after almost twenty
years in the best theatre in the world. Standing on
stage for the last two nights looking out at an almost
full house gave me a lovely *déjà vu* of the old days
of *The Front Page*, *Long Day's Journey Into Night*,
School for Scandal, etc, when one never seemed to
see an empty seat.

Thank you both for coming to the rescue of this
charming, unpretentious, funny and romantic
comedy. It's giving people so much pleasure.

Thank you also for the splendid bouquet which
sparkles in my dressing-room and brightened up the
First Night considerably.'

On the whole, the run was fun and the play grew in con-
fidence and audience reaction responded accordingly. In
retrospect, our production was more realistic, more centred,
than its New York counterpart, but consequently it lost some
of its light heart and good humour. In a comedy, if the
performances are at all heavy, then the play looks more trivial,
less worthwhile. There were bad patches when the audiences
suddenly, alarmingly disappeared a couple of weeks before
and after Christmas and there is a feeling of near guilt when
you stand on stage and there are, quite suddenly, 250 people
instead of 800 or 900. We played for six happy and respectable
months during which I hardly cried more than – ooh – once
or twice a week.

'You really have to learn to build a wall around yourself,
Mo,' said Janet one day after a particularly charged exchange.
'It's the only way to get through life.' She was right, I know,

but how can one be funny – or sad – through a wall?

I'm still fathoming the review which said, 'About Maureen Lipman I have a problem. Ten seconds into any Lipman performance I begin to giggle helplessly. While this might – should she opt to play Medea, Phaedra or Hedda Gabler – suggest in one or the other of us an unsuitability for our chosen profession, as long as she plays comedy our relationship goes swimmingly.'

Oh Mr, if you only knew . . .

Outside Edgy

My place at the crease went AWOL on the day I lunched at the Ivy with producer Paula Burden and Paul Spencer, the new head of comedy at Central TV.

Paula had worked on *About Face*. She is a short, neat, attractive and enthusiastic woman, whose school reports must have been stunning in terms of hard work, responsibility and friendliness. We were pleased to see one another and she was complimentary beyond the call of duty on the topic of my rosy good health. We ordered and I asked her what she was doing at the moment.

'*Outside Edge*,' she replied. 'It's very exciting.'

It certainly excited her lunch guest. I was over the green cheese with the cow with the crumpled horn by the idea. After all, it had been my long-cherished idea for Julia McKenzie and me to repeat our stage performances in the play, in a TV series, and Julia had badgered Richard Harris to write Miriam and Maggie, the 'odd couple' of the play into a sitcom ever since we'd played it so happily for six months at the Queen's Theatre in 1981.

Then, when STV filmed the play, Julia was working on a tight schedule at the National Theatre so Prunella Scales took her part. To compare the two Miriams would be like comparing caviar and, well, caviar, but Jules and I began the friendship which remains rock-solid to this day, and we longed to repeat the experience.

So Richard Harris wrote a pilot episode for producer Humphrey Barclay but Julia and I were vaguely disappointed, expressly because we knew the play so well and realized that the series was a slowed-down version of the stage play. It was an awkward situation, which never grew troublesome since no TV company showed interest in the idea and, like the best projects, it sat in an out-tray somewhere, growing a culture.

Fade in ... the Ivy restaurant a couple of years later when Paula's beaming face says, 'I'm doing a series about a cricket club called *Outside Edge*.'

I joined her beam and crowed, 'Oh, Paula, that's wonderful, how exciting!' high-jumping to the conclusion that this must be the purpose of the lunch. 'When do you start?'

'We've just finished Episode Two,' she replied.

There was no way to cover up my shock. Too late. My face said it all. Several changes of colour and, inevitably, a rush of unwanted moisture to the eyes (and an even *more* obvious rush of woman to the loo later), I managed to grasp that Brenda Blethyn and Josie Lawrence would be playing *our* parts. It was my first experience of Youthism and for that awful moment it cut through any front of *politesse* I thought I possessed. I've had better lunches in my time and the Ivy's menu had very little to do with that.

I presume conversation resumed, although I can't remember any of it. All I recall of that day was embarrassment, suppressed fury and the strain of waiting to get to a phone to call Julia.

'Are you sitting down, Jules? Because you are not going to believe this ...' I blurted out from the car, only to be met by a weary resignation.

'Yes,' she said. 'I've known about it for a while. I thought you knew.'

'But it was our idea!' I yelled.

'Yes, but we wanted it another way – not just sticking to the play and ...'

'Yes, but the TV companies agreed nobody wanted it that way ...'

'I know but then Central liked it and, well, Richard wanted to go ahead with it ...'

Jane Asher and me, *Honey* magazine 1968, before either of us were associated with fruit cake.

Me as Judith: Anthony Grant's composite of me as my favourite Gustav Klimt painting. (*Anthony Grant*)

'Super Model and last year's model' – Elle 'the Body' McPherson and 'I'. (*Mark Manson/Today*)

'I've been to the land of Noddy'. As Enid Blyton in Ken Howard's *Sunny Stories*, BBC2, 1993. (*BBC/Landseer Productions*)

Actor Chris Luscombe nervously waits his turn in a cleavage and crowns competition. Raquel Welch and me at the SWET Awards. (*Dave Benett/Daily Mail*)

O'Toole and O'heck ... two long faces light up when given Variety Club Awards. (*Richard Young*)

The dress that came equipped with the quip: 'Good evening, I've come as a pint of Guinness'. (*Mail Newspapers*)

The *Ag-Ag* Gang. *Back row*: Doon MacKichan, David Harewood,
Valerie Edmonds; *Front row*: Sacha Grunpeter, A Woman in Agony,
Maria Charles and Niall Buggy.

A modest man and three over-excited admirers. Jack with his CBE.
(*Michael Stephens/Press Association*)

And to cap it all . . . *another* borrowed gown. Receiving an Honorary
Doctorate of Literature from Professor Wilberforce at Hull
University, 1994. (*Hull University*)

I couldn't understand why she didn't feel as proprietorial as I did. My gracelessness was only exceeded by my desire to stick kebab skewers into everyone concerned in the enterprise. I was an old-fashioned pressure cooker on full steam, about to send cabbage into the cladding at maximum velocity.

Frankly, if Julie Andrews had been of my temperament when the film of *My Fair Lady* was cast, I can only surmise that Audrey Hepburn would have been crushed by a flower stall. As it happened, Ms Andrews didn't get too liverish and along came Mary Poppins and much more and all was well. If you want the full story read *On the Street Where You Live* by Alan Jay Lerner. It's the best Broadway biography I've ever read.

And all *is* well. The show works well … it always did and always will, it touches a populist pulse in the same way that *Educating Rita* did. Everybody has encountered a club bully and his submissive workhouse-donkey wife, if not in the cricket club then at the office, the church bazaar committee or the PTA.

In a lifetime of work, the words I always see forming on pre-gush lips are, 'You know the one I always liked of yours – that – whatsit? *Inside Leg*? No, I'm wrong there, what was it, Marjorie? *Outsize Edge*? That was it … laugh? If Richard Harris wasn't down our Golf Club, then I don't know where he was. That Roger was a dead ringer for whatsisface … Marge? You know, thingummy, even down to the cowlick, spot on, that. Mind you, you don't see much of him as an actor now, do you?'

He did ring me, to be fair, old Richard Harris, and he did say that he was astonished to hear that we would still have been interested in the show and I sort of believed it, although the call was a few months late. I suppose, apart from 'age', we knew the original too well and were looking for the relationship to move on to something different. One day, I'll learn that what people love is something the *same*. The actors are very well cast and have made the characters utterly their own.

Humphrey Barclay has moved on to re-produce *Agony Again*, in which I'm doing something the same – so let's see if my theory works for *me*. Richard Harris has a thriller in town with Jenny Seagrove, and *Outside Edge*, the play, is on the road somewhere, as always.

It wasn't meant to be, and in some ways, rightly so. Our sell-by date had passed. Nobody can steal someone else's part, it just doesn't happen. In fact, some years ago, I sued an evening paper for falsely claiming that I had somehow stolen the part of Beattie from Maria Charles. According to the diarist, I'd swept into the agency, long after the part had been given to Maria, and, in full make-up and wig, demanded the part should be given to me.

You know. Like you do. Get kitted out, find out the office, the time and the people concerned and just barge your way in, basically, shouting, 'It's mine! It's got my name on it! Gimme it *now*!' And somehow they do.

It was settled out of court, in my favour, and the proceeds made a very nice gift for those who needed it, but I cherish the sheer ignorance of those people who still believe that if an actor wants a part he will tread his rivals into cannibal purée to get it. Haven't they heard who wields the power? Don't they know any directors? These are the guys you have to get past and they come very opinionated and very intractable. You can know writers (in all senses), pay writers, schmooze writers and even spend twenty-five years of your life *with* a writer, but when the scripts are down the director will say, 'Nice idea and I realize you've written it with her in mind (and, straight up, I'm a tremendous fan) but the thing about Julie is that she's bankable.' Fade out and freeze frame.

Meanwhile, Paula Burden and I have been flirting with the idea of another series, about a late developer. It's a good script. Mind you, it's gone a bit quiet on that front lately, now I come to think of it ... Listen, for all I know it's probably into its second series, the merchandise is in Woollies and Pauline Quirk and Linda Robson are already up for an Emmy or two ...

Repartee's Over

The other night I crawled into my bed slightly more dilapidated than usual. It had not been an easy day. I'd spent the morning preparing a speech for a lunch hosted by computer firms for their clients. Now, what I know about computers could be printed on one side of a Paracetamol. So I'd had to scour my computer-literate associates for a reference other than 'I thought having a cursor meant spending the night with Bernard Manning'. I'd faxed my brother who happened to be in Canada and, bless his permanently jet-lagged brain, he faxed back the joke about the world's computers (ATT, BT, IBM, MCI, etc.) all linking up in Silicone Valley to one vast highway internet. Dr Stephen Hawking prints in the question 'Is there a God?' The answer comes back 'There is *now*.' Fine. One minute gone. Forty-three still to write.

For good measure he threw in the one where God told Moses there was good news and bad news. The good news was that he was fed up with Pharaoh and would be sending down lice, plagues, rats, fire, floods and slaying of the first born. 'Then,' He continued, 'I shall send you and my people to the Red Sea which I will open for you to walk through. Pharaoh will follow with his hosts and I will close the sea upon them.'

Moses replied, as well he might, that this was great news but what was the bad news?

God replied, 'I can't start till you do the environmental impact assessment.'

Let me state my case. I didn't actually understand either

of the jokes enough to fall out of my chair and throw my paper hat in the air – but, thank God, and Moses, the guys from *Computer Weekly* fell about.

It took another phone call to find out what the initials IT stood for in the company brochure. Perhaps I was due to address a 'Conference of International Terrorists' and how would they react to my line in humour? 'What's the definition of a Jewish nymphomaniac? Someone who'll make love on the same day she's had her hair done.' 'Songs for Swinging Terrorists' perhaps? 'Yasser, That's My Baby', 'You're Sinn Fein, you probably think this song is about you', 'Rwanda Who's Kissing Her Now'? – No. Tasteless and not funny! Besides, IT means 'Information Technology' as any moron knows, except the one who's second name is Lipman.

I'd phoned Ronnie Corbett earlier to ask his advice, since he'd done the same gig the year before. 'Oh, I do lots of "sizist" jokes, dear,' he burred down the line. 'Tell them you weren't the first choice of speaker. Say Ronnie Corbett was going to do it but he had an accident – he fell off a ladder when he was painting the skirting board.'

I tried it, along with 'David Mellor was coming but something came up ...' but in fairness I felt rather odd making jokes about Ronnie's size – it sounded a bit mean coming from a 5 foot 7 inch woman who happens to be very fond of him.

Invariably, I bridle when a non-Jew tells a Jewish joke. So have I got the right to tell Irish jokes? By my own admission I have not, and the loud snort I got from a table at a recent Kidney Disease Research lunch told me that the Irishwoman seated there would strongly agree with me. It was a harmless enough joke about an Irish actor who took an intense course of elocution lessons to ensure his accent was flawlessly English. Convinced at last that his origins were imperceptible, he went into a shop and, pukka as the man who broke the bank at Monte Carlo, demanded 'a pecket of Benson & Hidges cigarettes, a box of Swan Vesta Metches and a copy of the *Daily Telegraph*.'

The assistant smiled and said, 'You're Irish aren't you?' Astonished, the man asked how she could possibly tell. ' 'Cos this is a bleedin' fish and chip shop,' she retorted.

Now if it hadn't been for the snort from table one I would have quickly redressed the balance with the story of the Irish man applying for a job on a building site who was asked the difference between a girder and a joist and replied, 'That's easy. Goethe wrote *Faust* and Joyce wrote *Ulysses*.' This sets the balance straight, I always feel.

All that's left after PC are political jokes and we're lucky to live in a democracy where we can make them and retain all of our limbs. Political jokes are as old as Herodotus – and some say older. Four men were discussing which was the world's oldest profession. The lawyer claimed it was his because when Cain killed Abel, he needed a lawyer. The doctor claimed seniority because God created Eve from Adam's rib and would therefore have needed a surgeon. The architect demurred since God needed plans to create the universe from chaos. 'Aha!' said the politician. 'And who created the chaos?'

So where was I? Thursday, 1.00 pm and I've compiled the speech in longhand for the following day, and driven to the Actors' Centre to spend an hour each with two young actors and their audition pieces. A comedy workshop you might call it – except the first actor had brought me Iago from *Othello*. This was quite a challenge. For both of us. How comedic can you make jealousy with intent to murder? From there to the Old Vic theatre where the *This Is Your Life* team had set up a camera in my dressing-room to film an excerpt for Lesley Joseph's *This Is Your Life*. I patted on some make-up and made up some patter. Had I told the viewers the *truth* of our misspent youth, they would have collapsed into their Marks & Spencer's breaded whiting fillets and the BBC would have lost its licence. So I told them about the oven in our flat which, we discovered after fifteen months, wasn't self-cleaning, and the eye surgeon/landlord whose idea of an early morning jape was to come into our kitchen with his eye out of its socket and hanging on his cheek. The crew left promising never in a million eternities to spring anything similar on *me* and I stayed to put on even more make-up for an evening of sisterly American comedy in the British theatre.

At the end of the show the cast took a collection for World Aids Day then reassembled in the bar to meet the forty-odd members of the *Sunday Times* Theatre Club for wine, cheesy grins and, to our faces at any rate, compliments. I drove home and at 12.30 am, wrote my last joke sitting up in bed with a cup of something luke-warm, a Hobnob and an attention-seeking cat on a tray. I felt as funny as a skillet of condemned veal. Perhaps that's when we are at our funniest. Mark Twain said that humour springs from sorrow not joy. 'There is,' he said, 'no humour in heaven.' The late Roy Castle, at the height of his illness, had a letter from a member of the public saying, 'I'd just like to say, it couldn't have happened to a nicer fellow.' Such joy. Such sorrow.

Bob Monkhouse, whose autobiography is one of the best I've read, says wryly, 'When I said I was going to be a comedian, they all laughed at me. Well, they're not laughing now!'

6

Actor at Large

The Book of Nemesis

'Raindrops on roses and whiskers on kittens, bright copper kettles and warm woollen mittens', these were a few of the wayward Nun, Maria's, favourite things and, with nothing more exciting to do of a morning than shin up a hill and be late for vespers, she was rather easily pleased. What would her *bêtes noires* have been, I wonder, and would Rodgers and Hammerstein have found a rhyme for *bêtes noires*? And could it be sung by the Met's choir?

There is a joke about the Pope visiting California where he is interviewed by Barbara Walters. 'Tell me, Your Eminence,' she gushes, 'is there anything in life which really gets up your nose?'

'I am sorry?' says the Pope.

She rephrases it. 'Is there anything which drives you crazy, irritates you beyond . . .'

'Oh, yes, sortainly,' breaks in the Pope. 'Zere are two zings vich I hate and despise. Von of zem is Polish jokes. Zay are racist, unfunny, insulting to a fine people and not based on any truth vatsoever.'

'I understand that, sir, and what is the second thing?'

'Smarties,' replies his Eminence.

'Smarties!?' exclaims his interviewer. 'You mean the little colour-covered chocolates?'

'Oh, yes,' insists the Primate. 'I hate and despise zem because zey are *zooo* difficult to peel.'

Affronted Catholics and chocolate makers, please don't write in and abuse me – I do Jewish jokes all the time, I know it's not PC, but it's MA – as in mildly amusing – and I'm

207

willing for my Hull/Lithuanian roots to be dug up and derided, whenever.

Personally, there are so many zings which get up my nose that I'm thinking of having an extension built on. Let me cite, for starters, 'childprufe' medicine bottles which are also grown-up-prufe, arthritic hand-prufe, profanity-inducing and leave depressions on the skin of your hand which refuse, after forty, to bounce back. Many is the middle-of-the-night pain left unrelieved whilst its recipient leaps up and down on top of a small, brown plastic container screaming, 'Open, you pernicious bastard, or I'll break every bone in your body!' It goes without saying that the only people with patience and ingenuity to open the ruddy things are children, particularly those educated at Montessori schools with access to Fisher Price toys.

I reserve the same blind fury for packaging in general. Moulded plastic packaging in particular. It takes two minutes to buy a new toothbrush and two days to remove the sodding thing from the packet. Most of my new tooth-brushes are bought en route to somewhere at which I realize, too late, I will need to smile. 'A packet of "Super-freshliplickinstalebreathdevouringwaterfallminty"   mints, please. Oh, and a medium toothbrush with narrow, adjustable head for those awkward places which show the spinach.'

Quick dive into the toilets at the appointed place, then attempt to wrench, wiggle, slide, tear and finally bludgeon toothbrush out of moulded plastic. Eventually, mouth foaming, but not with toothpaste, attack the packaging with teeth and remove not, alas, the toothbrush, but £400 worth of bridgework.

Incidentally, this lunacy also applies to most household gadgets which are packaged by sadists to alienate the infirm, the aged, and the pusher of this pen. Hang on, I'm just getting going.

Industrial toilet rolls now come in hand applicators the size of Pavarotti. Ever tried to find the end of one? Whilst on the loo? Hand curved back on itself like a Balinese temple dancer, flailing uselessly at a sealed perforation that you can neither see nor reach. Bumper fun for all the family and not an adorable puppy in sight to help you out, which is just as well, because if there were, you'd probably kick it.

And you've just recovered from this in time to fasten your *snap crotch body*, (so called because anybody trying to achieve this will become so crotchety that they will eventually snap), the effort of which causes physical distress in the loo and mental humiliation when you return to the crowded party with an attractive black tail hanging out over your cream linen trousers. For the myopic, now becoming longsighted person, the joys of being unable to see the *self-coloured* poppers which bind the snap crotch together are never ending. Why don't they use Velcro, or brightly coloured presstuds? Or U-Hu, for heaven's sake? Then I wouldn't have to stick my head between my legs like an orang-utang on heat and forever be fishing my glasses out of the toilet.

Onwards. In one sentence, the Americanization of our high streets, our television system, our language, and, like, our eating habits, man. I may not be a cool dude but I like to see *through* things, not thru' them, I like to *be* a parent (well, not always, but occasionally) not 'to parent' and the double ll sound in surveillance is not music to my years. I could go on – and I do.

As for Cable Television, quite seriously, if *I* wanted to dig up the pavement outside my house and replace it with a load of lumpy tar in a winding and treacherous strip, then replace the tar with paving stones in a different style and hue from the remaining stones, all the while diverting and endangering traffic and pedestrians alike for several months of the year, do you think *they'd* let me do it? No, they bloody wouldn't. It was hard enough getting *them* to grant me a new soil stack so I could fumble with my snap crotch in the privacy of my own privy. It took weeks of negotiations. But along comes Mr Cable, or Glark, as I like to call him, wafting zillions of dollars around and the promise of acreage of dreary, violent videos and *What I Keep in my Inglenook* by Michael Winner and –

Hey Presto! – pounding drills, juddering flesh and tottering grannies with broken wheelies all over the high street. Bah! Humbug! Speaking of which, why don't *they* taste like they used to?

> Leaflets which fall out of fat Sunday papers,
> Burgers and Doners but nowhere a drapers,
> Monstrous white sneakers with gas in their springs,
> These represent my unfavourite things.

> Twenty-inch pepper pots, twenty-pound phone
>   books,
> Too many satellites, traffic cones, Sloane cooks,
> A mobile in a theatre which suddenly rings,
> These are some more truly horrible things.

> When the cat purrs, when the kids ring,
> When I'm feeling glad,
> I simply recall these unspeakable things
> To *drive myself barking mad!*

PS Jewellery fasteners (requiring three hands and a dental mirror); Sleeping Policemen (may the force *not* be with us); baseball caps worn backwards (they weren't dumb enough worn forwards?); cricketers in red and green strip with Harpic emblazoned across the front; Cheapo TV with the public as stars; politicians making 'one thing perfectly clear' . . .

It's no good. I must stop . . . I've another book to write in two years' time . . .

Last Year's Model

I keep seeing them. Everywhere. Nubile, powerful, skinny, feline-featured women with jutting jawlines, disproportionate breasts and lips like scatter cushions. And they're not just striding ferociously up the catwalks or bestriding the pages of the kind of magazines which require a second mortgage or frolicking across the bits you flick through rapidly at the back of *Hello!*. Oh no. Dear me no. *Pas du tout.*

They are everywhere else as well. They fill the pages of the tabloid press, they cause paparazzi riots at Heathrow Airport and paperback panic in Selfridges' basement, they flit through the movie colony and the international jet set, they take tea with Dalai Lamas and Des O'Connor, they pose in Calvin Klein leggings amongst the starving in Somalia and in the ravished rain forests. They are the darlings of the gossip columns and we are on first-name terms with them all. We know Cindy and Claudia and Cheryl and Carla and Christie, as well as we know Diana and Hillary. As well as we *knew* Fergie and Glenys. We know where to buy their videos, their calendars and their swimsuits. We know all their consorts too ... who dated De Niro, who mated Gere, who Iman-cipated Bowie and Infant-icipated Rod. We know that Gianni's Evangelical for Linda and Armani's Emporical for Naomi. We saw Yasmin's bijou le bonbon before her gynaecologist did. We're very familiar with Jerry's precious stone. These girls are not just social, they're sociological. They are superwomen.

OK. No sour grapes round this particular fruit dish. Good luck to 'em. Distorted limbs and distorted salaries are nothing new. I love Wimbledon as much as the next man. But hang

211

on a sec. The skill, training and commitment of a tennis ace is beyond dispute. Likewise your average round-the-globe female aviator, engineer, sculptress, dancer, equestrian eventist, culinary guru, spacewoman, scientist, picket-crossing protester, midwife, *housewife*, for God's sake. I don't begrudge them an inch of print, a handful of dollars, or all the romance in the *Tales from the Arabian Nights*.

But modelling? *This* is what the Pankhursts chained and Gloria and Germaine burned for? *This* should be the height of female wish fulfilment? Women gifted with bodies which resemble less than two per cent of the bodies of the average woman, with legs longer than the length of the average woman. With knockers firmer than the average woman's – firmer than the average *man's*, to be honest. Women to whom God handed out facial bones which leap out and embrace the merest hint of an arc lamp and teeth which are handpicked and matched like pearls from the sea bed. Women who, for sensational salaries, do one thing brilliantly. *They walk*. Up and down a couple of trestle tables. Don't get me wrong. Sometimes they turn around too. Or shed a garment. Or change expressions. But mostly they walk. Fast. Slow. Seductive. Aggressive. It's tough, I grant you. They also walk tall.

And, while they're doing it, they wear clothes. For the most part, unwearable clothes. Clothes which designers would love to see on beautiful boys. Clothes conceived by, designed by, cut out by, sewn together by and placed upon their bodies by other people. Ordinary looking, fat, slouched, balding, scraggy, paunchy, creative, skilled and talented human beings. Then make-up artists paint, hairdressers primp and the supermodel sends forward her perfectly narrowed hips through the curtains and a couple of minutes later, the rest of her follows. 'Oooh, aaah, oooh, la-la!'

Oh I know. They do photographic shoots and commercials too. In studios and exotic locations, as often as not accompanied by an endangered species or a primitive tribesman and a deal of ethnic jewellery. Here the creative team involves a gifted and self-important photographer to whom our superchick is often married, if not before the exotic location, then after, the equally exotic advertising team, copy-writers, clients, and desert-catering crew. Our girl's job is to snarl, sneer, straddle and smoulder, not necessarily in that order and elongate her already elongated limbs into positions heretofore only ever attempted by teams of Chinese acrobats and the odd lady of the night in Phuket.

Meanwhile, back in the bedsits and offices and tube com-partments and high rises and dentists' waiting rooms of home, others can peruse these pages sitting on their sofa beds in their Next copies of Janet Reger lounging pyjamas, eating their Marks & Spencer's cottage cheese and pineapple chunks and wondering idly if last year's Lycra mini skirt could be stretched into this year's split-thigh midi skirt with the inven-tive use of a spanner and a course of liposuction and whether anyone will come along to lick the Häagen-Dazs off their knee or should they use a J-cloth.

We'll never get into those high-thigh swimsuits of Jerry Hall's. Not without emerging doubled over from the changing room clutching a towelling robe round our hips and hitting the water at seventy miles an hour still clutching the robe. We'll never wear the slit to the waist, transparent black chiffon body with nothing underneath, without recourse to several rolls of double-sided Elastoplast and an animated but somewhat sheepish discussion about which stretch mark was from which child. And we'll never wear the floor-length, stretch-velour evening dress with the shoestring back because the only time we put it on, our partner fell off the bed laughing and said we looked like a roll of boned and stuffed brisket.

Surely the Trade's Description Act can be evoked in situ-ations like this? These girls are making fools out of us women. With our scholarships and our degrees and our careers and our memberships of women's groups and gyms that worked the arses off us and then bored them back on again three weeks after paying the premiums. They are giving us an image to live up to that we can't afford, don't want and couldn't walk in. These are our sisters, sister? Role Models? I think not.

Dandy Lying and
Murdoch

Sometimes a single sentence can make you hug yourself with joy. I was flying to Edinburgh when I heard the announcement: 'Sir Jeffrey Archer will be signing copies of his new book in W H Smiths on the second floor.' That was all.

It's not that I've got anything against book signings. Many's the time I've sat, solitary, before a cardboard cut-out of myself, willing the floor to open and drop me into the Home Brewing and Dead Languages Department. No, what brought a bark to my lips was the concept that Sir Jeffrey may have been flying off somewhere for the annual summer sojourn with the scented spouse, when the thought struck him: 'I say! There's a bloody bookshop at Heathrow, isn't there? Check-in's at 10.00. Flight's at 11.30. Mmmm ... seems a shame to waste the hour...'

This is pure supposition, I hasten to allege, and unfair on the grounds that Jeffrey is such an easy target and is therefore unworthy of attack. As is Jason. And Esther. And Claire. And Beadle. And Grossman. For are they not honourable men? Albeit with one common trait. The desire to be liked. A desire which shows.

But wait. Is this a crime? Don't performers perform in order to be appreciated? Didn't Beethoven and Olivier and Callas and Bernstein? Didn't Van Gogh and Schumann want appreciation *during* their lifetime? Didn't Veronese hope the Doge would pay for his 'Last Supper' and didn't Noël Coward wait up for early morning reviews?

I pose the question, dear reader, because I am troubled by the current fad for character assassination with pen *and*

215

sword, which is engulfing popular and grown-up periodicals alike. Death by tape recorder, I call it. In my *Independent on Sunday*, I see Jason being pinned to a board by William Reith. In my *Guardian*, Emma Thompson is quietly shredded by Catherine Bennett. Elsewhere Sir Andrew is decimated in an article which suggests that even his mother may not like him. Since when did talent and likeability have to go hand in hand?

Should one expect an artist to be a great human being? Would anyone really expect Mozart's company, on a week's chalet holiday in Leipzig, to be as entertaining as the same chalet with thirty of his best CDs, a red setter and a good bottle of cognac? There is scarcely a poet, composer, playwright or painter whose life is not a compendium of broken love affairs, madness, cruelty, drug dependence, poverty or profligacy. We want it that way. How else would Ken Russell earn a living? Perhaps the talent itself is a compensation for some lack of quality of soul. Perhaps artistic creation is part of a fretful search for happiness which others find quite naturally in living. 'I am not interested in the pursuit of happiness,' said Joyce Grenfell, 'but only in the discovery of joy.' She had made a discovery which, if bottled and preserved, could have changed the face of biography.

I first noticed this abusive trend in the photographers who gather at charity premières. 'Over here, Beattie!' they'd yell at me, not unkindly, and the cross-eyed grimace which ensued captured eighteen months' dental work, last night's vegetable biryani and a close-up of my uvula for the Sunday colour mag with the caption: 'Do us a favour, Mo ... termouth. Keep it closed.' This intellectual exercise alerted me to a spate of 'Twenty Naff Things You Never Knew About Hugh' and 'Anneka – the Dodgy Bits', all of them compiled by a disgruntled office-boy with an aegrotat degree in humour from Uppsala Poly.

Could Ghengis Khan (no relation, Jemima, worry not) have survived Jeremy Paxman? Can we take anything seriously enough, or concentrate on it for long enough, to wish to fight for it? Occasionally, I long for an alien invasion. By gum, we'd soon forget border skirmishes and petty religious differences if something huge, green and knobbly hovered over St Paul's or St Petersburg for an hour or two – 'Invasion of the Killer Gherkins'. My Sunday newspaper, the *Observer*, said the following with a straight face ' "Nasty Grandma", Yuko Aoshima, the transvestite actor and writer who tomorrow takes over as governor of Tokyo ...' 'You cannot be SERIOUS!' I want to yell.

I feel more and more like my late father, God rest his soul, who, suffering from memory loss, would turn over the pages of the *Express* or watch the TV news with the same expression of beaten disbelief and, clucking his tongue, would murmur, 'You can't bloody believe it, can you?'

'Who or what is God to you?' said a *Guardian* reporter to me last week after the obligatory apologies for bothering one in one's own home of a weekend. I was uncharacteristically serious as I strove to describe a feeling of peace, a freedom from worry, a sense of well-being and security ... when the reporter continued: 'I mean, some people have said Jurgen Klinsmann and others have said Sting.' I felt unaccountably depressed and asked the young lady, rather acidly, if she was happy in her work.

You get used to the inconsequential trivialities, but you never get used to the ones like the call which came, two days later, to ask us if we were aware that our friend, Nigel Hawthorne, was homosexual and would we describe his partner, Trevor, as a nice person?

I'll tell you, you don't know whether to laugh or cry. Cancel your phone subscription or your paper. What should have been the happiest week of Nigel's distinguished career, the week leading up to his appearance at the Oscars ceremony as a nominee, became a witch hunt. 'The Gayness of King George' and 'The Madness of Queen George' were tabloid headlines and elderly relatives in South Africa were telephoned to ask 'how they felt'.

I was passing a Granada Rental shop when I saw eight or nine screens full of Nigel, so I went inside to ask if they would turn up the sound for me. Karen Keating was posing the questions and Nigel's replies were moving and dignified. 'We've been together for seventeen years and expect to be together until we die,' he said wryly. 'We lead a quiet life, very mundane, and we wouldn't have expected that to be of much interest to anyone.' Then he added darkly, 'However, Karen, there is something that I feel I should share with you and with your viewers. I've never told anyone this before, but given the opportunity to use your programme as a platform, may I tell you that ...' he paused emotionally, and we held our breaths '... I feel I must tell you that ... that, I have ... a hole in my left sock.' It took a while, but most people got his point.

Back home, I faxed him our solidarity and congratulations 'from all of us with previously undisclosed holes', and two days later it was just another dead donkey – but at what cost to two of the most gentle men in the universe and to Nigel's searing, brave performance in *The Madness of George III*?

I'm trying to understand whether the rot set in before the Rotweillers got out. Are the press giving the public what it wants? Or are the public being pressured by the press? Does the appetite for junk food increase on a junk food diet? The Sid Vicious school of writers prepare their angle before they reach their subject's door chimes. Happy marriage? Humbug! Normal childhood? Bo-o-o-o-oring. Politics? Bad copy! They reveal the skeleton in the dressing-room and wait for promotion, reputation and, probably, their own alternative underwater quiz show on GMTV.

Julia McKenzie told a reporter recently that her friend Maureen had suggested she should begin the interview by confessing a nineteen-year-old passionate affair with Frank Bruno. Anything to avoid the face as flat as a fish's which asks, 'So, Julia, same marriage, same suburban life, do you ever long for excitement?'

And the *hatred*, oh, the hatred. Give a reporter their own column and call it 'The Martin Barbed Interview' or 'Lynn Probe on the Line' and you can be sure of only one thing:

you will learn, in the next one thousand words, a great deal
more about the interviewer than about his or her subject.
The interview will begin with a couple of paragraphs relating
to the difficulties of setting up the meeting, a description of
the restaurant and its pretentious/folksy clientele. Then we
are treated to a description of the victim (with or without
surgical history) and their class-revealing choice of food. By
now, we know that the celebrity has an attitude problem,
although it never occurs to the writer that this could, in any
way, relate to their *own* proximity. From here it's a short jump
to regaling the reader with the star's obvious attempts to plug
their own book or film which is why both people are there.
Ultimately, this leads to the angle on which the writer has been
waiting to pounce since grabbing the brief – the celebrity's
dependence on cyanide, fratricide, suicide or, if necessary
insecticide.

There was a time when *Private Eye* was the only harbinger
of gossip, tittle-tattle and cynicism. The bloodshed's now so
widespread that Lord Gnome may have to retitle his worthy
tome *Public Knowledge*.

I'm not advocating the *Hello!* school of writing: 'We get
to peek behind the magical scenes at her Hacienda-and-
Fontainebleau-style mansion where Jane, "This time it's for
ever" Seymour, weds her fourth husband.' In fact, this cock-
eyed optimism may have spawned the '*Hair* actress Weds
Fourth Victim' alternative style. As ballast. Maybe writers
are tired of famous personalities using *their* byline to plug
anything from Passion Plays to perfumed Y-fronts. 'Oh, Jeez,
I've got whatsisname from *Brooksiden-ders* at 2.00. He's
written, directed and starred in his first movie. He's fifteen!
I'll give him 200 words on that crap, then I'll hit him with
the troilism, the transvestism and the gerbil.'

Often celebrities don't help themselves. Take the trend
for expensive public confessionals: child abuse, alcoholism,
adultery, near fatal illness, obsessive attachment to *Cell Block
H*. Recently, Anthony Clare, interviewing Esther Rantzen,
asked her if she didn't feel she had a predilection for airing

her personal problems in public. A strange question for a radio psychiatrist to ask a woman who was airing them for eight million listeners ... and *him* ...

Unfortunately there's no YTS for handling success. Or failure. It's a surer test of character if you survive the latter than the former, but Kipling was right when he suggested that one should treat 'those two impostors' the same way.

In my experience, one minute you're dancing on a table top with a champagne cork in each ear, celebrating your first speaking role in an undiscovered Belgian farce for STV and the next minute you're marching, arm-in-arm, with Glenys Kinnock and Liza Minelli down Whitehall, demanding shorter working hours for Latvian seamstresses. It happens seamlessly and it's hard to handle.

My final word comes hotfoot from the kitchen. It is VE Day and I'm planting Fuchsia 'Winston Churchill' in my window-boxes. Jack comes out and says, wearily, 'It's the *News of the World*. They want to know what you think of the sacking of Will Carling as England's captain.'

I put down a handful of organic peat and wiped my brow, channelling soil into my new toric disposable lenses. 'Oh, for heaven's sake,' I groaned. 'Tell them I know nothing at all about rugby, but I like the cleft in his chin and I admire him for speaking out.'

Jack returned a moment later. 'You won't believe this. I told him what you said and when I got to the cleft in his chin, he said, "The what?" so I said, "The cleft" and he said, "Er, what is that? I mean, what does that actually mean? The *what* in his chin ... ?" '

What can you say? We are cleft apart, the *News of the World* and I, by more than just a five-letter word ... We are cleft apart by ignorance. Of Cary Grant and Bob Mitchum and Sarah Lancashire and ... Oh, what the hell ... he probably thought it was a baked lamb dish in a Greek restaurant and wondered what it was doing in Will Carling's chin.

Having said that, I'm oddly fond of journalists. I'm even quite proud when someone calls me one. I like their company and feel at ease with most of them. I just wish that when the wit hits the fan it wasn't 'them v us', because we plainly don't exist without each other. Times are hard for both professions. There are eleven national daily newspapers in a country which more and more relies on Ceefax and radio for its news. Perhaps the new killer journalism is merely a career move.

There is a story about President De Klerk and Archbishop Tutu having discussions about ending apartheid on a boat in the middle of a lake, with the world's press camped around the lake perimeter with zoom lenses trained on the couple. De Klerk's hat blows off on to the lake and Tutu calmly leaves the boat, walks across the water, retrieves the hat and brings it back to De Klerk. The next day, the newspaper headlines scream 'Desmond Tutu Cannot Swim'.

Still, I'm all right, Jack. Just dashing to Tesco's for some late-night shopping, and whilst I'm there I might as well sign a few of my books for the dumpbin . . .

Radio Daze

They make us. They break us. The public and their demo-
cratically elected representatives at the House of Wapping.
Actors are, like spectacles, growing more dispensable by the
minute. Particularly so since the advent of home videos. Quite
simply, the world of entertainment has discovered that the
most popular programmes are also the cheapest to make.
*Beadle, Blind Date, Confessions, Noel's House Party, Surprise
Surprise, Hearts of Gold, Don't Forget Your Brain* – sorry –
Toothbrush ... Common denomination? Yes, ma'am, you
guessed it, come right on down and collect an 'I'd eat Jeremy
Beadle's beard to get on the telly' T-shirt, and yes the answer
is the stars are 'the Public' – you at home.

Fair do's, it works. Barrymore's talent is to ape his guests
in the kindliest possible way, whilst inviting us through constant eye-to-camera contact, to join in the jape. It's nothing
short of towering. Bring me your toothless Elvis impersonator, your child contortionist/cymbal player, your team of
twenty-stone Batley transsexual unicyclists and I'll bring you
the very thing the British like best of all. An enthusiastic
amateur. Television thrives on them. Obsessives with just a
thread of unselfconscious lunacy.

TV eats them up, from David Bellamy, Barbara Wood-
house, Patrick Moore, Magnus Pyke, Peter Snow and his vast
swingometer, right through to the gloriously artistic Sister
Wendy. Who on earth could have thought up Sister Wendy?
Can you imagine the planning meeting in the bowels of the
BBC? 'What we need, Alan, luv, is a presenter who can relay
fantastic enthusiasm for art and real undisputed knowledge

of the subject with a certain ... well, eccentricity, well, no, more than that – all right, batty as a ... no, larger than life, sort of ... well, David Attenborough surveying a badger set, at twilight in a ballgown; or Loyd Grossman in a toga and a handlebar moustache, deep-frying bats; or Claire Rayner in a rubber wet-suit and flippers singing 'You Make Me Feel Karl Jung' or ... no, it's no good. What we *really* need to sell art to the masses is Chris Evans but we've as much chance of affording him as getting a nude-loving nun in bifocals with a wimple and an overbite!' Ba-boom! Wham, bam and thank you Sam! And TV history is made. It's Art but is it artless? What the hell? If it puts Rubenesque bums on seats, then God bless her and long may she stay in the picture.

Meanwhile the drama output gets less input. There are more and more drama schools springing up to accommodate more and more actors, to fill less and less roles in more and more sporadic productions. The alternative circuit is exempt from this vicious circle. They write their own stuff for themselves and their contemporaries and they produce it and package it and pat it and prick it and pop it in to Central Control and there you have it. Seven nights a week you have it. All you've ever wanted to see of Rik and Ben and Nige and Lenny and Ade and Jen and Dawn and Len and Dawn and Frank and Dave and Hugh and Stephen and Auntie Jo Wobbley and all. Which is fine. For these talented lads and lasses. Fine.

But where does it leave the poor bloody actors, trained from puberty to Wait To Be Asked? Then to turn up for an audition, polished and shiny and with a gleam on their shoes and a pan-lid on their eagerness to please. The ones who thank the casting team – but not *too* effusively, and phone their agent, not *too* soon though, for a hint of how *they* liked them and hang back and hang on and hang out, saying, 'Er ... just waiting to hear, actually, about some – er – costume drama at the Beeb. Not sure what it is, actually, only saw the couple of scenes I was involved in – er, that is, *might* be involved in – so, that's two apple pies, one iced tea, two decaffs and I'll bring you the check, shall I?'

In the eight weeks since my last stint in the theatre, I've seen more television than I had in the previous two years put together. Which is to say, I've seen more trolleys wired with drips, clattering through more swing doors, propelled by more actors in paper hats and masks, with more overlapping and unintelligible dialogue than I could possibly have seen if I'd spent eight weeks shadowing Stephen Dorrell shadowing Virginia Bottomley. (Sorry, bad analogy. It's unlikely that Virginia had actually set foot in a hospital, or even knew exactly what their function was. 'Of course, I knew what they were – they were *very* useful and *very* valuable plots of land, or they would have been if I'd been left to demolish what's standing on them!' VB.)

Still, my point remains. Human remains, carnage, mal-practice, overwork and seven or eight short, concurrent and largely unfinished storylines are the TV order of the day. *Cardiac Arrest*, *ER*, *Chicago Whatsit*, *Casualty* – the list goes on. They are the programme controllers' proffered alternative to the millions like my mother who 'Can't stand detectives. Nobody ever *wears* anything nice.' Either way, it's a helluva coup for the man in charge of prop blood and it invariably leaves the viewer wanting less.

Only radio continues to fire my imagination and fulfil my needs. The *Today* programme tells me all I know and all I need to know about the news of the day, nationally and internationally – and my word, you only have to spend two nights in an American hotel room to see how insular a country can be about its news. The American network news, during my last five-day stint in New York, during the height of the Rwandan massacres, the end of the Bosnian ceasefire, the antics of Winnie Mandela in South Africa and the murder of Israeli soldiers on the West Bank, made mention of one issue and one issue only and that was Princess Diana's predicted Time Share in New York. Other than that, it was OJ, OJ, and more OJ. You can OD on OJ and by the time you read this, he'll have walked away blot-free with the blank cheque in his DJ. The Simpsons: an everyday story of Family Life in the good ole' US of A.

Aside from the news, I am hooked on *The Moral Maze* to the extent that Michael Buerk has achieved superstar status to me. At the Sony Radio Awards, he came to my table to talk to the gentleman on my right, Mr Terry Waite, and I went a nice shade of bilberry when introduced and momentarily lost the power of speech.

What I love about *The Moral Maze* is its ability to provide real 'aggro' round the table and propel me out of my bed with righteous anger (sometimes I stand there and scream at my transistor), yet remain, in some way, gentlemanly. It's the discussion itself that is violent. Roger Scruton and David Starkey make Stalin look benevolent, turn Radovan Karadzic into John Betjeman. At the same Sony Awards, David Starkey, presenting, said, 'I'm usually employed to be very nasty to people, but today I'm here to be very nice to the person whose name is in this envelope.'

Correction, Mr Starkey. You are employed to debate a moral issue. It's because you *think* you are employed to be very nasty to people that you regularly do your cause the greatest possible harm by appearing to be as mad as a flapjack!

At any rate. It makes for excellent radio. On the subject of capital punishment, Roger Scruton demanded the death penalty on the grounds that punishment was not enough – one had to have *retribution*, thus, I would have suggested, doing God out of his traditional job ... and no redundancy pay! Although it has been conclusively proven that the death penalty in no way lowers the crime rate, the Scrutons of this world persist in feeling better when retribution, even in the form of the slow burning of human flesh actually takes place.

Janet Daly pointed out that it is only in murder cases when the biblical 'eye for an eye' occurs. We do not rape rapists, neither do we steal from thieves or assault muggers. Nevertheless, the right to slay continues to sway the righteous and the spectacle continues to attract the basest instincts of humankind. There will always be salivating spectators for witch-duckings, serial killers, child molesters and road accidents. Just as there will always be buyers for the former houses of serial killers, Adolf Hitler artefacts and marriage proposals by the sackful to condemned 'lifers'.

I would have thought that the greatest argument against capital punishment was, quite simply, the number of wrongful imprisonments revealed over the last few years. No further argument. In my book.

As I write this page, it's Good Friday and the first day of Passover and there are minute slivers of matzos all over the floor and inside my bra to prove it.

I have just put the phone down from apologizing to the Complaints Department of the BBC. I had been removing spoons from the waste-disposal machine as a prelude to asking Jack to remind me on what setting we have the dishwasher these days, and peacefully listening to *Gardener's Question Time* on, I thought, Radio 4. Now it was playing Bach's St John's Passion. The music was inspirational and the commentary both Germanic and vituperative. Scarcely a sentence went past without some reference to 'the Jew' and, it goes without saying, that it wasn't uttered as a term of endearment. As Jesus prepared for the Last Supper, the 'Jewish' police broke through the door to threaten him. Surely they were living in a Jewish state, albeit under the Romans, what else would the police be? Wasn't Jesus a Jew? Wasn't the Last Supper the Feast of the Passover? The text was racist and untenable in this or any day and age, and had the references been either Muslim or black, I reckon the Race Relations Board would have filed for damages and Johann Sebastian might have found himself *fatwa*'d.

So what do I do? I phone up the BBC and ask for the Complaints Department, then bend the ear of the gracious and understanding duty officer for ten minutes on how the commentary was insulting and should be updated in the light of current sensibilities. After all, it was 150 years after the death of Christ that Judas as betrayer entered a single historical manuscript, was it not? Hadn't the Pope officially and benevolently let us off the hook? And furthermore was it not perfectly obvious to scholars and laymen that some means had clearly to be found, after the death of Christ and the birth of Christianity, to separate Jesus the Messiah from his Jewish roots? Who better named to do the job than the ideally placed Judas? I for one was not about to blanch my sprouts to the sound of the BBC fanning the same tired old embers.

You get my drift? Yes. Well so did the sympathetic duty officer at Portland Place, as she took down my name and my address with care and equanimity.

'You did the right thing,' said Jack, as I prepared to leave the house on various errands. 'I couldn't bear to listen to it – good for you for telling them so.'

'Well done,' said my friend, Harriet. 'I left the choir I used to sing in because the commentary made me want to throw up.'

It was only when I got into my car sometime later and attempted to tune into the same BBC programme that I realized the St John's Passion, anti-Semitic narration and all, was not on Radio 4 but on Classic FM. It was the *Gardener's Question Time* which had thrown me, since it had been transferred lock-up, stocks and rainbarrel from Radio 4 to Classic FM.

So what now? Same grievance, different Complaints Department. I phoned the BBC and, with much self-deprecating badinage, explained that I was a sheet of bubblewrap and could they please pass it on. I then toyed with ringing Classic FM, but by now the white-hot fury was more 'white with a hint of yellow' and I'm afraid the point was never made. Why is it that whenever you stand up to be counted, it turns out that you are standing up at a convention for the severely innumerate?

Still, my radio accompanies me to every room in the house, occupies me whilst I cook, continues in my car and starts up again in my dressing-room. I write to the tune of Classic FM, switch to Melody when the adverts for Kleenex make me

puke, move back to Radio 2 for John Dunne and forwards
for *I'm Sorry I Haven't a Clue* and *Just a Minute*. Radio
soothes my troubled brain and stimulates its little cells at one
and the same time. My son recently explained to me at length
the way sound waves work, and I'm even more impressed
than ever by wirelessness. You need a private income to base
a career on appearing on it, but, my word, when you do the
thing you realize is that, compared to the one-eyed monster
in the living room, the *pictures* are so much better. And now,
at *enormous* expense, a recitation:

Watch This Space

Clap your hands if you're tired of the telly,
Cross your eyes if you're bored with the box.
If one more defective
Pre-menstrual detective
Makes you throw up all over your socks.

Does your console give no consolation?
Your remote make you even remoter?
Does nubile Vanessa
Seem 'Mother Confessor',
Or Cricklewood boxing promoter?

Does your video have machinations?
Are your tapes all unravelled ánd botched?
Are there shows which are lauded
You've carefully recorded,
But never quite sat down and watched?

Are you sick of the Soaps you have swallowed?
At Loyd Grossman invading your home?
If that's what you'd like on
And Cilla's your icon –
You shouldn't be reading this poem!

If you can't take a mini-series seriously,
And for want of a play you could die.
If your cathode ray tube
Seems a terrible boob,
Then kiss the offender goodbye!

You think every home has to have one?
Well, not everyone would agree.
Sir John Logie Baird
Never thought he'd be paired
With those pillocks on GMTV!

If Barrymore, Brucie and Beadle
Are not what you want from your Licence,
Cross Shepherd's Bush Green
And smash in your screen
With a punch reminiscent of Tyson's.

See football on grounds not on Sky,
Take a walk in the woods with the wife.
Plan a trip, plant a seed,
Have a bloody good read!
Get un-set in your ways – Get a Life!

Turn the sound down on game shows and quizzes,
Don't credit the crap that you hear.
They're laying down Cable,
As fast as they're able,
You'll have multiple crap by next year!

Roll your eyes if your telly's a turn-off.
End your quest – so romantic and tireless.
Give a yawn, have a stretch – if it helps you,
    just KVETCH*
And turn on the handiest wireless!

---

* *For non-Yiddish-speaking readers, substitute 'retch'. For quick learners, kvetching is grumbling (a lot!).*

A Nice Cup of Cha-Cha

Are you a secret *Come Dancing* watcher? Admit it. You don't mean to watch but you hear the hidden Alan Bennett timbre in Rosemarie Ford's voice, you see two patent leather men with bums on cantilevers and two women with hair like they've stuck one wet thumb in the light socket and a quarter of a dress, and you are hooked. You are in Ballroomland, a State of Never-Never inhabited by desperate people in numbered clothes.

The Latin American section is particularly amusing. In an attempt at what aficionados barely attempt to describe, they strut and pout and smoulder and wiggle and they are about as sensual as Rod Hull and Emu. Yet in *Tango Argentina*, or its current equivalent, *Tango Forever*, at the Strand Theatre, the place is burning with passion. Sparks fly from the feet of each couple. Some of the men are way into their sixties and I swear you would faint if one of them so much as asked you for a light. (Remember the tango in *Scent of a Woman*? Blind man, Al Pacino, takes Gabrielle Anwar on to the floor and the result is torrid. OK. Double it and take away the number you first danced to, and you've got it.)

Each couple create a dramatic scenario. One grey-haired papa holds his sultry childwoman at arm's length, her tousled black hair falls louchely over her face – she is totally in his thrall. Their feet and legs dart in and out of each other like sewing machine needles in silk. Another stocky Albert Finney lookalike holds his woman like a ragdoll somehow sewn to his body. She is a dark reflective shadow of his machismo force. There is little room for equality in the tango, although the women are intensely powerful.

It was the sexiest evening you could hope to have in the theatre. Even my mother was first in the ice-cream queue. I've been promising for years to take her next door to the Waldorf Hotel for their weekly tea dance. How different from the home life of our own dear Queen?

Although they existed in Edwardian times, tea dances peaked in the Twenties and Thirties: daring and modern, they were one of the few events one could respectably take a gel to and actually get physical with her. Joyce Grenfell's father, Paul Phipps, and his Astor cousin were the first men in London to introduce the racy 'reverse step' into the waltz. Presumably before that you just got going in one direction until you collapsed back to your table. Hats and gloves were obligatory and chaperones the order of the day.

At worst, a tea dance means a stewed pot, a curled white sandwich and a five-piece band which rehearsed for the first time a week last Tuesday with a 'dep' trumpeter. At best, it can personify *joie de vivre*, intimacy, the refreshment of unreachable parts and the perfect pick-me-up.

Now, as far as I understand it, the only tea dance in London is on Saturday and Sunday afternoons at the Waldorf Hotel on the Strand. When *Lost in Yonkers* was at the Strand Theatre, I thought I'd pop in, between shows, and leaf through it. All I can tell you is that the whole experience was riveting. I am, as you know, a committed people-watcher. I can sit on a New York sidewalk or beside a Spanish fountain and earwig for Europe! Sit me in a hotel restaurant for two nights running and I'll give you a rundown on the state of every marriage and suspect alliance in my aural vicinity. Not without straining did Joyce Grenfell once overhear one waltzing matron say to another, 'How is poor Ethel? I was *terribly* worried when I heard she was tap dancing again!'

The Waldorf tea dance was a whole new ballroom. In fact, I'd go as far as to say that all human life was there, if you knew how to look and you looked with affection and without malice. Also, the tea is splendid. A choice of Indian, Ceylon, Darjeeling, Earl Grey, or, if you've an alternative disposition, there are those teas which have floral names like camomile, rose hip and peppermint. To go bopping in between two exhausting performances should have been enervating. Normally, I would just close my curtains, put an hypnotic tape into the machine, lie on the lumpy day-bed and feign sleep, but on this occasion I gathered together Sally, my dresser, and actor Tim Pepper and we headed next door for some serious light fantastic.

Like other baby boomers of my generation, I had attended the Muriel Riley Academy of Ballroom Dancing for a couple of pre-pubescent years and Bernice Marcus, née Segal, owes practically all her dancing skills to being partnered by her tall friend, Maureen. Unfortunately, my skills have remained constant. I can still only be the man. And, as the saying goes, 'Ginger did everything Fred did. Only backwards.'

Added to which, the man I married has many formidable skills, one of them, he assures me, being the 'wing and whisk' down the side of the ballroom. (Another is to approach a young lady with a view to asking for a dance while buttoning up your single-breasted and combing your quiff.) However, he has not, on the whole, kept up or improved upon these accomplishments and, what's more, has reduced his steps to a mournful shuffle in one direction, which, combined with my ruthless attempts to lead, mean we cover about seven centimetres of the floor only and list dangerously towards the bandstand.

We of the *Yonkers* company engaged the weekly services of that most distinguished choreographer, Geraldine Stephenson, who, as a favour, coached us five floors up, above the Strand, every Wednesday between shows. Hopelessly keen, we covered waltz, cha-cha, quickstep and samba before keenness turned to lethargy as, one by one, our men began to go AWOL. Within weeks I was back to square one, pushing Sally round the floor and twirling an imaginary moustache.

The Waldorf, however, would be different. From my first glance at the ornate wrought-iron balcony studded with tiny fairy lights which framed the generous dance floor, I was aware of some gentle magic taking place. We were ushered to our white linen-covered table, boasting fine china and fresh flowers, by a smiling and courteous maître d', and presented with the menu. High tea is not low price but I'm convinced you get what you pay for. Personally, I could hardly find my chair, let alone choose my choux because the dance floor entertainment was so completely mesmerizing.

The young quintet – piano, bass, drums, sax and clarinet – and girl singer were playing, let us say, 'I Get A Kick Out Of You' and couples of every possible size, shape and hue were giving it the *Come Dancing* touch, minus only the hair gel and frontless frocks.

Very quickly, we began to sift the pros, who are there to show, from the couples who are playing out a familiar, familial theme, and the pranksters who perhaps thought it a good way to entertain overseas visitors and ended up mopping their palms and murdering their Maud Frizons.

There was a gorgeous pair, who looked rather glum and frigid in repose and, if I dare say so, somewhat past their sell-by date, but positively leaped to their feet at the mere scent of a slow foxtrot and proceeded to do virtual exhibition dancing for a two or three-tune set. It was astounding. Synchronized and ritualistic as some tribal scene from *Disappearing World*, they covered the floor at a rate which left *my* heart pounding and even brought the house to a standstill with their dramatic and somewhat louche version of the jive. He, ramrod straight, pink-faced and bespectacled, swung her, blasé in powder blue and pearls, round and about him, and their professionally shod feet kicked up and across in a way which could have made Tina Turner beg for mercy. On the far side, a couple who were almost their clones, give or take fifty years, were skilled but so precious you wanted to hold up two zeros and haul 'em off.

A smattering of applause. A murmur of approval. Then

onwards to the Latin American section. Yes, a middle-aged lady in an orange chiffon cocktail dress and looped hair is on the floor almost a fraction too quickly. Her companion, I hesitate to use the word long-suffering – perhaps it was just a hot day, and a man in shirtsleeves will inevitably look like he's suffering besides the rhythmic and insistent thrust of an orange chiffon-clad mate – took one last gulp of his Lapsang Souchong, though, and he was up and away. The throb of the tango, the lure of the lady – they are acting out a long-established pattern of sultry seduction, spawned in Seville and pruriently and diligently matured in Maidenhead.

The waltz and the quickstep will almost always seduce a middle-aged boy and his mother on to the floor. Is he still living at home, I want to know? Is this his bi-weekly treat to her? Will he ever waltz with another woman with everything to find out about him? Tune in to next week's fascinating episode. Same spot on the dial.

Some of the silver wedding and golden wedding couples make me misty the moment they rise from their tea tables. You can tell so much about people from the way they dance, the way they hold each other back. The rhythm that flows or the one that judders. Sometimes a couple just melt into one and you start to wonder if that unity still flows into the bedroom. The pros are the ones with the special dancing shoes, well worn but, seemingly, sprung. The ones who do it for sheer pleasure and slip into nostalgia like a well-loved dressing gown are the ones for whom I have to wring out my glasses.

I should add that whilst observing this living mural, I imbibed several cups of tea, each one stronger than the last. Too rapt to use the silver strainer provided, I ate the tea leaves. They harmonized quite nicely with several scones, crisp on the outside and crumbling within, cream and conserves and a selection of dainty pastries on an even daintier cake stand. My little finger arched to match my eyebrows. I was hooked.

Three or more times I returned to the Waldorf tea dance.

Finally, I just murmured something about an in-depth piece I'm writing on ... er ... 'The tea dance, then and now' – and they let me sit there and gawp for nothing. But next time my mother comes up from Hull, we girls are going dancing at the Waldorf. *A deux*. Stately as a galleon – or in our case, a couple of trawlers. You askin'? We're dancin'.

Artful Dodging

There are times when I'm confused about the role of the Arts in life. Sometimes those times coincide with the very moment when I'm up on a platform somewhere, flanked by fellow luvvies, pleading for more Government funding for them. Hand on heart, I'm praising an obscure theatre company, a mobile art gallery, a video project about inner-city sewerage in Chorlton-cum-Hardy. 'We judge a civilization,' I hear myself rant, 'by its culture,' pause for effect and continue. 'What kind of heritage are we bequeathing our children if we cut the very lifeblood which feeds these projects?'

Don't get me entirely wrong. I mean it. I want, desperately, libraries to stay open and exhibitions to flourish and today's students of film to be tomorrow's Mike Leighs. It's just I can't help wondering. Would it really disturb the average woman in the street if the Royal Academy of Art closed its doors tomorrow and became a Japanese multi-suchi-bar complex? I'm not saying there wouldn't be a protest, there obviously would. *Daily Telegraph* readers would probably chain themselves to the state of the art elevator, pour turpentine on themselves and an elderly relative from Falmouth and self-immolate, but I doubt whether it would be a fight of veal-crate proportions.

(Then again, Guys Hospital has gone and Bart's is on its way out and there's a desperate shortage of hospital beds in London, yet the demonstrations are not loud enough to save them from savage closure. Perhaps it's just that this generation has lost the will to fight. During her first term at University, I kept saying to my daughter, to the point of tedium on my

236

part and whites-of-eyes stoicism on hers, 'But darling, haven't
you been on a march yet?', 'Can I help you make a placard?'
and 'Would you like to borrow my leather jacket? You can
paint obscenities on it if you like.' The fact is, they don't.
Protest that is. They seem to have lost the knack. Or the
need. Or the belief. On the whole they just drink. Get pissed.
Rat-arsed. Legless. Even the most self-interested subjects,
like student grants, the iniquity of cuts therein, lead them not
to the Dean's Office or Whitehall but to the Union Bar. A
universal belief in the powerlessness of the masses to change
anything at all has descended, like an LA smog.)

Sorry, I'm digressing.

But Art? What's it for? When I hear art critic Brian Sewell
mewing and caterwauling at me from the TV screen, archer
than a brick viaduct, I want to set fire to every canvas in the
land, starting with the uppers on his loafers. 'What's that got
to do with the price of cherry tomatoes?' I want to screech,
and 'Get back to Jurassic Park, you deviate!' Yet I only have
to spend four minutes alone in front of a Hockney, a Van
Gogh or a Dali and I'm anybody's. And I can't explain why.

Often it's the sheer sweat of getting to the gallery that
constitutes my problem. How often have the words 'Shall we
go to an exhibition/museum/gallery this afternoon?' crossed
my lips of a Saturday afternoon, to be met by the kind of
enthusiasm which would greet 'Who's for a salt-water enema
and some minor gum surgery?'! It's familial. My daughter
and I once carted my mother to the National Portrait Gallery
for an afternoon of the kind of challenge and opportunity one
doesn't find in the Brent Cross C & A designer floor. As we
entered the magnificent lobby with its myriad portraits, Mum
stopped in her tracks, allowed her jaw to falter from the set
stance and said, in that over-emphatic tone she has elevated
to an art form, '*Don't* tell me these are all *pictures*?' Encour-
aged by this reaction we started on the first room, only to
lose Mum to a bench in the middle of the hall and a lovely
chat with 'ever such a nice woman from Horsham who's up
for the Ideal Homes Water Bed Display'. To some people,

people are more representative than representation.

I'd be the first to admit there's something overly self-conscious about viewing. When my son and I did the Poussins at the Royal Academy he pointed out to me the 'standing in front of one picture for an aeon' syndrome, where you hover there looking, trying to take in as much as you can and next to you, shoulder to shoulder, is this total stranger, doing the same thing. You don't want to move away before they do, because it might appear you are giving it only cursory attention. So you go into a glaze and stand there looking interested. They, of course, are doing precisely the same thing and the decent interval turns into a couple of lifetimes, before one of you, eventually, steps backwards as though to increase your perspective, whereupon the other one scurries off sideways like a soft-shell crab on a populated shingle.

This took me back three decades to the Ferens Art Gallery in Hull where I would hang out in the hope of seeing a particularly enticing Art Historian, of Dutch origins, who set my art history class's collective heart aflame (not too difficult a task in a 1964 all girls school – all you needed really was to be under eighty and wear trousers). Invariably I would gravitate to a favourite picture of mine called 'The Card Player' by Meredith Frampton, which held a peculiar fascination for me. Once there I would stare fixedly at it for an obscenely long time in the vain hope that someone, *anyone*, would become equally fascinated by my fascination and involve me in a romantic discussion concerning my sad, suffering expression. It was a form of self-awareness masquerading as unselfconsciousness which afflicts the very young and very posey.

I watched it in Central Park, New York, a few weeks ago, where I was the only person amongst five thousand afflicted with a strange disability. I had no wheels beneath my feet. I perambulated. They glided. And swerved and looped and arabesqued and waltzed and slalomed. It was a sport which included the spectator. More like a zoo. It was gorgeous, enviable, mind-expanding, but was it Art? Well, in a way, yes it was, because it made me meditate on a whole range of sociological issues, about American obsession with image, about one-upmanship, about joy and freedom. Did it move me? Not nearly as much as it moved them, patently, but it was refreshing.

The Poussin Exhibition did the same. We came out as you do from a great film or play, feeling 'worked'. It was in no way the vaguely guilty feeling you get after a hedonistic few hours in front of the television. I didn't even particularly like the paintings, although I couldn't help but be in awe of their brilliance. I'm always discomfited by paintings with religious and biblical themes. Sacrilegiously, I wonder what magic the painter might have weaved had he not been working on a job lot for Cardinal Richelieu with a deadline come Michaelmas. 'Dawn at the Fishdocks' or 'A Day Spent With Auntie Vi and her Schnauzer' by Nicolas Poussin will always engage my heart more than the 'Garden of Gethsemane' or yet another flying assumption. 'Oh, ye Gods!' I can hear him mutter. 'Not the blessed "Last Supper" again! Still – what the hell, it'll pay the school fees.' The painterly equivalent of another batch of Vauxhall car commercials for Tom Conti, I guess. And there we have it again, Jesus and his Disciples, as plainly as the nose on my face, having a Passover meal – everyone leaning and the door wide open – and, yes, you've guessed it, He's just said 'One of you will betray me', and here am I, four hundred years after Poussin took that commission, a middle-aged woman of slightly anarchic tendencies meditating on a 2,000-year-old theme, in an ornate room somewhere off Piccadilly. That's Art and, like I said, it's refreshing.

I *want* Art to be remembered by the Lottery Committee as much as the next man, which probably varies, of course, depending on which hamlet the next man is sitting in – Tower Hamlets or the National Theatre's Hamlet. Do I want £13 million to be spent on a box of letters, or £55 million rising to £80 million on an Opera House? No, I bloody don't. Or maybe, yes, I bloody do, provided I see twice that money going to medical research, to hospital equipment, to inner-city schools, hospices and, well, my list is endless.

Make no mistake, these profits are iniquitous, coming as they do from pandering to our lowest instincts. The prize money is obscenely high for one reason only: to provoke the kind of tabloid frenzy and envy which sells more tickets – and the man responsible for allocating the money seems seriously suspect on the basis of some of his provocative statements. The die was cast from the moment they gave the franchise to Camelot, a commercially structured organization, instead of Richard Branson, whom I believe would have done something special with the proceeds, to better society.

We took *Re: Joyce!* to Scarborough for a week of benefits for Alan Ayckbourn's new theatre which is in the process of being built. We performed in the Spa Theatre at the end of Scarborough Pier. We raised £28,000 and had fun doing it. Why did I do it? Well, at the time, for the reasons I wrote in the programme.

It was midway through the run of *The Sisters Rosensweig* at the Old Vic that I received a letter from the Whitby home of actor Ian Carmichael. I'd met Ian and his wife, Kate, for the first time, oddly, last year when touring with Rosemary Harris in *Lost in Yonkers*. I say oddly because Ian and I are fellow comedians and fellow Hullovians – although I have a feeling he hails from Beverley, which is definitely one or two up the pecking order from Anlaby Road.

Ian's letter was asking a favour on behalf of Alan Ayckbourn's new theatre. He explained the financial crisis, about Alan's own input and about how much was still needed. He told me Victoria Wood had done a benefit for a night (and her from Lancs! There's noble for you!) and wondered if I would do *Re: Joyce!* for the same cause. I thought it over for – ooh, ages, and rang him, ooh – five minutes later – to suggest we do a whole *week* in Scarborough of *Re: Joyce!* and that way we would, as my mother might say of a vest, 'really feel the benefit'.

Why? Why not? I've always had a soft spot for Scarborough from the days we took our annual draughty holidays there as children. I love the faded splendour of English seaside resorts. In fact my husband and I took our honeymoon in Bognor Regis some twenty-two years ago, and we've been trying to better it ever since ... I'm writing this from my holiday hotel in Eilat, the cranes outside are chugging away, the French are screaming down by the pool and Scarborough seems a dear and distant dream.

Also, because I admire the way Alan runs his seaside ship there, using London to feed Scarborough, as opposed to the other way round. Because I admire his journeyman approach to theatre as writer and director, his 'hands-on' small family business for the community at large – the mixed metaphors have now gone mad!

Because he likes and admires actors. Because he's created such wonderful parts for us – particularly for women – throughout his prolific career. Because this seemed like a great opportunity to give something back, and for once one would be giving a present the receiver genuinely wanted and giving one that the giver could easily give.

And let's face it: this is the nearest I've ever got to playing Hull. I've always heard that the good folk of Hull don't turn out for their own, according to Mr Courtenay and Mr Alderton, (as in, 'If he's that good what's he doin' 'ere?) so it seemed like a bit of a challenge.

On the last night, working on a reserve tank, I would swear on a stack of judges that Joyce came in and did the show for me. I remember walking on stage and I remember walking off, but the middle was a mystery. I just floated above it. Members of the audience felt it, as did my pianist and I. It was rare and magical. Also, we stayed with Alan and Heather in gorgeous Scarborough, swimming-pooled luxury for a week, so I'll never regret it, and the theatre will be one of the most exciting buildings in the world when finished.

Still, a minor twinge affected me when they received £2½ million from the Millennium Fund. I'm delighted for everyone concerned, yet one eighth of me is saying, £28,000? That's a year's salary for a therapist to visit a hospice each day, or fourteen computers for a sixth form, or safe haven for how many refugees?

It's all a tricky moral issue. Recently, on my way to the rehearsal rooms in Acton, I cut through Harlesden from the North Circular and was stunned into braking point at the sight of something like an Eighth Wonder of the World in a small suburban street. There, rising from the dusty, scaffolded cladding, is a £60 million Hindu temple, every inch carved intricately out of white marble, with a dome of solid gold. Alongside it is a low oriental building, in which, I understand, 3,000 people are fed, for free, each day. I sat there blinking and watched the agile Indian construction workers, rumoured to have been sent over on a payment of £4 a day, buzzing from one ornate tower to another like worker bees, until finally I made myself late for rehearsals.

I stopped every day to marvel at this feat of engineering mastery. All the money has been raised by donations apparently and it will stand there for centuries for the world to admire a gentle, spiritual culture. I can't think that anything can have been built in this fashion since the Victorian era. I'm told that when Indian dignitaries come over to oversee the progress, they throw gold rings into the site to be melted down and used for the golden dome. It's very beautiful, very practical and, I imagine, very authentic. Is it worth it? Is it Art? Is it £60 million well spent? Compared to the content and longevity of the $200 million spent on Kevin Costner's *Waterworld* I'd say yes to all three questions.

Critique

I don't suppose that 'When I grow up I want to be a critic' is one of the ten foremost phrases heard by doting parents across the land. But to Mrs Wardle, and Mrs Tinker and Tynan, and Mrs Banks-Smith, and Mrs Agate, and even Mrs Hazlitt, the words might have been irritatingly familiar. 'Ooooh for heaven's *sake*, Irving,' she may have groaned, 'will you stop messing with that Pollock's Toy Theatre and concentrate on your "Life Cycle of the Ichneumon Fly". Don't you want to be something in life, like a dentist? . . . or a butcher? People will always need meat, Irving. It's basic.'

It isn't, of course, a vocation, like being a female priest or a male nurse. It's something you drift into, courtesy of journalism, and by way of shorthand, short staffing and short-sight. However, though it may be true that nobody ever erected a statue to a critic, I'm not about to endanger my career by writing a diatribe about the whole dire tribe.

John Osborne, the old softie, claimed that critics are, 'those who would send Hedda Gabler to a marriage guidance clinic', but he could afford to do so. He was a man and a grumpy and malevolent one to boot, but he wrote like an angel, so reprisals were unlikely.

I'll save my wrath till I've left the country with a seven-picture deal in LA and a personal introduction to Kenneth Branagh.

Joyce Grenfell became a radio critic by sitting next to a newspaper owner at a dinner party and telling him of the great joy of being a radio listener. Nothing wrong with that. She was gifted, articulate and any hors d'oeuvre-eating

243

newspaper magnate would have been a fool to himself not to
see her potential. Similarly, Ken Tynan, arguably the possessor of one of the greatest writing styles of any twentieth-
century critic, became one because 'The sheer complexity of
writing a play always had dazzled me. In an effort to understand it, I became a critic.'

Roughly as many people love being criticized as love having
root canal work. I'm no exception. It upsets my digestion for
weeks. When a local London critic described my performance
in *Lost in Yonkers* as 'Winsome – perhaps a shade too winsome', it repeated on me like a kipper. Here I was in the most
complex and difficult role of my career and all I could hear
in my head for days was, 'Was that winsome? Whoops ...
winsome again!' Still, that's showbiz ... you win some ...
you lose some.

The criticism of *The Sisters Rosensweig* was often patronizing. The *Sunday Express* critic wrote that Larry Lamb didn't
'look sufficiently Semitic' to play Merv the Furrier. I sent off
a furious missive to his editor on the grounds that this was,
at best, a pretty lousy criterion on which to judge a performance and, at worst, racist. What sort of looks did he
want? Topol's? Lew Grade's? or the blond, blue-eyed Aryan
look of today's young Israeli sabras? The letter was printed
and Hirschorn replied in print that the actor in New York,
Robert Klein, had *looked* more the part and, good heavens,
he would never make a racist remark, being Jewish himself.

It reminded me of when we had had a Royal Gala at
Richmond the year before, whilst touring *Lost in Yonkers*
there. Princess Margaret attended and during our introduction remarked that I looked a lot happier than when she'd
last seen me. I coloured, remembering the last hot-making
meeting in Derek Nimmo's dressing-room during the run of
a play we were both in called *The Cabinet Minister*, which had
just received some pretty vituperous press. I guess I'd been
stinging a bit from the notices – some of which claimed
the play, by Sir Arthur Wing Pinero, was anti-Semitic. She
remembered my annoyance on this occasion and I said I

hoped I hadn't been graceless when we'd last met, but perhaps I'd been upset by the accusations.

'Do you know what anti-Semitic means?' she demanded.

'Er ... I most certainly think so Ma'am,' I replied.

She beckoned me to follow her behind a pillar. She was wearing grey-green chiffon and there was something ghostly about following her. She paused for a while in the semi-gloom and said, meaningfully, 'Anti-Semitism means prejudice against Arabs.' There was nothing I could say to contradict this and we returned to the rest of the company forthwith. She was right, of course, but the derivation of linguistics is often quite different from their modern perception. After all, the Swastika started out as a Christian symbol.

The problem remains in all branches of entertainment: that if you put prejudice into the mouths of ignorant people, like the ghastly Twombley family in *The Cabinet Minister*, it should, in theory, mean that the author is on the side of the victim. Unfortunately what happens in practice, particularly in a country where prejudice is as badly hidden as a winter crocus is to a hungry squirrel, the public becomes enamoured of the bigoted perpetrator, not the victim. Margot, Victor Meldrew, Mrs Bucket (pronounced Bouquet), Alf Garnet, all the way back to Andy Capp and Lady Bracknell. We idolize the person who speaks the lie we dare not utter ourselves.

Occasionally, in script conferences for my TV series, *Agony Again*, lines would be cut because of black sensitivity or gay sensitivity, usually at the behest of those of that proclivity. On one occasion I threw in the towel saying, 'But there are endless Jewish jokes and I have never objected to them! If I'm prepared to take the flak, then we all must be.' Rule of Lenny Bruce – same shit for all, everyone gets education, no one gets hurt. I'm sure the differing sensitivity derives honestly from the feeling that, fifty years after the war, the Jews are OK now. Mainstream society and no need of protection, whereas for blacks and gays, the revolution is still taking place and nerves are more exposed. Except it doesn't feel that way to me. The right-wing fanatics are just a stone's throw away and we set up a Jewish stereotype, which, in *Agony Again*, we have in Jane's mother, Bea (rightly, because that's when she's funniest). We accept that anything she says will in some way cause offence to someone, then she always get her come-uppance, and all is well.

At the press launch for *Agony Again*, a fresh-faced young woman from the Hull *Daily Mail*, asked me if I thought Jane Lucas was a soft touch.

I replied that I thought she probably was.

'And is your mother like that?' asked the girl, who couldn't have been more than twenty-two.

'Er, not really,' I replied. 'I mean, she's kind but . . .' I didn't really understand the relevance of the question, but I burbled on, as one does. 'Actually, my father was the generous-to-a-fault one. He had a Gent's Outfitters in Hull and he would give people shirts, ties, socks, whatever was going. He sup-ported more needy people in *his* life than anyone I've ever . . .'

'Really?' she interrupted, blue eyes wide and smile broad. 'And that's not really what you'd expect at all from a Jewish shopkeeper, is it?'

Fifty years this year. The end of the last bout but one of ethnic cleansing. This Yorkshire Lois Lane out of Jessica Mitford, was scarcely a glint in her grandfather's eye, yet she'd ingested ignorance and prejudice with her Farex.

Oh, for Eric Cantona's feet!

Small wonder that my teeth were already gritted for the reviews of *Agony Again*. Not only has television changed drastically in the fifteen years since *Agony* was aired, but criticism has changed. Back then, the show would be men-tioned, sometimes praised, sometimes dismissed, and Nancy Banks-Smith would talk about her cat and how she once wrote an agony column by mistake and all would be well. Nowadays, it would be no surprise to pick up the London *Evening Standard* and read, 'Maureen Lipman is a pretentious old bag with the talent of a tuning fork and her show is as predictable as vomit from a grass-eating cat.' And that's a *reasonable* review! Fortunately, Nancy BS will still write about her cat again, so do what I shall do and swap to the *Guardian*. I considered writing to the Hull *Daily Mail* but decided that the reporter was foolish rather than malicious. When the article appeared she had paraphrased her question and added, 'Miss Lipman shot me an icy glance down the length of her long nose . . .' I think that said it all.

Sixteen years after he wrote *The Knowledge*, Jack received the review of his life for the repeat showing in August 1995. It posed the unanswerable question: 'Is this the best television play ever written?' To this critic it was, and to the next cabbie I meet who says, 'Nah, it was nothing like that – far-fetched', it wasn't. And who can criticize his right to say that?

Joyce Grenfell, as ever the wisest bird I know, was once asked on *Any Questions* whether critics served any purpose. She admitted that they did but added that, in an ideal world, the critic would read the script to get a sound knowledge of what the author's input was, as distinct from the director's. He would then attend an early rehearsal to see what the intention of the production was and then he would return – not on a first night when it's all nerves and flowers and unreality – but some time during the first week of playing to see how far that intention had been achieved. It's so simple, so brilliant, and it will, of course, never happen.

Worse still, how are you on implied criticism? Enter the author's mother, stage left, wafting a pile of bone-dry and deeply crumpled laundry. 'Do *you* think it's worthwhile tumble-drying things, for all that money, when it's a lovely blowy day outside and the line's empty and just been wiped down?' or, 'Funny, isn't it, how Amy hasn't joined any clubs and societies much at University? Do you think she's meeting nice boys and everything? You're not *worried* at all are you?'

You've got to keep your sense of proportion polished up and your good humour buffed for this one. God knows, I grinned stoically through perfect strangers greeting me with, 'By gum, my phone bills haven't half shot up since BT started paying your salary, Maureen!' But I'm not sure it wasn't preferable to, 'Haven't seen *you* on the telly for a while,

Maureen' and 'Whatever happened to that woman who played whatsit in the Beattie commercials?'

Of course, when you're on nodding and shaking terms with the critics, then your opinion of them is likely to be more subjective. They have foibles and prejudices and fallibilities like the rest of us. They get fed up of seeing the same faces from the same row of the same stalls in pot-boilers presented by the same angst-ridden authors. It's this 'déjà-view' existence which makes them over-react to a new face and turn bilious over an old one. Old Chinese Proverb states: 'Those who have free ticket for the play hiss first.'

One night on the *Late Show*, I watched a ballet critic dismissing the work of Maurice Béjart in derogatory terms. He was hilarious. A TV natural. Pink as a new-born piglet, pompous as Pooh Bear and wearing a perky little bow tie, he didn't just mince words. He minced for Europe. Béjart was 'vulgar'. His choreography 'simply ghastly – no purity, no line!' He was fuelled by petulance, archer than Ambridge, every centimetre the bourjolais gentil-homme – and so keen to condescend to the cognoscenti, that this particular viewer became desperate to see a Béjart ballet – *any* Béjart ballet – if this silly person said I *shouldn't*. I knew, as surely as I knew the state of my husband's toilet bag, that this fellow's opinions, his politics and probably even his recipe for shepherd's pie, could *never* tally with mine.

Maybe that's the answer to how you pick your taste arbiter. Put 'em all on Ceefax. A critic's forum. Show me the critic face to fascia and you can set his prejudices against your own. Two minutes of his mannerisms and you'll suss out the snob from the sycophant and the buff from the buffoon. The following day you can not only choose your future entertainment with ease, you can turn to the arts page of your favoured tome and read a critical critique of *The Critics*. Imagine how they'd wince.

Wonder-Barbra

The circus left town long ago, leaving nothing behind it but a string of disgruntled critics, a million out-of-pocket but delirious fans, several thousand metres of white satin and a carpet custom-cut to fill Wembley Arena.

I'm referring, of course, to the State Visit of Barbra Streisand (equal emphasis, Strei and sand, soft s) legend, superstar, icon and musical phenomenon. She of the voice which flowed through my adolescence like hormones in honey and gave me the only intimations since Alma Cogan that there was hope and maybe even glory for other 'funny girls' with, let's say, irregular features.

My one previous, and much-chronicled, encounter with my heroine was when, during the time my husband was writing *Yentl*, our six-year-old son informed her that her voice was too loud. 'It really hurts my ears, your voice,' he bleated pleasantly. His star-struck mother then added injury to insult by trying to point out a mistake in the orchestration in 'Memory'. The star's baby blue eyes gazed at the writer's wife for a *very* long time and the rest is silence, of the black hole variety.

It was in the mid-sixties when I read in *Time* magazine about her 'Miss Marmelstein' in the show *I Can Get It For You Wholesale*. Instant identification. Later, 'People' from *Funny Girl* became my mantra for months before it acquired a tune (Broadway soundtracks were not easy to track down in downtown Hull in '63). By the time I'd acquired *My Name is Barbra* and *Colour Me Barbra* in vinyl, most of the world knew not only that this girl could snake her way into your

249

soul with one note of that most beautiful of instruments, her voice, but also that she had an even more formidable talent for alienating 'People' who needed her.

The story goes that when she was a struggling actress, she was in the apartment of her friend then, and still today, Cis Corman, and began to sing to herself in the kitchen. Corman came in and commented on the brilliance of her voice. Barbra immediately stopped singing. The only way she would ever sing again for Cis and her husband was to stand at the other end of the kitchen and turn her back on them. Pardon my psychobabble but I don't think that phobia has ever really left her. She just finds subtler ways of turning her back.

After *Funny Girl*, director William Wyler, when asked what it was like working with Barbra Streisand, replied that she was quite brilliant considering it was the first film she'd ever *directed*. A cynical comment, perhaps justified, but in the light of *Prince of Tides* and *Yentl* it was an early indication of a real director's eye. Maybe even two.

There were other films where this theory falls apart and perhaps her desire for total control is perfectionism gone AWOL. But consider. To be a superstar in the US for three decades takes more than talent. It takes fortitude, stamina, the skin of an armadillo and a kind of madness to want it. Who else is still there? Shirley MacLaine? Liz? Liza? Not in movies, records, TV *and* stage. No one. And she's done it by demanding the best, moving one step ahead of every trend, fast, and taking no prisoners. In so doing she's got right up the nasal passages of a great many people who would, otherwise, have nothing up there but very finely cut white powder.

So, if I were to state my bias in the she's a genius/she's a monster debate, I would certainly come out in the same camp as most of the 12,000 loving fans who gave their diva a standing, stomping, salaaming reception, which made my last trip to Wembley, to see a cup final, sound like a day spent in the Fossil Department of the British Museum.

The tabloid press sounded off differently. For weeks before

she arrived, the speculation grew increasingly strident. Hysteria greeted the news that top ticket prices would be £250 (normal price for Pavarotti or Glyndebourne) and – shock-horror-have-they-gone-raving-mad? – barmaids from Bootle were willing to pay bootleg prices for a mere two hours of their heroine's time. Full typographical Tourette's syndrome, however, was reserved for the news of her autocue. 'Every line a prompt!' they screamed, 'News At Ten comes to Wembley at £250 a ticket'. The fear and loathing factor was at fever pitch. She was, characteristically, granting no interviews, so each headline was accompanied by snatched street snaps of uniform unkindness.

Her fans knew about the autocue. She'd already used it in Las Vegas. After the press attacks here, she told her audience that twenty-eight years ago, singing to 125,000 people in Central Park, she'd 'dried' as dead as Daedalus and could think of nothing witty to excuse it. As a result of that, she'd stayed off stage for twenty-eight years. We could take her, security blanket and all, or we could leave her. Instant standing ovation, then she caressed her way through classics and songs she had made into classics and I swear, hand on fan club badge, she never looked at her security blanket once.

Afterwards, in the dressing-room, she talked of her fear of performing live. 'But you must feel better now you've done these concerts?' someone ventured. The baby blue eyes hardened momentarily. 'Not a bit. It gets harder.' She's right. It does.

'What I say to myself is ...' I heard myself burble, ' "Maureen, in three hours' time you'll be in bed." '

She considered it for a millisecond. 'No. Wouldn't work for me.'

I toyed with adding 'and home by five', but I didn't.

Afterwards, my Hull chum, Valerie, and I were like the couple of schoolkids who'd just swapped one 'Best Wishes, Helen Shapiro' for two barbershop snippings of Cliff Richard's quiff. It was, in truth, Val's fault I was there at all. We'd considered buying tickets but, to be honest, decided they

were a tidge on the expensive side. 'If it was for a charity . . .'
I mumbled, parsimoniously.

'Wembley?' said Jack, who reads only the political and
sports pages. 'No. Every time I go, they lose.'

'For God's sake,' shrieked Val. 'You *know* her. Ring somebody up! Gedda discount! Whatsa matter with you?' I rang
someone, they rang someone, someone rang me, and I
managed, Eureka! to get two seats for – yes, you've guessed
it – exactly the same price as advertised. Maureen 'I can get
it for you retail' Lipman.

So Val and I were all set for Wednesday night. Tuesday
evening, I'm in bed resting my neck for the occasion, when
the phone announces, 'Hi, this is Kim, Barbra Streisand's
assistant. Ms Streisand wondered if Mr Rosenthal and yourself would like to be her guests for the last concert.'

My mind is going like an Apple Mac on print-out. 'Ooooo-
er-gosh, thank you, but I'm already coming tomorrow night.'

'Oh, is Jack going to be with you?'

'Er – yes,' I lied. 'But we'd love to see it twice. *Thank* you.'

Phone down. Address book up. Who do I know who'd pay
£500 for two seats in eighteen hours' time? No one. What do
I do? I cajole Jack into buying another seat for the last night
for Val. So, by now, we're up to £750 for three seats and I'm
envisaging myself touting Wednesday's seats, outside
Wembley, in a flasher's mac and beard. Six hours before
curtain up, we sell at a philanthropic loss.

I wish I could report that the loss was deadly. I wish I
could send up the set, the clothes, the fans, the car parking
arrangements. It would make funnier reading.

In fact, it was worth twice the price. It was priceless. I
could carp about her philosophical patter, perhaps wish her
freer, wilder and more spontaneous. But you don't hire Nigel
Kennedy for his table manners, you hire him for his talent.
Perfect pitch, modulation, phrasing – the voice pours out like
mozzarella. She is fascinating and fine like porcelain. What
do the critics want – plasma? Or maybe drama queens? Liza,
Judy, Shirley spilling out their guts, sleeves dripping heart,

equally for 'Rain Or Shine' or 'Thumbelina'. Instead they got a reluctant diva, not working the house, but working through her angst. Not drowning but wavering. On this night, we were seeing a reflected image of a past. Ours and hers. Not quite the real thing but, in the time it took to get here, an image of the real thing. Astronomically speaking, A Star.

On the drive home, I looked at my programme. It said 'For Maureen. In three hours' time, I'll be in bed.' I hope she had a great supper. She sang for it, beautifully.

Be a Sport

Actors, journalists, sportsmen are all in the business of communication. I count myself among the first two – I know this because we share the same prohibitive car insurance. (I suppose insurance brokers assume we finish a show or an interview, drink a bottle of vodka, rev up and head for home. I suggest they check out the drinking routine of your average city gent, civil servant or doctor.)

A sportsman, though, I've never claimed to be. I was art and drama, my brother was science and sport. As distinct as Trivial Pursuit categories, we were pigeonholed at primary school and remained so for forty odd years. He played rugby till his nose refused point-blank to be broken any more, leaving him, after the last re-set, with the only straight nose in the family. Then he transferred his prowess to playing equally lethal tennis. I played nothing. Instead I claimed to have a painful period twice a week. I'm a lousy tennis player. I can't run for toffee, nor can I ride, ski on land or water, climb or catch round things.

What I *can* do, now, is watch. Football and cricket are no longer mysterious moving mandalas, densely populated by faceless, numberless insects. I've learned that to enjoy a match you must first be prejudiced in favour of one or the other side. A smattering of the house rules will not come amiss, of course, but though I will never understand the offside rules, I can now be utterly compelled by, and really care about, the outcome of a Test match or a league game.

This helps in more ways than you'd think. I am able to communicate with my son on subjects which don't make him regard me as an alien. Like our usual exchanges:

Me: Who will be with you, when you go to China?
Him: Ngeugh?

and:

Me: Have most of your friends got holiday jobs?
Him: Ngeugh? Eugh. Noreawha?

No good at all. But on sports grounds, at times, we have fabulous communication:

Me: Sampras is incredible, isn't he? Unbelievable tennis.
Him: All serve. I really like Becker. Can't stand Sampras's game.
Me: Yeah ... right.

or:

Me: Dominic Cork! Hat trick! Phenomenal! I think we're in with a chance. West Indies are really all out and we're ninety-four ahead ... We're gonna do it ...
Him: They have got another innings, you know, Mom.
Me: ... Yeah, but ...

and I peter out, knowing I'm only being humoured. It takes a real sportsman to spot a hanger-on, a game groupie.

He and I went to the 1994 Milk Cup and the FA Cup 1995 at Wembley. Our team, Manchester United, were playing Arsenal in 1994 and, the next year, Everton, and I was a celebrity reporter for the *Daily Express*. It was massively exciting to walk into that roaring amphitheatre. It took my breath away.

Nothing can take away from live theatre. Watching the Lads in Red at Wembley was live theatre – the good guys against the bad guys. The thrill of real conflict. My husband hasn't been to Wembley since he saw Manchester United lose two successive finals – he thinks he's a jinx. I come from a Rugby League family – Hull Kingston Rovers – my dad was an outfitter who made blazers for, amongst others, the legendary soccer hero Raich Carter and his team. As I went out for tea at half time, a man came up, shook my hand and said, 'I want to shake the hand of the daughter of the man who made David Whitfield's suits.' My eyes filled up. My father would have loved that moment.

I became a fan of the Lads in Red when I met Jack in 1969 at Granada TV in Manchester. It was part of the courtship routine to pretend I was a football supporter, and I was a decent enough actress to pull it off, but it has taken twenty odd years for me to authenticate the hoax.

My man and I are horrified by the Ferguson purges. Personally affronted by his ditsy decision to transfer Paul Ince and Mark Hughes, the heart and stomach of the team, and thus lose the life blood of Cantona. Jack is bewildered. He doesn't know where to turn. It's not easy being a red. It makes you blue.

Last year was bad enough, when Cantona took a flying leap at a noxious spectator. Of course, he was out of line to assault his insulter; it brings the game into disrepute and encourages hooliganism. It also, unfortunately, reflects the game. He should have shrugged off the abuse, as black players have to do all the time, but his temperament is Gallic and *voilà!* 'He didn't understand what the ref said,' goes the joke. 'He thought he said "Get off the pitch and put your feet up." '

It's the concentration on goals, goal average, goal bonuses that is at fault. Any sex therapist will tell you that goal orientation destroys love-making. Public shows of clinches, cuddling and canoodling are by no means signs of a happy marriage or a contented sex life. *Au contraire, mon ami, au* bloody *contraire*.

It's the game as money-making machine which should be looking deep into itself. It's the television dilemma again. If ratings are the only criterion, then the programmes will be, largely, rubbish. It's a problem of society, not just of sport, and perhaps going back to sport for the sake of pleasure and leisure is just a fantasy.

Because Fantasy Football is gaining supporters, as is Fantasy Cricket. Last year my Celebrity Fantasy Cricket Team, 'The Kricheters', came top of the *Daily Telegraph* C.F.C. League. I was over the moon, Brian. Ninety points ahead of nearest rivals, Rory Bremner and Dickie Bird.

They were called 'The Kricheters' because of the Yiddish word to 'krich', or move slowly and creakily – the ch is guttural like the Scots' 'loch'. Basically, your players are selected from any team, from within an appropriate sum of money, and their scores from county and Test matches are converted into points. You can buy or sell players and the prizes for the regular public's team are all manner of holidays, champagne and tickets to Lord's. The prize for the celebrity team winner is bugger all, but at least you get the *Daily Telegraph* ringing you up to ask for the secret of your success.

'My lads done good,' I told them. 'They showed character, read the game well and paid heed to my superior game-plan.' When pushed, I also admitted that a wee drop of credit could go to my friend, Colin Shindler, who did nothing short of structuring my entire team from the depths of a hot, soapy and ruminative bath. In fact, we just stopped short of calling our team 'Shindler's List'.

There were lazy summer afternoons when I would come home from *Agony Again* rehearsals and collapse, fatigued and with a hot brain, in front of a Test match or a Wimbledon final or even an international golf tournament (this only when I'm desperate, you understand, and the opposition is showing a British spy movie or old *Poldarks*) and time passed by quite blissfully.

A soporific commentary, Geoff Boycott fantasizing that he's still at the crease, the sound of willow on leather or grunt on centre court and yes, it's still England, I'm still the optimistic side of fifty and there may even be honey left for tea ... And when I drive back from the theatre after an eight-show week and *Match of the Day* plus highlights, plus multi-crapola from the mouths of Lynam and Lineker is what's there to greet me, I can snuggle on the sofa, next to the rapt spectator – and when he says, 'How did it go, love?' I can say, 'Shsh ... Please! I'm trying to watch the penalties!'

Actually, last night just about sums up the whole trans-formation. We came home from a marvellous Prom at the Albert Hall. The building was evacuated as the concert ended because of an LEB power cut and our hosts, Duke and Susan Hussey and the BBC, had fifty-three tables laid for a dinner which nobody could eat. I actually picked up an enormous platter of coronation chicken, held it high over my head and yelled, 'Everyone back to my place!' Nobody laughed but Jack. Anyway, the point being that once back home, over beans on toast, he explained the offside rules to me, with reference to a diagram, ad nauseam, and I still don't bloody understand them.

My new-found little 'knowledge' saw me as a speaker on the top table at a special tribute dinner to Sir Stanley Matthews on his eightieth birthday. The other speaker was Tony Blair, whose wife, Cherie, and Sir Stanley's fascinating Hungarian wife, Meela, were elegant illustrations of how you can stand by your man without standing on him or under him. Meela is a psychotherapist who had never even *seen* a game of football before she fell for Sir Stanley.

My job was to toast the Ladies present and I told them: 'Ladies, we have been graciously allowed into the heady testosterone-charged environment for this fabulous fixture. Let us face facts, men are a complete mystery. They think they know us inside out. Wasn't it P J O'Rourke who said, "There are a number of mechanical devices which increase sexual arousal, particularly in women. Chief amongst these is the Mercedes Benz 380L convertible!" Well, tonight is Ladies' Night, I am your lady of the night and though I know it's not fancy dress, in honour of equality [and here I must point out for those of you who are reading in black and white, that I was wearing the black velvet Wim Hemmink dress with the huge white satin stand-up collar], I have come as a pint of Guinness.

'When I met my husband, he made it clear it was "Love me, love my team". Twenty-four years later, is it too late to admit I've been faking it all these years? Now, to be honest, I really do get a genuine thrill when I see the Lads in Red – or is it fuchsia pink and pistachio with navy epaulettes? I haven't seen *this week's* strip yet.

'Men are, as I said, a mystery. After all they spit, they punch, they scream, they rant, they kick each other when they're down and think nothing of putting their hands down their shorts and fiddling about. Of course, if they did it in the street they'd be arrested – but if they do it on a pitch they're worth £7 million!'

I left them, as a Yorkshirewoman, with the joke about the prostitute who claimed to do anything for £10 if it could be described in three words. The Cockney went in, said, 'Lick my body', paid £10 and came out delighted. The Scouser went in and said, 'Grope me everywhere', paid his tenner and came out thrilled. The Yorkshireman held on to his money, looked her square in the face and said, 'Paint my house.'

Cone-senting Adults

Who's doing well in these recessive days? I mused as I watched steam issue from beneath the bonnet of my car. It was protest steam at the sheer indignity of being stuck in a two-mile tailback when what it wanted to do was the one thing it was created to do, namely motor me from A to B, then sit patiently on the tarmac, ticking contentedly, till it got the nod to drive me back to A.

I'll tell you who's doing well. Bollard makers. If there's a bollard makers' union they must be rubbing their little cone-shaped hands together and stifling collective smirks. Never was business more booming. Summer in the city and rows of pantomime-bloomer-striped witches' hats are *everywhere*. Like wire coat hangers, these falsely merry symbols of procrastination seem to propagate with no regard whatever to population control.

Diversion! Single Lane Traffic Only! Some Delay Expected ... Work Will Continue till July 1999. The jaundice-yellow signs only tell you this when you are actually stuck in the mayhem they've created. Not before. Oh, the envy I felt after a two and a half hour crawl in a boiling vehicle to a surprise party in Hampshire, to see Eve Pollard glide down glacially, loftily almost, on to the lawn. For it was in the time of her editorship of the *Sunday Express* and this was the *Express* helicopter.

Will somebody tell me whether the tarmac industry is contributing huge amounts of dosh to the Conservative Party? This is the only rationale I can conjure up for the mindless mess of road building and traffic diverting which typifies every junction in London and the Home Counties. Give me a tailback for forty-five minutes on a stretch of narrowed single-lane traffic and I'll give you two red and white fences, 240 orange and white cones and *no* workmen, save one jaunty jovial cove in a hard hat, seated in a miniature crane laughing his head off into a mobile phone. 'You wanna see this lot, Doris. They're steamin' at the gills. There's blokes havin' coronaries in Corniches here. Laugh? I almost bought the scratch cards!'

How lovely to be above it all. Uninvolved. With your own private chopper, so to speak. Instead of fussing and fuming in an orange-and-white striped straightjacket. How could you not feel lofty? Maybe it's a family firm, 'Bollard and Daughter', only the signwriter's pen slipped. Or maybe it's a row of striped *Pollards* that I see in front of me at every juncture.

The North Circular Road, the most user-unfriendly stretch of tarmac since Traitor's Walk, is in its usual summer turmoil. Smooth as a macadamia nut till Henleys Corner, where it suddenly becomes a theme park ride. Arrows and signs join the myriad puffing steam vehicles, chugging bulldozers, pounding, pumping power drills and rows of hard-hatted fellows · with risible, visible bum-cracks, chomping their baguettes and laughing at the spectacle of the British on the move. Or not, as the case must be. I understand that there is a group in existence called the North Circular Road Appreciation Society', an oxymoron if ever I've heard one. They organize coach trips to North London and marvel at its ever-changing splendour: 'Look, everyone! There on the left, a new Galaxy of Leather emporium! *Those* suites have got simulated onyx inlay, I prefer it to the jade leatherette, don't you? And cheaper than the ones in Leatherama Land on that last bend, by the big hole in the road. Ooooh! There it is! IKEA! On the right with the blue and yellow flag – wave everyone! – you can just see it behind that sixty-foot crane – quick! Quiet please! Can I have your attention? A quiz. How many Homebases are there between here and Toys 'R Us?

Time's up. Yes – Geoff? You're right again – just the three. And you've won the free guided tour of the Window and Door Hyperstore, so we'll drop you off at Hanger Lane and pick up you, and your free sliding patio window frame, after a compulsory stop for refreshments at the Bart Simpson pizzeria and crèche in the Tesco Superstore.'

The other growing industry, besides bollards and super-stores, is the 'sleeping policeman' business. Someone, somewhere at the Ministry of Trade and Industry must have done a deal and imported several million tons of unprocessed concrete, probably in return for a couple of butter mountains and some redundant coal, and since then the Minister for ministering to the unemployment figures has been jolly busy figuring out how to use it: 'I say, sir,' the Under-Secretary to the Civil Servant chirps to the Minister of Transport. 'What if we mount a scheme to put two or three huge, useless bumps across every side street in every town in England? It will only cost £1,500 a bump, it will give lots of work to lots of redundant coves who can't keep up the payments on their gas-filled Reboks and keep all the cars off the little short-cut residential streets and on the main thoroughfares, where we've placed all the stripy cones.'

'Bravo, Hargreaves-Mayhem! Excellent wheeze! Just the scheme we're looking for, to go with "Pay & Display", "Road Up", "Wheel Clamp & Tow". We'll drive the driver utterly insane. Off the roads and into the mental hospitals. There's enough of 'em empty now, eh? eh? I said – "nough of 'em empty"! Ha, ha! What? Take a rise, Hargreaves-Mayhem. Go out and buy the little woman a Peugeot.'

Pardon me, friendly reader, while I wipe away the froth from my forehead. I'll be all right in a minute. I'm just a tidge overheated, that's all.

My newspaper of the 31 July 1995 tells me that, 'the Cones Hotline has been abandoned (cost to the taxpayer of £5,000 a year rental), because calls are in the region of only two an hour. Only five sets of unnecessary cones have been removed from roadworks in the whole of Britain as a result of calls to the hotline.'

Right. So Major has admitted he was wrong? It's been a cause of embarrassment to him? Well, not exactly.

'The scheme has a unique accounting system covering up the real cost to the taxpayer. While most Whitehall costs are monitored in detail, no charges are made for staff manning the "cones" line, on the grounds that they also cover other duties. Nor are records kept at the Highways Agency, which runs the service, of the hundreds of thousands of pounds a year of putting up signs at the end of every trunk road and motorway scheme.' Wait, there's more.

The Agency records every phone call – 17,700 per month – but admits that this rate of thirty to forty a day includes those *not* asking about cones.

Just the £5,000 per year rental then. Plus. Since 1992. I reckon the real culprits are those perennial villains, teenage single mothers! Sitting at home all day *not* phoning the Cones Hotline. It's a public disgrace. Cut their benefits – put their children into care. Then, with the saving on all those £29 benefits per week, we could send the Chairman of British Gas away for a nice couple of weeks in the Seychelles.

Although, I must admit, the North Circular is much better these days. You can positively whizz round from Finchley to Hanger Lane since the bulldozers and the cones left town. Course, you then sit in Hanger Lane for a couple of lifetimes ... not to mention that should you wish to go in the opposite direction, ie eastwards, you will sit in a half a mile long tailback from now till Michaelmas.

At present the blockage is merely a double row of defiantly casual cones, but the men in hard hats with the crack in their bums showing are due any day soon. It's a promise. And from then on it can only get worse. Conical, isn't it?

Yesterday, the local Total and I had a run in. They call it a service station. Inside, two men watched as the lead-free pump leaked four star down my arm, my jacket, the forecourt and everywhere but my petrol tank. I rushed into the booth to tell them I was switching pumps. This time the pump cut out every five seconds and managed just a dribble of fuel. I beckoned wildly for help. In the service station they viewed me impassively. Again I raced in, my voice up an octave, my right arm smelling toxic: 'Your tank must be full,' was the manager's assessment.

'My tank is empty! That's why I'm in your ******* garage,' I squeaked. Then, Cleese-like, 'Right. That's it. I'm going to another garage.'

'What about paying for the petrol you've already had?' was the last sentence I heard over the sound of my own curses.

Our local police are not sleeping. They arrived this morning at 11.00. They were sweet, but if I didn't pay the £7.70, they would have to write a criminal offence report. Being a mature woman in my forties, I'm off to the Post Office for £8 of pennies.

It's hot out there and I keep expecting two men in white bearing a jacket with extremely long sleeves, to come up the drive. Thank God this is England and the most offensive weapon I'm carrying is my pen.

The Agony & the Epilogue

I've been filming for the new series of *Agony*. It's almost fifteen years since I played the fictional television Agony Aunt Jane Lucas in the last series and, since then, a lot of bridging loans have gone underwater. Some of you may never have heard of it. In which case you're smug juveniles. Never fear though, I'm not embittered and I think laugh lines are fetching, even though they remain there when I stop laughing. The critics may say '*Agony* is back with Maureen Lipman and a lot of new lines.'

The new series is called *Agony Again* and co-stars Maria Charles as my mother Bea, Sacha Grunpeter as my son Michael, with the odd guest appearance of the divine Simon Williams as my ex-husband, Laurence. Honest, I'm not really plugging the show, I'm setting the scene for the week when all the filmed 'inserts' are made. These are the bits which couldn't be shot in a studio in front of an audience and which will be spliced into the completed episode.

These include all the driving sequences. When the camera has to film you from the front, they put the car on a lorry called a low-loader, the camera crew sit in front of the car and the lorry driver drives you around and around on nice quiet roads. That's the theory anyway. The actor just makes 'vrmm-vrmm' movements with the steering wheel and is therefore free to do the sort of things one is called upon to do in the whacky world of sitcom – in my case, changing out of a shirt and skirt and into a large woolly dress whilst the lights change from red to green.

I had mentioned to the production team that I had only

driven automatics since my driving test twenty-one years ago, when, somewhat disabled by an eight-month-old distension containing the future Ms Amy Rosenthal, I managed to pass, despite refusal to do an emergency stop and much stressing of the possibility of a waters-breaking scenario. But things being what they are in TV, the word 'automatic' failed to penetrate office ears, added to which my fervent wish for something battered, unkempt, bumped and overspilling as befits Jane Lucas, a woman for whom a car is merely an extension of her office, failed to materialize.

Consequently, I got a sparkly new Renault Clio – manual drive only. We did not take to one another. I would have happily driven over both Nicole and her Gallic old goat of a father, if only I could have got into first gear. I was fine on the low-loader, miming away like a graduate from the Marcel Marceau school of motoring, but left to my own devices to drive past a stationary camera and stop on a piece of double-sided tape, I was useless.

It goes without saying that the locations were busy. Finchley and Totteridge seemed to be having Le Mans style rallies on the days we were there. As Props men smeared brown liquid and soot over the bodywork to make it look more 'Lucas-like', the first assistant crackled through a dodgy walkie-talkie, 'Drive past the camera, Maureen, then turn around as soon as you can, so that we can do it again if we need to.' At this point I'd had ten minutes gear practice after a twenty-one year lay-off. My foot was jerking up and down like a Country & Western Singer at a hoe-down and the unfamiliar co-ordination was giving me cramp in one calf. Still, actors are trained to obey orders, mostly in order to show that the casting director wasn't a congenital idiot, and, tugging my doorlock, I set, jumpily, off.

I managed to pass the camera and drove on till the traffic lights stopped me, rather abruptly, in third gear. A few embarrassing hops later, I was forced by the traffic flow to turn left down a narrow, steep gradient with the gears making elephant noises as I struggled from first to second. I was being hotly pursued by an Escort Cabriolet and a removal van on their way either *to* a pressing appointment with Baroness Thatcher or *from* a press conference with Sinead O'Connor. On a patience scale, they came out at minus ten. I started to sweat as I got further and further from the crew into unknown territory, and contact with them broke down because I daren't take my hand off the wheel for long enough to press the button which activated my end of the walkie-talkie. There were no side streets in which to execute the faultless three-point turns I once excelled at, when the world was young and my foetus didn't answer back.

About three miles down the road, with my make-up running down my neck and my ears sweating, I swerved violently into a private driveway. The private driveway was on an even steeper slope than the hill. It was here that I conducted the first ever 105-point turn. I couldn't find reverse or do a hill-start. When I finally left the driveway, steam was coming out of the tyres and the *Guinness Book of Records* was hovering on the melting tarmac.

When I finally got back to the camera crew, I felt as though I had just survived a shell attack in enemy territory. I drew pitifully and shudderingly to a halt and awaited some kind of testimonial dinner. Unfortunately, as far as the crew were concerned, I'd just been off turning the car round whilst they'd been having a coffee and re-angling the camera. I felt like the Japanese soldier who staggered out of the jungle, twenty-five years after the war was over, and surrendered.

The next day's location was at Tally-Ho Corner, which is like Trafalgar Square but with people dropping things instead of pigeons. There was an outdoor market nearby and the sound man was going crazy trying to hear anything over the racket of buses and vendors. The shot was easy. Just getting in and out of a car. While thus occupied, an elderly, very distrait gentleman arrived with two large and pathetically mangy dogs on leads. Somehow he persuaded Vandra, our kindly stage manager, to hold on to his dogs whilst he shopped for a few items in the market. He then disappeared for long enough for us to consider a distress flare to Linda McCartney. We were ready to move on to the next location when he finally meandered back. It was quite a surprise to see he was accompanied by a band of grim-faced cops.

As usual, the lefty liberal thespians were convinced that the police were about to maltreat a victim of Carelessness in the Community and were poised to alert Helena Kennedy, QC, until we watched them relieve the innocent old codger of the largest knife I've ever seen outside of an animated short of *Scaramouche*. As the Finchley police carted him off in one van and his poor arthritic dogs went off in another, the crew and I were still attempting to get one four-second shot of a distraught Agony Aunt climbing into a Renault Clio.

The next day we filmed in the Fulham Road about twenty yards from Anne, my agent's, office. During a set-up she and I went for a coffee and found Valerie Singleton at the next table. We chatted amiably for a while and I wasn't sure whether or not to tell her that the following day the script demanded me to shout, 'I'm *not* a dinosaur! I'm the same age as Valerie Singleton!'

The series was recorded in an unusual way for me (but not, I gather, unusual in today's budgeted TV world), in that we rehearsed two episodes at the same time. We began on the Sunday with a readthru' of two scripts, then spent Monday to Thursday blocking (the moves) and learning both episodes. On Thursday, the producers attended a runthru', which felt more like a 'faint-thru'', then on Sunday the technical crew arrived, camera plans in hand, for a collapse-thru'. Then on Monday we rehearsed the *first* episode only and on Tuesday we worked all day in the studio, a technical rehearsal at 10.00 am, a dress rehearsal at 4 o'clock and, at 7.00 pm a full show in front of a studio audience, with re-takes, when necessary, until 10.00 o'clock. Episode One in the can. The following morning we returned to the studio at 9.00 o'clock to technical and dress rehearsals, and eventually, played the remaining episode which we last rehearsed on the previous Sunday before *another* audience.

I'm not saying it was difficult. I'm saying it was an effing impossibility. You are learning an hour's dialogue in four days and performing it in ten. It made weekly rep look idle. An ITV comedy, of course, is twenty-four minutes. This is the BBC, *sans* commercials, and it comes out at twenty-nine minutes. Needless to say, we did it, so some poor sod is going to have to do it after us, and when they collapse with hives, herpes and hernia, they will be told, 'Well, Maureen Lipman did it on *Agony Again!*' (we've now taken to calling it *Ag-Ag*) and very soon they'll be asking actors to record three episodes on one afternoon.

We did, of course, have the best team, the dream team, in our *Ag-Ag* cast. The brilliant and dynamic Doon MacKichan who plays Debra, the beastly producer of Jane Lucas's TV Show. She was an acclaimed Princess Di in Sue Townsend's *The Queen and I* and has a wicked sense of comic deliniation and is destined for stardom. 'If I didn't like her so much,' I told director Bob Spiers, 'I'd bloody kill her!'

The Scots influence continued through Valerie Edmonds, who plays my over-zealous secretary, Catherine. Here I should point out that I'm intensely proud of Valerie to the point of considering her 'my creation'. She auditioned for my production of *The Sunshine Boys* in Edinburgh. Six foot tall with the bones of a Slav, the legs of a supermodel and the heart of a small fawn, she was going to be discovered soon, if not by me, then by *everyone*. Lovely comic timing in a small part proved once again that there are no small parts, only small actors. When *Ag-Ag* was casting I urged Kate Day, casting director, to see Valerie for any of the odd cameos, and she ended up with a running role, which she built brilliantly each week. If we do another series (God and Mr Yentob willing), the possibilities for her are endless.

What's more, when 'Mother here's' lack of courage became overwrought, over-emotional or overbearing, Ms MacKichan and Ms Edmonds would disappear into the Acton smog and return with a posy of stunning pansies and lilies, or a heavenly aromatherapy oil and all would be well.

Niall Buggy is as Irish as peat and has the healing properties of a day trip to Lourdes. Niall plays the homeless ex-bank manager derelict, whom Jane defends on her TV programme, then, in a fit of fervour, takes home to live with her. Having him around every day just lightened the load and the memory of his rendition of 'New York, New York' at the last-night party accompanied by assorted high-kicking women, will live on, whenever the past confronts the future, for ever in my mind.

I have a son and a lover in the show. It's unusual for me to have sex. On screen that is. Or off, I hear you ponder, on her schedule? Normally, I'm the best friend who doesn't get the man, the mother who thinks sex is something men carry coal in, or the maiden aunt with knots in her knickers. Here I get to bed with a delicious black actor, David Harewood *and* I get to neck with Simon Williams.

David is gorgeous and considerably younger than I am, although his next job, playing Anthony in a production of *Anthony and Cleopatra* with a Bosnian director and Vanessa Redgrave, should soon take care of that. He had never seen *Agony* and I suppose his picture of me was similar to the picture familiar to most tabloid newspapers – sixty-five, grey-haired, cadaverous and generally past it.

After David had talked to us at the audition, it was clear he could play the part and producer, Humphrey Barclay, asked him if he had any questions.

'No, not really,' he said. 'It's very funny stuff. Oh, yes,' he added. 'There is one thing – who's playing Jane?'

It was a classic moment which he will replay over and over (if *I* have anything to do with it) for a few hundred years and, poor chap, he was mortified. We all covered up manfully – once I'd been prised off the table top – and fortunately he has a great sense of humour and will be able to tell it on the *Jimmy Tarbuck Show* when the series hits the air.

On one day in the studio, I seemed to spend the entire day snogging one or the other of them. I'm here to tell you that, on a scale of one to ten, it beats the hell out of reading Gerard

Manley Hopkins on Radio 4. Simon has aged disgustingly well, in the wood, you might say, and I got quite weepy over the '*temps perdu*' in our scenes together. Every time they put Peter Skellern's *You're a Lady* on the turntable for the beginning of our scene, I was awash and had to be hosed down, fanned and re-powdered. I wouldn't care but *You're a Lady* has no more meaning to me than *Knees Up Mother Brown*. I suppose it was just that the last time we played those scenes together our kids were at the sixes and sevens stage and were at the beginnings not in the middle of our expectations.

Maria Charles returned as Bea, the Mother from Hell with whom a regular exchange would be:

> Jane: I thought you always told me it was not the winning that was important but the taking part?
>
> Bea: I was sparing your feelings. What would *you* have ever won?

With the transparent frailty of a dragonfly, she packs more energy, more punch and more spluttering into a performance than the combined weight of the Three Tenors performing live at Wembley Stadium. It was good to be back at sparring pitch and with mutual concern and respect.

The new boy was Sacha Grunpeter, fresh out of Cambridge. We saw many eighteen-year-olds for the part and Sacha won it at the eleventh hour and was told the news by Kate Day in the bicycle shop where he was working. He was quite pleased. It was tough for him being thrown into the zippy world of sitcom and over the next seven weeks he was forced to sacrifice Stanislavsky in favour of Stan Laurel. It worked.

The final night-shoot was in Battersea Park, by the river, where I was to walk with my potential love interest, David Harewood. Sally, my assistant, and I arrived to find the crew were still filming elsewhere and there was no one around but the catering van. We needed a balmy night – but I didn't anticipate just how barmy it would become.

We decided to walk across the park in search of a loo and within the maze of curious erections – by which I mean pagodas and sunken sculptures – we came upon a straggly group of tents and roped-off enclosures, peopled by parents, their children and an over-the-odds number of dogs. We were sauntering past when a young woman ran up and breathlessly asked if I was Maureen Lipman. When I confessed that I was, she grinned sheepishly and said, 'We were wondering if you would mind judging our Dog Show. It's for a very good cause!'

'I'm sure it is,' I howled, noting the 'Proceeds to Battersea Dogs Home' logo. 'But what I know about dogs could be written on a worming tablet . . . and I don't think . . .'

'Oh, that doesn't matter a jot,' said a hearty voice, and up strode the Colonel who'd been, it seemed, judging the rest of the day's canines. 'Just pick the one you like the look of.'

And so it was that, whilst looking for a lavatory in a park, before filming a romantic tête-à-tête for an ancient sitcom, I found myself facing eight pleading eyes and four lolling tongues panting to be picked . . . And their dogs were quite eager too!

Ten seconds later I was pinning a rosette on a retriever and apologizing to a blind chihuahua, an ancient mongrel in a knitted coat and, my absolute all time prejudice, an English bull terrier with one pink eye. The whole experience was over in four minutes and left me feeling as if I'd passed through a dream sequence.

Walking along the river bank hand-in-frozen-hand with David, I was colder than I've ever been. It was slap in the middle of what I laughingly call English summertime and my feet were immobilized into numb and feelingless blocks. If you can believe, when you see the episode, that I'm serene and flushed with a rosy glow, then I'm a better actress than you think I am.

I have videos of the first three episodes downstairs in a plain brown envelope and I still haven't been able to watch them. By the time you read this they will have been on air. Which is fine. I'll watch them then when everybody else does. There is something strange and stale about sitting down to watch videos of your work, at the wrong time of day, in the wrong setting. It feels masturbatory – not that I'm against masturbation or anything you do in the privacy of your own home, as long as you don't do it in the street and frighten the sleeping policemen.

In fact, *Ag-Ag* is one of the most difficult, technical performances I've ever had to give, simply because all the characters who surround Jane play at different levels and in very different acting styles and somehow Jane has to stay at the same level of reality throughout.

Debra, the producer of Jane's television show, is all diamond hard, fast, hard-edged, vampy, review-style panache. Bea, Jane's mother, is fantastical Vaudeville; Michael, the son, mainline moody; and assorted guests – lodgers, guests on her TV programme and rival chat show hosts – vary from over-the-top to 'Eat your heart out, Alton Towers'! I'm grateful and relieved that the critics realized how bloody hard it is to make things look easy and liked the show.

Jane Lucas, well left of centre, is obsessed with the liberal issues of life and supporting those who can't help themselves. She can cope well with healing the world's problems but makes a giant mess of her own. She claims to be a slob, many of the people surrounding her describe her as plain, and yet most of her clothes are designer wear and her hair and make-up are carefully done. She claims to be out of practice and hopelessly inept in the world of sexual mores, but she doesn't seem to get too many complaints from the men she beds. She has no time to spend with her own children but their relationship is full of trust and friendship. She claims to be serious and sober and plodding but most of the time she speaks, people laugh. Her life is disorganized, chaotic and she is imposed upon by everyone she encounters, yet she somehow seems to deliver the goods. Her life is such sweet agony. I wonder whether she found me, or I found her ...? You tell me – After all, you've read me like a book...